CW00794147

Confessions

The WISH List

(Warwick Interdisciplinary Studies in the Humanities)

SERIES EDITORS **Jonathan Bate, Stella Bruzzi,**
Thomas Docherty and Margot Finn

In the twenty-first century, the traditional disciplinary boundaries of higher education are dissolving at remarkable speed. The last decade has seen the flourishing of scores of new interdisciplinary research centres at universities around the world and there has also been a move towards more interdisciplinary teaching.

The WISH List is a collaboration between Bloomsbury Academic and the University of Warwick, a university that has been, from its foundation, at the forefront of interdisciplinary innovation in academia. The series aims to establish a framework for innovative forms of interdisciplinary publishing within the humanities, between the humanities and social sciences and even between the humanities and the hard sciences.

Also in *The WISH List*:

Reading and Rhetoric in Montaigne and Shakespeare
Peter Mack
ISBN 978-1-84966-061-7 (Hardback); e-ISBN 978-1-84966-060-0

The Public Value of the Humanities
Edited by Jonathan Bate
ISBN 978-1-84966-471-4 (Hardback); ISBN 978-1-84966-062-4 (Paperback);
e-ISBN 978-1-84966-063-1

Raising Milton's Ghost
John Milton and the Sublime of Terror in the Early Romantic Period
Joseph Crawford
ISBN 978-1-84966-332-8 (Hardback); e-ISBN 978-1-84966-419-6

Open-space Learning
A Study in Transdisciplinary Pedagogy
Nicholas Monk
ISBN 978-1-84966-054-9 (Hardback); e-ISBN 978-1-84966-055-6

Confessions
The Philosophy of Transparency

Thomas Docherty

BLOOMSBURY
LONDON • NEW DELHI • NEW YORK • SYDNEY

Bloomsbury Academic
An imprint of Bloomsbury Publishing Plc

50 Bedford Square
London
WC1B 3DP
UK

1385 Broadway
New York
NY 10018
USA

www.bloomsbury.com

Bloomsbury is a registered trade mark of Bloomsbury Publishing Plc

First published in 2012
Paperback edition first published 2013

© Thomas Docherty 2012

This work is published subject to a Creative Commons Attribution Non-Commercial Licence. You may share this work for non-commercial purposes only, provided you give attribution to the copyright holder and the publisher. For permission to publish commercial versions please contact Bloomsbury Academic.

No responsibility for loss caused to any individual or organization acting on or refraining from action as a result of the material in this publication can be accepted by Bloomsbury or the author.

British Library Cataloguing-in-Publication Data
A catalogue record for this book is available from the British Library.

ISBN: HB: 978-1-8496-6659-6
PB: 978-1-4725-5745-2

Library of Congress Cataloging-in-Publication Data
A catalog record for this book is available from the Library of Congress.

Cover design: Burge Agency

Printed and bound in Great Britain

For Valentine Cunningham

Advance praise for Confessions

Thomas Docherty has long been not only one of our most significant, provocative and original cultural critics, but one of the most consistent. In this book he deploys some of his key concepts — the event, radical historicity, becoming as heterogeneous flux — as a basis for a sustained interrogation of the history and supposed virtue of the idea of confession. The result is a learned, sophisticated and powerful counterblast to a culture whose demand for immediate transparency is inseparable from a range of disabling fetishes, from management and security to space and speed, 'truth and reconciliation' and, above all, identity and identity-politics. Everyone should read it.

— **Andrew Gibson**, Research Professor of Modern Literature and Theory, Royal Holloway, University of London

In this virtuoso work, Thomas Docherty uses the idea of confession to reach to the core of contemporary concerns about the subject and its responsibilities. With breathtaking boldness, and dizzying sweep and swerve of thought, Docherty mounts a devastating denunciation of the culture of transparency, in which everything must be made immediately available for consumption. Drawing on thinkers from Augustine to Beckett, he builds an impassioned case for an aesthetic democracy founded upon singularity. Rarely has theoretical reflection been conducted with such brio and scorching brilliance.

— **Steven Connor**, Birkbeck College, University of London

We live in an age where 'transparency' is everything, or its illusion at least, from the *mea maxima culpa* of the disgraced politician, to the pseudodoxia of institutional accountability. Tele-technologies, kiss-n-tell biographies and massmediatic intrusiveness have rendered confession meaningless to such a great degree, that to read so finely attuned a 'confessional' as Thomas Docherty's is to be reminded of an ethical imperative that is as inescapable as it is misunderstood in our wilfully stupid secular culture. Docherty begins with disarmingly straightforward questions concerning what it might mean 'to confess', and what the role of the subject is in this practice, opening out his exquisitely crafted meditation with a breadth of scope that belies the filigree-work of its arguments, explorations and interrogations. Docherty demands that we take responsibility for that which is often beyond any mere 'economic' weighing of benefit or harm. The book is a reminder that ideas which have been glibly consigned to 'literary theory' can still have disquieting power in the hands of an original and provocative thinker.

— **Julian Wolfreys**, Professor of Modern Literature and Culture, Loughborough University

I have to confess to liking this book a lot. It is a literary, theoretical and autobiographical *tour de force*. Docherty's acute critical sense ranges across the philosophical and cultural landscape to read Paul de Man, Giorgio Agamben, Hannah Arendt and the Lisbon Lions. A few more books like this and the humanities might be worth fighting for after all.

— **Martin McQuillan**, Professor of Literary Theory and Cultural Analysis and Dean of Faculty of Arts and Social Sciences, Kingston University, London

Contents

Series Editor's Preface

Living in the twenty-first century's confessional culture is at once alarming and soporific. On the one hand, we are subjected to unprecedented technologies of surveillance, calculated to compel exposure of our innermost failings to public view; on the other, we are cocooned by a pervasive media miasma of celebrity exposé, designed in no small part to divert attention from the fundamental challenges facing contemporary society, politics and the environment. As modern governments increasingly fetishise 'transparency', Thomas Docherty resoundingly demonstrates in this volume, they manipulate a longstanding confessional drive in novel ways, and thereby endanger the very communicative practices upon which democratic cultures have been built in the modern era.

In keeping with the WISH List's underlying premises, *Confessions: The Philosophy of Transparency* opens up a dialogue across the disciplines that highlights the ability of scholarship in the Humanities to illuminate (and critique) not only texts and contexts but also political praxis—as it plays out both within and beyond conventional academic debates and formations. Readers of Docherty's treatise will encounter Augustine's *Confessions*, Hegel's *Phenomenology*, Zola's *J'accuse* and Lowell's *Life Studies*, each subjected to a searching philosophical analysis that recognises its specific intellectual genealogy. But they will also find these (and a rich array of other works) resituated by Docherty, deployed to probe the problematic, interwoven paradigms of—for example—disaster capitalism, identity politics and literary criticism.

Lauded as an unproblematic virtue in much religious literature, the cult of individualised confession emerges from these pages instead as a potent threat: when transparency borne of an atomised confessional culture runs amok in democratic cultures, Docherty asserts, governments' (and citizens') communicative modalities are fundamentally compromised. Framed by astute analyses of classic texts and honed by judicious applications of continental theory, these arguments speak eloquently to the challenges of performing the self in the twenty-first century. For if confessional texts ostensibly proclaim the self, Docherty concludes, the process of confession all too often reduces the individual to an impoverished iteration of normative identities inimical alike to difference and democracy.

Margot Finn
University of Warwick

Preface

'I confess.' This is seemingly a straightforward statement, but as soon as it has any content at all, it becomes charged with difficulty. What might be the content of a confession; and what ought it to contain if it is to constitute 'confession' rather than just 'statement': is there a difference between 'I stole the ribbon' as a statement, and 'I stole the ribbon' in the mode of confession? Clearly, yes; and what makes the difference is the context and the accusatory demand, expressed or tacit, for confession rather than statement. Guilt, anguish and responsibility all immediately enter the frame. Further, the context is one that immediately places the confessing subject in a relation to others, to an audience of sorts for the confessional act. It thus becomes intrinsically a social act of some kind. And who might be the subject of the confession? When I say *I* stole the ribbon, is the confessing and speaking I to be identified with the I who committed the action, the I who is now rather displaced and distanced from the speaker?

These kinds of question lie at the heart of this inquiry. Out of a simple questioning came a complexity of issues ranging from matters of narrative to memory, from authenticity to sociability, from hearing to testimony, from evidence to authority. Such questions are potentially enormous; but they are held together and controlled here by the presiding demand to engage with ideas of a transparent culture and a culture that sees a prerogative for expression – free expression – of the self. The nexus of these things is a problem concerning modernity and its political formation as democracy. If the book has a purpose beyond the matters of literary critique, it is as a contribution to our possibilities for living together in democratic organization. That, too, turns out to be extremely difficult to achieve; but it would be good if a society could ever manage to try it out, and this book is an urging towards such an essay.

Parts of it have been tried out, across a number of years, before many audiences and individuals. I want to thank colleagues in the Universities of Glasgow, Edinburgh, Rosario, Utrecht, Dublin, Harvard, Sheffield Hallam and Leeds. From all of these, I have gained enormously; and to colleagues and students in these institutions, as also in the institutions where I have taught, I confess my indebtedness.

Introduction:
The Philosophy of Transparency

On 13 January 1898, Émile Zola published his famous letter to Félix Faure, then President of France, accusing the French government of anti-semitism. *J'accuse* makes a number of demands, but, implicit within these opening words of the letter is the demand for a confession: *J'accuse* calls for the reply '*I confess*'. In this book, I want to consider how the modern and contemporary world has responded to such a demand. We live increasingly in what might be called a 'confessional culture'; and there are serious consequences in this for the nature of community and for the idea of a personal identity. As Peter Brooks pointed out in his book on legal issues regarding confession, *Troubling Confessions*, we seem to be fascinated by the almost everyday nature of confessional discourse; but when confession becomes a matter of reality TV shows, we have perhaps reached a point where 'televised confession demonstrates the banalization of confessional practices'.[1]

Confession, which in legal terms can be a matter of potentially massive significance – even of life and death, at times – is in danger of being reduced to kitsch; confession, which in religious terms is seen for the believer also as a matter of life and death or of salvation, is in danger of being reduced to the trivialities of salacious celebrity gossip. However, there are serious issues here still. Agamben has argued in recent times that it is becoming common, especially in the public sphere, for confession of wrong-doing to supplant admission to legal guilt: 'the contrite assumption of moral responsibilities is invoked at every occasion as an exemption from the responsibilities demanded by law'.[2]

These, however, are not just recent phenomena. There is, obviously, a long history of confessional writing that dates back long before the Fourth Lateran Council of 1215 when the Roman Catholic Church, then the single most dominant power shaping everyday life across Europe, required an annual act of confessing from its adherents. This history lingers on into present times, but it has assumed a different form and has had a different series of consequences. We might recognize this most immediately in the contemporary demand for what we might call a 'culture of transparency' in all aspects of public life and governance. The fact that we now require governments, businesses and (above all) publicly funded bodies to 'reveal' their inner workings and decision-making processes is but one aspect of this new norm. Transparency has become our rather shrunken substitute for truth; but within this demand for transparency there lies an assumption that, without transparent revelation, individuals and organizations might behave in ways that are unjust, unethical or simply unfair. The philosophy of transparency goes hand in hand with a demand for accountability in our decisions and judgements.

While there may be some social benefits from this (the emphasis here is on the words 'may be'), there is a further corollary that is of importance to this present study. The other side of transparency is surveillance. Where a culture of transparency is the norm, it can start to permeate the everyday life of the citizen as well, such that we lose the right to any form of privacy. The intimacies that help us to shape ourselves as constituent parties to the public sphere are no longer intimate, so to speak; and we lose our right to a private life.[3] There are far-reaching consequences for us as subjects and as citizens in the establishment of a transparent society.[4] The question of surveillance as the sinister counterpart to transparency becomes all the more pressing when it is further internalized: that is to say, when we all start to 'look within' and to focus the grounds of our social and cultural being upon our sense of our own interiority or 'selfhood' and identity. The net result is one wherein we essentially are in danger of focusing endlessly on the question of 'who we are'; and this leads, in cultural criticism, to identity-politics as the ground of critique that now dominates much of our everyday critical activities. There are serious and grave consequences for a democratic culture in this.

These problems and consequences of what we can call the confessional drive or impetus require some exploration and explanation; and this has assumed a much more pressing importance in the culture of the last fifty years or so. That culture has its roots in a moment of what I describe later in this book as cold-war democracy. It has a kind of counterpart in more recent formulations of capitalist activity in what Naomi Klein calls the 'shock doctrine'. Klein's case is that what she calls disaster capitalism works by trying to capitalize, literally, on natural (or in many cases politically generated) disasters. A disaster such as Hurricane Katrina, which devastated New Orleans in 2005, gives disaster capitalists the opportunity to raze all existing arrangements of the social sphere to the ground in the interests of an entirely 'new start'. In this, 'shock' operates in precisely the same way as the more muted 'confession': confession seeks to establish a kind of *tabula rasa* for the self, by humiliating the self to a point where it is a kind of 'zero-point', so that it can be rehabilitated, but essentially with a new and refreshed identity. For disaster capital, read 'redemption'.[5]

In this collocation of confession with capital, I mean to indicate that what is important for the work of this book is not so much a desire to treat, discretely, matters of legal confession or of religious confession (though these are important); rather, it is to explore the ways in which a culture of confession has a set of consequences for our polity, and especially for the relation of human subjects or citizens to the public sphere and to intimate human relatedness. In short, confession, as something that ostensibly is primarily a matter of *conscience*, is something that exists in a profound relation to the *communication* that is constitutive of the possibility of democracy. The argument of this book is that we do not achieve democracy through the confessing of our selves: that is to say, through a kind of 'deliberation', in the agora or public sphere, of points of view that are revealed as being matters of atomized or individuated consciences. Democracy does indeed have a relation to a confessional culture, but it is a relation that depends primarily upon the modes of communication and the modes of human relatedness – intimacies and public actions – that are endangered by a transparent society.

* * *

In 1959, M.L. Rosenthal reviewed Robert Lowell's collection, *Life Studies*, in the *Nation*. Almost in passing, he noted what he called a major thrust towards biographical self-revelation and self-humiliation in Lowell's writings, and he used the term 'confessional poetry' to describe this phenomenon. As he himself noted very soon after, confessional poetry is not at all new. Rosenthal traces it back at least as far as Thomas Wyatt's 'They flee from me that sometime did me seek' in the sixteenth century; and, indeed, if we think of it as *confessional writing* more generally construed, it might be said to have a much longer history and one that is not limited to the anglophone world. That history has not yet been adequately examined. More specifically, the fundamental philosophical and theoretical conditions governing the drive for such a mode of writing have not been addressed; and this important dimension of writing and of culture more generally now requires fuller understanding. This is all the more important given our contemporary demand for a culture of transparency in the public sphere, a culture that disturbs the usual dimensions of, or relations between, what might constitute the private and the public, and a culture that thereby threatens a social order based precisely upon clear demarcations between these two domains.

This book explores what is at stake in the confessional culture. We have seen different key moments of explicitly 'confessional' writing (as in Augustine or Jean-Jacques Rousseau), of 'testamentary' writing (François Villon), of 'essays' in presenting the self (Michel de Montaigne), of more or less autobiographical revelation in that group of poets that so interested Rosenthal in cold-war America (Robert Lowell, John Berryman, Sylvia Plath, Elizabeth Bishop, Theodore Roethke), or even of self-revelation in recent philosophical writing (as in Jacques Derrida's 'Circonfession'), not to mention the so-called 'confessional turn' in literary and cultural criticism. In all of this writing, there is a certain philosophical foundation or substratum – the conditions under which it is possible to assert a confessional mode – that needs exploration and explication. In a sense, this is the counterpart to Zola's great *J'accuse*: in the face of self-accusation, how is it possible to assert that *I confess*? Indeed, is confession even possible; and if so, what would be its grounds?

As I tease out some answers to these questions, we are also able to arrive at a philosophy of confession that has pertinence for a contemporary political culture (as also of a dominant contemporary ideology), based on the notion of 'transparency'. Few have followed seriously Gianni Vattimo's observations on the 'transparent society', which he saw as a way of understanding or explaining what he called the postmodern; and key to this was the idea that a contemporary, technologically advanced society was able to confound the real and its representations, as if G.W.F. Hegel's Spirit had come to full self-knowing or self-consciousness. In this society, the self coincides with its self-representations. Such a position would appear to be central to the idea of authenticity and truth-telling in confessional writing: it is the basis of saying, truthfully, 'here I take my stand'. The question is: what other consequences might there be of an assumption of the primacy of transparency?

Long predating this, however, Molière frequently considered explicitly the idea of transparency in his plays. Most especially in *Le misanthrope*, he was concerned to explore what it might mean in terms of being able to tell the truth. Rousseau was later to follow this up in philosophical fashion; and the question then becomes whether it is possible to tell the truth while at the same time maintaining sociability. Without sociability, of course, 'telling' anyone anything is impossible.[6] One way of putting this is to ask the question: can the words 'transparent' and 'society' properly sit together at all? That is to say: what these texts show is that the very communication that is at the core of social life depends upon the miscommunications required in those kinds of truth-evasion. One cannot 'confess' oneself and, at the same time, remain a member of a social community.

Despite these historical precedents, transparency is usually regarded as a general social and ethical good; and this is probably especially so historically, particularly since the days of the cold war when, not only in political espionage but also in public life, confessions as to one's political allegiances were required, at least implicitly. This book widens the political arena and uses the understanding of confessional writing to explore the consequences for private life in the public sphere, for a culture of surveillance and especially of an interiorized surveillance, that generates modern and postmodern anguish or guilt. The claim is that this guilt has extreme consequences for the contemporary notion of authority and autonomy; and, since the assertion of autonomy is fundamental to modernity, the book exposes certain fundamental flaws within the formation of modern cultural life. In short, confessional discourse, far from endorsing the idea of a strong identity or selfhood, is precisely responsible for a weakening of individual liberal autonomy and freedom in the face of the pressure to 'reveal'.

Confession (in both writing and speech) has some key priority areas that can be considered as determining its intrinsic shape: especially and above all, the religious and the juridical. The book looks particularly at the religious base for this kind of writing, but prefers to see this in more secular terms. In doing so, it argues that confession requires an anorexic 'reduction' of the self to a kind of 'zero-state', in which the act of confessing becomes axiomatic to human relatedness. However, that act is shown to be one in which actual historical and material experience is precluded: the self can proclaim its relation to others (what we call love or society), but can only do so at the cost of reducing historical experience merely to official forms of identity. When it addresses the political realm, the book not only considers the politics of 'confession-without-penance' that shapes movements such as those for 'truth and reconciliation', but also examines how a contemporary culture of transparency engenders a society in which autonomy (or the very authority of the subject that proclaims 'I confess') is grounded in guilt, reparation and victimhood.

* * *

The book comes in two main sections, with a concluding third part. The first part (Chapters 1–3) has to do with the assertion of identity and what that can be based upon; and the second (Chapters 4–6) is an examination of what we might call the fundamental humiliation of the self that is central to the act of confession. In this second part, we are looking at what I call the ecology of anguish: the reduction or kenosis of the self or the subject that is necessary for a confession to take hold. The paradox is that the writing of a confession asserts selfhood, while the substance of the confession diminishes the self.

The argument of these two sections leads to the final part (Chapters 7–8). The first chapter of this section is the straightforward political summation of the argument; and it relates to what has happened to the idea and material substance of the public sphere within a confessional culture. The second (Chapter 8) is an exercise in literary confession: it relates my own experience of Shakespeare and how I come to write the very book that we have just read. More importantly, it relates the argument of the whole to what has happened in recent decades in the educational practices surrounding literary and cultural criticism, and argues that the predominant modes of this education have been profoundly anti-democratic, despite their ostensibly emancipatory credentials.

Confession, then, turns out to be a necessary response to *J'accuse*; but it turns out to be much more than that response. The book explores the foundations of modernity in terms of a whole philosophy of revelation, transparency and truth-telling. This last, needless to say, is never straightforward.

PART ONE

1

Now

Or, On Memory and the Contemporary

and he wonders if it is worth hoping for a future when there is no future,
and from now on, he tells himself, he will stop hoping for anything and
live only for now, this moment, this passing moment, the now that
is here and then not here, the now that is gone forever.
Paul Auster, *Sunset Park*[1]

To tell the truth

In 1958, amid the heady excitements of post-war European aesthetic experimentalism, and just after the signing of the Treaty of Rome the previous year, Alain Robbe-Grillet opened his well-known 'new novel', the Kafkaesque *Dans le labyrinthe*, with a basic truism: '*Je suis seul ici, maintenant*':[2] I am alone, here, now. This is truistic for the simple reason that, virtually by definition, 'I' must always be 'here', 'now'; and, insofar as I am self-aware enough to talk about 'I', then this 'I' is also, in a profound sense, alone or at least distinguished from all else. While the political scene is marking a supposed unity of various geographical entities (the very making of a labyrinth, in at least one sense), Robbe-Grillet asserts solitude. *Dans le labyrinthe*, of course, is also a self-consciously *nouveau roman*, a self-conscious departure for the novel as a literary form: it presupposes novelty, a change, and an experiment in which any 'now' – and most specifically the 'now' that opens the novel itself – is very definitely different from a 'then', a past or an already existing state of affairs. This now, like every now that is self-conscious, is determined by its difference from its immediate past. It is 'modern', and self-consciously so, in making this break and in characterizing itself precisely as a break with the immediate past.

I want to try here to think through what is at stake in this. What are the implications of our thinking that the *content* of 'I' is given by the substance of whatever is the 'here-now'? The question can be phrased in some different ways, depending on one's preferred inflection of the problem. What is 'now', and what might its content be? How might we understand 'the contemporary'? Perhaps of greater socio-cultural consequence is the concomitant question: 'What is modernity?' Within this, we should ask the question, 'How is *change* possible such that "now" differs from "then" or from its immediately preceding "now"?' This last mutates more generally into a much more far-reaching and fundamental question – in some ways the political question that shapes the post-war political settlement that shapes 'the west' – a question that will shape this entire study: 'How is history possible; or what might it mean to be genuinely secular?'

It has always been difficult to assert a genuine secularity and perhaps nowhere more so, paradoxically, than when one asks questions regarding the very substantive constitution of history itself. In the neo-theological terms within which the question has traditionally been posed, it has been thought of as a question about creation or about the world itself: why is there something rather than nothing? This, in turn, is translated into literature, where it is inflected as a problem concerning authority and legitimacy, by one such as King Lear, for example, arguing that 'Nothing can come of nothing'. In broader terms, it is the question of 'beginnings', as Edward Said once insisted.[3] It is translated into more abstract form in mathematics when one asks the question concerning 'zero' and its relation to both a cardinal and ordinal number: how do we get from zero to one, or what is the relation of zero to 'the first', for example.[4]

Behind all of this is a fundamental issue that is at the heart of my inquiry in this opening chapter: what constitutes the substance of 'now'? How would we characterize the present moment, the presence or the substantiality of the '*je*' who is '*ici, maintenant*' in Robbe-Grillet's labyrinth? At one level, the '*je*' is precisely defined and determined as a specific conjunction of '*ici, maintenant*'; and so, we can say with some precision, what is at stake is the very condition of the subject of modernity or of the subject in modernity.

In what follows, I shall explore this under various headings. It has become, in diverse ways, a pressing issue for some contemporary philosophy, for sociology, and for literary and other forms of aesthetic and cultural critique. Indeed, any form of criticism that thinks of itself as contributing to historical change of any kind – that is, any criticism that would see part of its purview as being 'political' – must find an answer to the question of what constitutes the now.

Walter Benjamin certainly thought this, in his 'Theses on the Philosophy of History'. There, he argues a preference for a kind of criticism that is, in his terms, properly identified as a historical materialism. Such a criticism needs to attend to what he regards as a 'messianic moment', which he describes as the *Jetztzeit* or 'time of the now'.[5] Rather than seeing time as a mere succession in which this is followed by that (one damned thing after another, as it were; or the narrative of 'and then ... and then ...'), Benjamin argues that the historical materialist needs explicitly a moment that is, in a very precise sense, outside of time while yet being of that time: a present that is *arrested*, or a moment in which time stands still while still being of the order of the temporal. In this way, the 'continuum of history' is 'blasted apart', as he graphically describes it;[6]

and in that moment of drastic analysis or dissolution and fragmentation, the historical materialist can come to understand their now as a moment in a wider narrative. That is, the arresting of time allows for the comprehension of the now as a specific moment in or aspect of a 'constellation' or a shape that gives a form to the content of history itself as a whole.

Jean-François Lyotard offered something similar when he considered the operation of memory in Augustine, one of the confessional writers whose work will help shape this inquiry. In his posthumously published book on *La confession d'Augustin*, Lyotard described the operation of memory in Augustine as a seemingly self-contradictory 'negative-affirmative force' that calls to presence that which is not there, or that *re-presents* objects that are absent and then organizes those objects as if they constituted an entire world. He summed up by saying that, for Augustine, memory is 'the friend of time ... One thing after another, certainly; but the first is conserved in the second, and this latter is engorged with the former.'[7]

The thinking involved in the formulations of Lyotard, and the thought that shapes Benjamin's attitude to history, have perhaps not been fully understood. Certainly, it is a commonplace to think of Benjamin as a Marxist whose views are coloured by forms of mysticism and religiosity, such as those we might see in Augustine; but we should take seriously the question of *Messianic* time as expressed and explored here.[8] Too often, the mysticism is forgotten or elided as we try to co-opt Benjamin for all sorts of historicisms – including, fatally, the very historicism against which he himself wrote in his Theses.

Behind Benjamin lurks Hegel, another philosopher marked by the signs of religion, in his case specifically Christianity. At the start of his *Phenomenology*, Hegel ponders what is given to us in sense-perception as the condition of our being-in-the-world. That is to say, he ponders the state of the 'here, now' that constitutes human consciousness at any given instant; and he finds a problem related to truth. Late one evening, he suggests, write down on a sheet of paper the phrase 'now it is night'. That phrase, measured against the facts of the given world, is true. Read it the following morning, validating it in the same way; suddenly, the same phrase has become false, untrue. Yet the matter is a good deal more complicated, as always in Hegel:

> The Now that is Night is *preserved*, i.e. it is treated as what it professes to be, as something that *is*; but it proves itself to be, on the contrary, something that is *not*. The Now does indeed preserve itself, but as something that is *not* Night; equally, it preserves itself in face of the Day that it now is, as something that is also not Day[9]

In other words, something that is linguistically true at one moment ('Now it is night') becomes either false (because now it is day) or, at least, *fictional*. In reading 'Now it is night' at some other moment than the night on which it is written, we enter the terrain of what constitutes the fictional itself.

What became, for Hegel, the opening to the question of *negation* becomes, firstly and more fundamentally, precisely the construction of fiction: the construction of a mode of truth-telling whose validity is *not* to be measured against the world that is given to us, but rather to be legitimized in some other way.

In other words, we have a now that both *is* and *is not* a now, and a now that problematizes the idea of truth, if we consider truth to be a function of referential linguistic propositions about an actual historically material state of affairs.[10] What follows from this – as we know from our understanding of fictions themselves – is that truth cannot be so easily considered purely as a function of linguistic propositions. That would lead us simply to a referential version of truth; but, as references vary in time, so also we lose the substantive idea of the transpositionality, the absolutism, of truth.

For Hegel, truth is either true or not true, so to speak. The referential version of truth is one where truth becomes dependent upon location, upon the locatedness of the '*ici-maintenant*' or the '*je*', and thus a purely subjective sensation, the feeling that the I has here-now, wherever this here-now may be. Given, further, that the here-now is entirely specific to one configuration or constellation of subjectivity (that is, by definition it cannot be occupied by any other I), then at this point truth becomes not merely relativistic, but also empty and entirely unverifiable. It is reduced to a pure manifestation of I-ness: *je suis seul ici, maintenant*. The resulting *solitude*, akin to an isolation, becomes total, and the material reality of the world is reduced to solipsistic fantasy.

The position is one that was satirized by Swift, in his examination of an earlier moment of self-conscious 'modernity', when he critiqued the 'modern' author in his 'Tale of a Tub'. There, we have a modern author who indicates that all that has preceded him – the ancient authors and the entire classical tradition – is, by definition, untrue, since it has failed to take account of the author's contemporary moment. It cannot account for it for the simple reason that, when the ancients wrote, this modern was the future and therefore unknown. Thus it is that he can claim, in Section V of the tale, that 'I here think fit to lay hold on that great and honourable privilege of being the last writer. I claim an absolute authority in right, as the freshest modern, which gives me a despotic power over all authors before me.'[11] Almost equally satirically, the position is criticized more recently by Michel Serres, when he wonders about the eternally optimistic or Whiggish notion of historical process that leads us to assume that the past was another country where people lived in error whereas '*Ouf! Nous sommes enfin entrés dans le vrai*' – finally, we have entered into the realm of the true – by virtue simply of being in the present moment, the most recent 'modern', purged of previous error.[12]

Hannah Arendt has considered something pertinent here, in a piece that looks at truth-telling: her essay on 'Lying in Politics'. She points out that truth and politics are uneasy bedfellows and always have been.[13] She indicates that 'A characteristic of human action is that it always begins something new';[14] but that it does not follow from this that we can ever make something out of nothing. In other words, she is addressing the fundamental question of my present argument: how does something happen; how can we be fully human in this making something new, and even in making ourselves anew and thus 'authoring' ourselves or asserting autonomy? Arendt's argument, indebted to Heideggerian notions of *Destruktion* and to Hegelian notions of negation, really depends upon our capacity for imagination, for seeing a now that both *is* and *is not* at once:

> In order to make room for one's own action, something that was there before must be removed or destroyed, and things as they were before are changed. Such change would be impossible if we could not mentally remove ourselves from where we are physically located and *imagine* that things might as well be different from what they actually are. In other words, the deliberate denial of factual truth – the ability to lie – and the capacity to change facts – the ability to act – are interconnected; they owe their existence to the same source: imagination.[15]

History, we might say following this, depends upon two things: displacing the here-now and lying *or* fiction. This is interesting for anyone who would be a historical materialist, for it contains within itself a remnant of idealism. Rather than accepting that imagination is simply shaped by history (i.e. that imagination is determined by the material economies of the historical process), it is arguing that history depends upon the capacities of imagination, upon our ability to see a now that both *is* night and *is not* night all at once. For Arendt, this is also an indication of our potential for freedom itself. In the same essay from which I have been liberally quoting, she concludes that 'while we are well-equipped for the world, sensually as well as mentally, we are not fitted or embedded into it as one of its inalienable parts. We are *free* to change the world and to start something new in it.'[16]

It is important, thus, that we add to our question (basically a question concerning the linguistic function of the deictic) this problem concerning truth or the impossibility of our telling the truth 'now'. Can we tell the truth? This is the basic question here but, in the context of a study of confession, it is important to get the inflection and intonation right: can we *tell* the truth? Given that 'we' are in a 'present' position, how is truth possible?

Such a question is obviously of great importance in any text that would be 'confessional', be it Augustine acknowledging sin and relating the story of a conversion, or Montaigne trying to paint 'my self' (and acknowledging Augustine in his essay 'On Liars'), or be it Rousseau determinedly and seemingly perversely revealing things about himself (including his lying) that become a source of temporary shame.[17] It is vital to any text that seeks to establish and legitimize a form of natural authenticity, such as we find in certain central strands of British romanticism. It is important for any text that presents a testimony or testament of some kind, as in Villon's 'Le testament', for example;[18] it is equally important in a text that proposes an exemplary kind of confession, as with the tales in John Gower's *Confessio Amantis*; and, very differently of course, it is pertinent also in the circumlocutions that constitute a text like Derrida's 'Circonfession'.[19] It is also, obviously, vital to any text that sees itself as a corrective to other forms of thought (and thus all rhetorical texts, all persuasive texts, including any and all concerned with the business of literary criticism). And it is obviously vital to any text that regards itself as being historically accurate or that sees its role as being one of revealing the truths of history or of the historical process.

We now have, therefore, not just one question but rather two interlinked fundamental questions here: not only the question of how history might be possible, but also a question of how or whether truth or truth-telling might be possible.

Augustine's conversion: kenosis and the empty turning-point

Let us begin the investigation of these questions by looking directly at a confessional text: the *Confessions* of Augustine. This is a text that narrates, among other things, the trajectory of change itself, of *conversion*, and thus of Augustine's 'starting something new', in the phrasing used by Arendt. In it, Augustine ponders the question of responsibility for his sins. Among the many topics that he covers, he asks two key questions related to this issue of responsibility, or 'answerability': first is the ostensibly reasonable question of whether he can genuinely be held responsible for actions committed without his mature consciousness of them, actions carried out when he was an immature infant or even a baby; and second is the equally pertinent question of whether his desires, as seemingly elaborated in dreams when he is asleep, are as sinful as they might be were he conscious and awake.

The implied corollaries of these questions are very serious. Firstly, should a child be held accountable for actions that an adult, possessed of a full consciousness of the norms that govern their world, characterizes as immoral, prior to their knowledge of morality itself? Behind this is a juridical issue, but one whose philosophical basis is thus laid bare: does consciousness determine history, and does intent thereby determine guilt (or innocence)? Secondly, can one commit a sin unconsciously? The relevant example for us here would be Augustine's dreams, for instance (another of Augustine's abiding worries). He feels happy to have purged himself of concupiscence in his waking life, but he remarks that he still has dreams that include matters seemingly revealing an intrinsic lust and immorality in his character, or at least in what we would now call his unconscious. Let us imagine a dream of lust: is this an instance of the dreamer sinning? Or, even more pertinently for present purposes, let us suppose that as a child, I take an apple from a tree, under certain conditions: a) without knowing that the tree does not belong to me; b) without knowing the laws governing private property or ownership; c) without any concern for consequences for anyone else other than myself, since, at this stage, I have an underdeveloped sense of alterity. Is this a sin?

That Augustinian question is answered by Lyotard, who replies to it in his posthumously published book on Augustine's *Confessions*; he responds by saying that it is indeed a sin, *though not a sin committed by a subject*. It is a sin committed by time itself, by *le retard* – by delay – as Lyotard puts it: '*c'est le péché du retard*' ('it is a belated sin').[20] That which *was not* a sin *becomes* one. That which *is not* turns out to *be*. This, of course, is Hegel's 'now' revisited again – a now that has its own forerunner in Augustine, and that has its legacy in Lyotard. We have an act that *is* and *is not* a sin, all at once. How can we understand this? It is a pressing question for the law, of course, concerned as it must be with the age of criminal responsibility, not to mention with the possibilities of mercy, redemption, regret, grace and forgiveness.

In the light of this, we may need to look slightly differently at the question of the 'now'. Recall that, in Hegel, it is not the case that the 'Now it is night' simply becomes false; rather, it is the case that the night-time that is 'contained' in the now is, as it were, preserved and maintained in the later 'now', the now of the morning. Thus, the now contains a present *and* a past. This is different from a Derridean trace, for what is at stake here is *narrative* itself and the possibilities of establishing a narrative truth. Bearing this in mind, let us look more closely at Augustine.

In Augustine, the now becomes equated with the evanescence of the present moment. He effectively tries to understand it by inserting it into a narrative construction: beginning (past), middle (now) and end (future). As he develops his thought, these will respectively become enlarged as memory (past), attention (present) and expectation (future). In Book XI, Chapter 15 of the *Confessions*, he tries to locate and to meditate upon the present (in my terms here, the now). He starts by asking about 'the present century'. However, he immediately realizes that there is no such thing as 'the present century', given that a century cannot be present all at once, but is comprised of its constituent years. In the same manner, the 'present year', made up of constituent months, cannot be 'present'. Further, the present month is made up of a series of days; and the day is made up of hours and so on, until the now evaporates into the purest emptiness of a transitional moment – a moment of change – between future and past:

> In fact, the only time that can be called present is an instant, if we can conceive of such, that cannot be divided even into the most minute fractions, and a point of time as small as this passes so rapidly from the future to the past that its duration is without length. For if its duration were prolonged, it could be divided into past and future. When it is present it has no duration.[21]

The now is defined as that moment of change itself, a moment of *conversion*, as it were, and thus totally of the essence of Augustine's project in his book.

Yet, in voiding it of duration – that is, in voiding this time of time itself – Augustine has also voided it of any substantive *content* at all in this. What he does is to maintain the *formal* substance of a now (as a median or mediating point linking a past with a future and thereby enabling a narrative) while evacuating it of any substance in terms of content. This is a sleight of hand, of course; but it is vital to our understanding of our basic questions: what is the now and how is history possible? If the now is empty, then how can it be characterized by the substance of a conversion?

What eventuates from this is that history becomes possible solely as a *formal narrative* or as a structure; but the present moment within it remains unavailable or at least empty in terms of having any substantive *content*. We have the *form* of the now but without any *content*. It is this kenosis that shapes Augustinian ideas of substantive time. Correspondingly, we have the forms of history (narrative), which are of necessity fictions; and the now, as a something that actually happens, or as a change in the material conditions of the given world, evades our grasp.

We can partly explain this through a consideration of Benjamin's philosophies of historical critique. As we know, Benjamin argues for historical materialism against mere historicism. Historicism, according to Benjamin, thinks of history in terms of a simple progression from past to future; but here, this is a history that proceeds smoothly, without the irruption of any substantive event and thus without any real change. This kind of historicist grasps 'the sequence of events like the beads of a rosary'.[22] In this, each bead would represent a now, but one that has no real content, since it is but a repetition of the same and a consolidation of a static constellation; and thus, it allows a history that can be told from the point of view of one who positions himself in the role of the victor, the teller of the beads.[23] With this state of affairs, the present moment is homogeneous (always the same), but homogeneous precisely because it is empty (it has no possibility of change or of anything really happening that might disturb the whole). Against this is the kind of history explored by the historical materialist, for whom, as Benjamin puts it, 'History is the subject of a structure whose site is not homogeneous, empty time, but time filled by the presence of the now.'[24] The example he offers is that of the French Revolution which 'viewed itself as Rome incarnate. It evoked ancient Rome the way fashion evokes costumes of the past.'[25] Here, the now of ancient Rome persists in or is contained in the now of the Revolution. The Revolution thus becomes one of those moments that actually have substance: it does what Arendt sees as bringing about something new.

Benjamin's 'rosary beads' are, in microcosm, a metaphor or model of what we might call the law of habit; and habit is the enemy of history. In the structure of the habitual, the 'next' occurrence of that which is habitual has always already happened, in a paradoxical sense; and it therefore can have no status as an event in history. Lyotard is clear on this: in a certain sense, 'the next time' has already happened: '*Ce futur antérieur au négatif indèxe l'avenir sur une impuissance toujours déjà accomplie*' ('This negative future anterior pegs the future on a powerlessness that has always already been fulfilled').[26] Habit predetermines the future, such that it cannot ever surprise us: the next bead of the rosary is the same as always, same as it ever was, and always already prefigured in the beads that we tell now, in the present. Under the sign of habit, what is mistakenly called history is but repetition or ritual; and, as Hans Blumenberg argued in 1966, genuine history knows no repetition.[27]

What Benjamin is seeking, although he uses a different vocabulary, is the *content* of an event, the substance of a moment of transition that would give a solidity and a historical reality to the present or to the now-time. But an event here is to be understood in the terms given to us by Lyotard and Alain Badiou, for example. An event is something that happens, certainly; but it is a happening that could not have been predicted as the outcome of the set of circumstances that immediately precede it. The event is, as it were, history in the form of that which is conditioned by surprise. Jean-Luc Nancy offers us a language for this: 'There is, then, something to be thought – the event – the very nature of which – event-ness – can only be a matter of surprise, can only take thinking by surprise.'[28] As he puts it, in a fuller definition where it takes its place alongside a meditation on the experience of freedom:

> Surprise as surprise does not come up in order to add itself to the course of events and to modify it. It offers another course, or, more decisively, it offers in the 'course' itself the withdrawal of the course of time, the withdrawal of all its presence. In fact, we could say that surprise is already inscribed in the heart of all philosophical analyses of temporality and, in a singular manner, in the analyses of the present instant: on the limit between the already-having-been and the not-yet-being, the present has also always proved to be the limit of presence – the already-having-passed of what has-not-yet-come. This is the structure of the surprise ... it takes place without having happened; it will therefore not have taken place, but will have opened time, through a schematism of the surprise whose 'I' would surprise itself[29]

In these observations, the event is tied to freedom; and this is also of importance as we will see later. It is important to note here that we now have a series of collocations, thanks to Arendt and to Nancy, that link the event to both truth and freedom. That is to say, we have a clear identification of the now – once it is given substantial reality (which means historically materialist reality) – with both truth and freedom.

Now, what is the event in the present moment? It is only a point of transition between and a then and a future, between past and future. It is the now of the freedom of the Eliotic individual talent; it is the location of Nancy's surprise; it is the moment when time needs to be arrested, as in Benjamin.

These formulations bring us to the recent work of Giorgio Agamben, and specifically to his essay on the question of 'what is a contemporary?'

For Agamben – whose thinking on this is very deeply influenced and shaped by Benjamin, even to the point of a shared vocabulary at times – the contemporary (essentially Agamben's different word for what I have been calling the now) is marked by a certain untimeliness or, better, an intrinsic and interiorized anachronism. The genuinely contemporary (by which Agamben means the genuinely contemporary individual) is one who is never at home in the present moment, one who, though alive to that moment, is not fully encapsulated or assimilated by it. In the same way as Arendt suggests that we are not fully encompassed by the present space of the world, so, likewise, for Agamben's contemporary, we are not fully assimilated to the temporal present:

> Those who are truly contemporary, who truly belong to their time, are those who neither perfectly coincide with it nor adjust themselves to its demands. They are thus in this sense irrelevant. But precisely because of this condition, precisely through this disconnection and this anachronism, they are more capable than others of perceiving and grasping their own time.[30]

It follows from this that 'contemporaries are rare'. Interestingly, as he works this through, Agamben starts to pick up a vocabulary that very directly echoes Benjamin. When Benjamin considered the relation of the French Revolution to ancient Rome (as we have already seen above), he compares the persistence of ancient Rome's now to fashion: The Revolution 'evoked ancient Rome the way fashion evokes costumes of the past. Fashion has a flair for the topical, no matter where it stirs in the thickets of long ago'.[31] Alongside this, let us place Agamben:

> Fashion can be defined as the introduction into time of a particular discontinuity that divides it according to its relevance or irrelevance, its being-in-fashion or no-longer-being-in-fashion. This caesura, as subtle as it may be, is remarkable in the sense that those who need to make note of it do so infallibly; and in so doing they attest to their own being in fashion. But if we try to objectify and fix this caesura within chronological time, it reveals itself as ungraspable. In the first place, the 'now' of fashion, the instant in which it comes into being, is not identifiable via any kind of chronometer … The time of fashion … constitutively anticipates itself and consequently is also always too late. It takes the form of an ungraspable threshold between a 'not yet' and a 'no more' … But the temporality of fashion has another character that relates it to contemporariness. Following the same gesture by which the present divides time according to a 'no more' and a 'not yet', it also establishes a peculiar relationship with these 'other times' – certainly with the past, and perhaps also with the future. Fashion can therefore 'cite', and in this way make relevant again, any moment from the past.[32]

This, though, is exactly what Augustine has already argued as a fundamental condition of the possibility of his making his *Confessions*. There, he cites his past – his sins – in order to transform the self through the transitory moment, breaking through in an event (or a 'moment of being', better understood as a 'moment of becoming') called a conversion, into a future that will differ from the past. This is, as it were, the opposite of Stanley Fish's characterization of

John Milton's Satan, 'surprised by sin'; here, we have Augustine 'surprised by the event that is grace', so to speak.[33] And this happens *all the time* and *at every moment* in *Confessions*.

Lyotard expresses this well. He points out that confessional writing is marked by a kind of rupture (*une fêlure*, as he calls it) between what I once was (a sinner) and what I now hope to be (redeemed). In these circumstances, conversion is not something that happens like a one-off thunderbolt; rather:

> *le coup de la conversion n'est pas un seul coup porté une fois pour toutes, et pas non plus une grêle de coups répétés. Non, l'écriture confessive porte la fêlure avec soi. Augustin confesse son Dieu et se confesse non parce qu'il est converti, il se convertit ou tente de se convertir tout en se confessant*

> the conversion moment is not a single once-and-for-all blow, and neither is it a hail of repeated blows. No, confessional writing carries a fracture within itself. Augustine confesses his God and confesses himself not because he has converted, but rather he converts or tries to convert while confessing himself[34]

He goes on, in a phrase that once again recalls the passage from Hegel's *Phenomenology* where we began, to state that, in these conditions, '*Il n'y aura plus pour le confessant une nuit et un jour, mais désormais du jour fêlé, de la nuit fêlée*' ('There will no more be a night followed by a day for he who confesses, but from now on only broken day, broken night').[35] In this way, Lyotard helps us realize part of the point and power of writing, and specifically of writing a confessional text: the resulting text is *not* the description of a conversion that has already taken place: the script actually *is* the conversion happening *in the present* – and that present approximates, as a time of the now, to the eternal.

In any confessional text, it seems axiomatic that the subject making the confession confirms her or his presence before the act itself: 'here I take my stand. I can no more,' as it were. That is to say, the confessing subject confirms that they are 'here, now'. The now in question, however, turns out to be a now that *must* be characterized as a moment of conversion, a kind of revolutionary moment between a past and a future. Yet it further turns out that such a now can have no actual *content*. In sum, the now exists as a formal requirement for the construction of a narrative that *explains* the conversion; and, in so doing, it reduces the status of the conversion – the status of history itself – from that of an event to that of a mere 'happening'. It is impossible to confess to an event.

Alias and survival: confessing in the name of another

There is a political dimension to this, obviously, and a useful starting-point for our investigation of the political effect of such a concentration on 'the now' is, as we will see, the work of Alain Badiou on Saint Paul. Let us first sum up where we are so far, for we have a series of interlinked problems that are generating the political issue and giving it a specific shape. Firstly, we have a now that simultaneously both *is* and *is not* now; secondly, we have an I that *is* and *is not* I (a conjunction of time and space, or an *ici-maintenant* that is and is not an *ici-maintenant*); and finally, we have the present characterized as a moment of transitory fashion, the site of change par excellence, but a change that, while *formally* there, nonetheless lacks substance or *content*, for the present moment must of necessity disappear. We can narrate the change, as it were; but we cannot live or experience it.

With all this 'being' and 'not being' at once, we could, of course, call this a Hamlet question: the soliloquy of his 'to be or not to be' in which the 'or' is not exclusive – in short, Hamlet wondering whether there is a certain being in not-being; and thus his speech is a meditation not about the possibilities of suicide but rather of being dead and alive both at once, a meditation on 'surviving oneself' or 'living on', as it were. If, like Paul, or like Augustine in Book 13, Chapter 11 of his *Civitas Dei*, we are bearing witness to an event that is called a resurrection from the dead, then we can call it the Christ question.[36] If resurrected, Christ both is and is not dead: he is and is not at once. He thus becomes precisely the kind of fulcrum figure that is at stake in our questioning of the now. It is for this reason, almost certainly, that Paul has become such a key figure in the work of Agamben, Badiou and (to a lesser extent) Slavoj Žižek in recent times.[37]

Badiou, the atheist, is interested in Paul for the simple reason that he sees in Paul one who is 'militant for truth'. Expressing this even more precisely, he sees in Paul a manifestation of the demand for truth precisely *as* militancy. That is to say, he sees in Paul a version of what Badiou himself thinks of as a kind of absoluteness of truth. This is important for Badiou's by now well-known stringent attitude to the question of truth, which he defines as a kind of 'fidelity to an event'; and, in Paul's case, the event in question is the Christ-event and the resurrection, the moment of being and not-being at once, the messianic moment of the now or *Jetztzeit*.

Badiou is opposed to the prevalent thinking in our contemporary state of affairs in which truth has been systematically reduced to forms of relativism. If my here-now is Night, and yours is Day, then (the relativist argument goes) we neither of us can have an absolute opening to truth as such; rather, we have truths that are conditioned precisely by our divergent subjectivities, by the particularity of our condition, our variant versions of, or historical conjunctures of, the *ici-maintenant*. Such a state of affairs would prioritize the particular over the general, as it were; and, in the end, the subscription to such relativism makes a *law* of the particular. Yet, if a law is always a law that legitimizes particulars, it can have no real force at all properly as a law; for laws must, by nature, have a generalizable applicability.

For Badiou, this is characteristic and typical of a more general state of affairs, in which the present world is actually hostile to truth or to '*les processus de vérité*' – 'methods of truth' – as he prefers to call it. He points out that we have seen what, in another context, Gianni Vattimo calls a kind of *kenosis*, an emptying out of substance from some key terms.[38] Badiou advances four key and (for him) axiomatic examples: a) art, he says, is reduced to culture; b) technique obliterates and replaces science; c) management replaces politics; and d) sexuality obliterates love. The result is that: 'Culture-technique-management-sexuality, which has the great merit of being assimilable to the market, and all of whose terms, further, signal a rubric of mercantile presentation, is the modern nominal recovering of the system of art-science-politics-love, which typically identifies the procedures of truth.'[39]

In this, then, truth is lost entirely under the existing market-capitalist procedures: it becomes a commodity whose value is open to negotiation and bargaining; and that value is always determined to some extent by the powerful, those who can 'buy' more truths, who can be in possession of more truths or who, more simply and crudely, can be more malleable with respect to their identity, as it were. Those market-procedures *produce* numerous 'identities', each of which can be aligned with a specific *ici-maintenant* or located subjectivity; and each now has a claim upon a series of what they will call truths, but what cannot ever be truths. In short, truth is reduced to a matter of the particularity of a localized 'opinion' and, paradoxically like Cardinal Newman a century earlier, Badiou is profoundly hostile to the proliferation of opinion, especially when such opinion becomes the basis for a supposed democracy.

According to Badiou, there is a kind of 'co-responsibility' between art and philosophy. The task of art is to produce truths and that of philosophy is to show them. To show these truths, if they are there in an artwork at all, is, he says, a 'very difficult task ... To show them means, essentially: to distinguish them from opinion. Such that the question today is this, and nothing but this ... is there anything other than our "democracies".'[40]

Our present state of affairs, argues Badiou, is characterized by the progressive reduction of the question of truth to the merest linguistic forms of judgement and opinion. For Badiou, this would be another way of describing what he sees as the scandal of a 'democracy' that encourages diversity of opinion and multiplicity of argumentations, while truth as such is ignored and circumvented. This prioritization of a democratic impulse, according to Badiou's philosophy, leads to cultural relativism, such that even mathematics is viewed as a 'western construct' (and this, despite even the manifest fact that much of what shapes mathematics is 'imported' from non-western cultures). The consequence of our accepting such cultural relativism is that we radically distinguish the subject from truth itself: truth becomes nothing more or less than the 'performance' or borrowing of superficial 'identities', names or opinions; and, surviving thus behind a succession of aliases, the subject as such avoids the confrontation with any 'fidelity to an event' or truth. The costs are massive.

As soon as we start thinking this way, we can start to identify sub-cultures (*sous-ensembles*, as Badiou calls them), each with their own particularized claims on their truths. Truth, in this, becomes a matter of contestation between particularities – and between particularized 'identities' – regardless of any absolute claim on historical eventuality or 'events'. In turn, this form of contestation of opinions reduces all criticism, indeed all thinking, to a series of *victimologies*. In this, the response, by those who lack authority, to the effect of power in the marketplace of truths is an assertion of victimhood and a call for recompense. It is the identity as victim that guarantees legitimacy (if not yet power). Yet the end result of this, as Badiou shows, is that each alleged identity, for each alleged victim, will have its own market or marketability:

> What an inexhaustible future for mercantile investment in this surging up, in the figure of redeemed communities and supposed cultural singularity: women, homosexuals, the disabled, Arabs! And then the infinite combinations of adjectives here: what a dawn! Black homosexuals, disabled Serbs, Catholic paedophiles, moderate Islamists, married priests, young green managers, oppressed unemployed, the already-old-young. Every time, a new social image authorizes new products, specialist magazines, adequate commercial centres, 'free' radio stations ... and so on.[41]

Badiou argues that in this state of affairs – a state of affairs that he characterizes as 'barbaric' and entirely consistent with the logic of capital – truth is systematically and organically simply impossible.[42] This state is 'organically without truth', as he puts it.[43] Paul, while noting social and cultural difference, is completely opposite to all this, according to Badiou; and it is this that attracts Badiou to him, and to his militancy for a truth that transcends relativist positioning, a truth that is *not conditioned by identity*, identity-politics, or a truth that is produced by the mere presence of the *je* or of the *ici-maintenant*. Rather, in Paul, truth is a matter of being faithful to the declaration of an event; and the event in question is that of the 'Christ-event' and the resurrection.

After Paul, then, asks Badiou, can we re-found any relation between truth – a truth that has a greater substance than mere opinion or judgement – and the subject at all? Truth, here, is an event *independent of my identity*. It follows from this that 'I' cannot 'tell' the truth, as it were: truth is not a matter of my speaking at all in that sense.[44] Badiou explains this by having recourse not to the question of particularity but rather to that of what he calls singularity (and what he will eventually call a 'universal singularity').

He rehearses the claim that, for Paul, truth is a matter of being faithful to the declaration of an event. Two things follow:

> First, truth being of the order of an event, or of the order of that which comes to pass, is therefore singular. It is neither structural, nor axiomatic, nor legal.

No available generality can give an account of it, nor could it structure the subject which lays claim to it. There could not possibly be therefore any law of truth. Further, truth being inscribed with effect from a declaration that is essentially subjective, no pre-constituted sub-group underpins it, nothing communitarian or historically established lends its substance to this process. Truth is diagonal with regard to all communitarian sub-groups, it does not authorize itself from a basis in any identity and (this is obviously the most delicate point) nor does it constitute one.[45]

With these two consequences in mind, Badiou removes truth from the question of identity-politics (and vice versa, in fact). Truth, then, is not a function of a linguistic proposition whose validity can be tested by being aligned with or placed alongside a non-linguistic fact. Nor is it a matter of who is speaking or of where the discourse comes from (these being now Foucauldian or Barthesian questions that have no claim on truth at all). This truth or fidelity to the declaration of an event – a *process* of truth for Badiou – is something that cannot recognize degree either. Either something is true or it is not. The result is that either you declare the truth and live with it or you remain outside of truth, and thus forever a stranger to it.[46]

Badiou's position up to this point seems relatively uncontestable. He has made it abundantly clear that a certain kind of relativism leads to an identity-politics in which the production of identities, each armed with their 'truths', leads simply to an enhancement of the capitalist marketplace. It would follow in this that the contemporary demand for confessional culture, all the way from demands for 'transparency' in public life to daytime TV shows where individuals parade stereotypically dramatized versions of their personal lives, is entirely consistent with a market-capitalism. If this is so, then confession is simply a literary and cultural mode that requires conformity with preset identities, identities that are given to individuals through established cultural norms; and the I that 'confesses' is necessarily simply playing out a role, their confession ripe for consumption in a marketized society. Is a more genuine confession – a confession that is informed by the necessities of *conversion* and difference or change rather than conformity and identity – at all possible?

At the core of this is the way in which Badiou deals with the great question of modernity: how do we reconcile the claims of the particular with the general; or, better perhaps, how do we *persuade* someone who does not share my particular view that it is not simply a particular view but rather a universalizable truth? That is to say, how do we *convert* others – as Saul/Paul was converted, as Augustine was converted – to the universalizable truth?

Yet we can also see the difficulty clearly emerging. Insofar as truth is not a matter for the subject, then one cannot 'tell' the truth; or, to put it slightly differently, one cannot possibly 'confess'. At the same time, insofar as truth is indivisible, insofar as one is either 'in' the truth or 'outside' of it, then *all* that one can do is to 'confess' or to be of a particular singular confession. We will use this difficulty to prise open further the issue of democracy and its relation to confession.

It has long been a commonplace that one way of thinking about aesthetics and its importance for a philosophy of modernity is to see its fundamental question as one in which we seek to regularize the claims of the particular against the universal. For Francis Hutcheson in the early eighteenth century, for example, beauty was described as a 'variety within uniformity' (or vice versa): that is, a specific particularity noted as particular or varied (and thus distinguished from the universal or uniform) while still being identifiably part of that universal or uniformity. For Badiou, this is an error. In fact, Badiou claims, these are not opposites but precisely part of the same intrinsic whole or structure. Against them, he finds what he calls not just singularity but a 'universal singular'.

This, he argues, is what allows us to assert a truth that is not based on opinion, democracy or even the subject who 'tells' the truth. The subtitle of his book on Paul, we should recall, is *La fondation de l'universalisme* – the foundation of universalism. However, given that this universalism depends upon the fidelity to an event, it becomes less a universalism and more a fundamentalism. For what happens when I am certainly faithful to an event, and you are too, but the events in question differ? In fact, it seems, Badiou is in some ways evading the problem that Lyotard once identified as that of a differend. A differend arises when two competing claims upon truth, each entirely reasonable within their own regimes of discourse, enter into a conflict with each other, and when we cannot find a third and overarching regime of discourse within whose terms both parties to the dispute can operate. It is a kind of impasse in thought or in argument. Badiou's position circumvents this, essentially by claiming a more fundamental viability for one of the potential parties: one event, as it were, has a greater claim on universalizability, or, in Badiou's terms, one *singularity* is *universal*.

Such a condition or claim for a singular universal is close to totalitarian. Against it, I will pose here the vexed question of the democratic space; or better, since we speak of the now, the democratic *moment*.

The moment and democracy

In my opening section here, I indicated that, for Augustine, the moment of the I, the 'here-now', is, in a certain sense, evacuated of content; it has a formal being, but, insofar as that being is characterized by transition, conversion or *becoming*, it can have no stable essence. Here, I want to see what happens if we try to consider the confessional moment precisely as a moment that *can* have a material and historical substance; and the effect of this will be to give us an idea of the relation of confession to democracy.

Jacques Rancière is useful here. In his essay on 'Politique et identité', he indicates that, in the frame of identity-politics, what happens is that '*on donne la parole aux gens uniquement dans le cadre d'une identité qu'ils auraient à réaliser ou même à exprimer'* ('a voice is granted to people solely within the framework of an identity that they would have to realize or even to express').[47] We certainly bring those who have been silent into voice, as it were: we try to legitimize and to authorize; but it is an alleged identity – not a subject – that is authorized thereby. Now, argues Rancière, correctly, *'la citoyenneté n'est pas la défense de sa culture ou de son groupe d'appartenance'* ('citizenship is not the defence of one's culture or of the group to which one belongs').[48]

Culture, we should note firstly, is not a state of affairs but rather an event, a 'something-that-happens'. It is episodic and rare. Further, culture is culture precisely because it *converts*: it is edifying, a moment of transformation or growth, *Bildung*.[49] As Rancière has it, *'la culture est toujours une forme de désidentification : la possibilité de parler autre chose que la langue de ses aïeux et de son groupe d'appartenance ou d'intérêt'* ('culture is always a form of dis-identification : the possibility of speaking otherwise than in the language of one's forebears and of one's community- or interest-group'). If there is a public sphere (or a possibility of democracy) at all, it is the space in which we speak other than what we are, in which we can differ from our forebears or from the identity that we have 'inherited' from the past. For Rancière, without this, politics itself does not even exist. If it is the case that confession is of necessity conversion, then we are close to saying that confession – but confession of *that which we are and are not at once* – is intrinsic to culture.

This is important for one who will want to salvage the public sphere as a *full* space, as a space with actual and material content, and not just the kind of 'transitional' formal and empty space that characterized Augustine's idea of 'the present'. This is, as it were, the crowded agora and not the formal but uninhabited piazza. However, it is not the agora simply as a space to be colonized by the market; rather, it is an agora whose very instability is of its essence. Badiou's position leaves us either in a totalitarian mode of conformity, or simply silent. If we reject this (while acknowledging its force as a critique of identity-politics), we can move further, beyond the limitations of identity itself.

In his posthumously published book, *The Memory Chalet*, Tony Judt reflects on what he calls 'edge people', those with 'identities' that are usually characterized as minority or tangential to the mainstream or, in my terms here, peripheral to the agora. He invites us to consider the response to this in the life of the academy or cultural criticism; and he points out that 'Undergraduates today can select from a swathe of identity studies: "gender studies," "women's studies," "Asian-Pacific-American studies," and dozens of others.' His argument against this is that these programmes encourage students 'to study *themselves* – thereby simultaneously negating the goals of a liberal education and reinforcing the sectarian and ghetto mentalities they purport to undermine'. The counter-desire – the democratic desire – would be one where, instead of confirming identity and conforming to established norms for that identity, we try to find ways of seeking alterity, difference or change: that is, the democratic moment is that moment where identity becomes filled with *becoming*, with a becoming that is 'confessed' as an act of conversion.

Judt goes on to point out, as we would expect from a historian, that:

> Most people [in the United States] no longer speak the language of their forebears or know much about their country of origin, especially if their family started out in Europe. But in the wake of a generation of boastful victimhood, they wear what little they do know as a proud badge of identity: you are what your grandparents suffered.[50]

The assumption of such historical victimhood is, of course, a proud denial of the present moment and of its possibilities for change, difference, confessional conversion. The democratic impulse is not one where we 'confess' to a pre-existing or normative identity, given to us by the voices of the past or the dead, nor to a stable identity at all; rather, the democratic filling of the agora is what happens when we enter that agora in pursuit of conversion, change and difference, when the I is identical-and-different at once.

A major problem with identity-politics in the end is that it atomizes the political will and its community. If we endlessly multiply identities, all we do is: a) give capitalism more markets; b) struggle among ourselves for victimhood (is one more of a victim – and does one have more counter-hegemonic, or simply *critical* legitimacy – if one identifies as Irish *and* a woman, say; or are these both trumped by being working-class or homosexual or both?). While the political right stands firm, and assumes the identity of confession with a transparency that encourages only conformity to pre-established historical norms, the left squabbles among itself for authentic being, an authenticity that is given to identities by marketization, by advertising, by capital itself. In short, leftist 'confession' is every bit as conservative as the very rightist ideologies that it seeks to confront. Political identity then becomes evacuated of content. It is imperative that we return content to the now of lived experience, the now of a conversion of identity, the now that depends upon the democratic community, a community that is always evolving, the historical still-to-come.

2

Official Identity and Clandestine Experience

Introduction

When Vincent Descombes ponders what it means to be a historical agent, he states pithily that 'To act in history is to work at *not being* what one is'; and this – acting in the world of *history* – is unlike the world of *nature*, where, as he puts it, 'being signifies identity'.[1] In essence, in that explicit opposition of worlds of history and of nature, we can see here the remnants of a rather Romantic sensibility. Descombes pits an established or stable world of exteriority (a 'state of affairs', as it were, the world as 'given' or '*was der Fall ist*' – 'everything that is the case' – in Ludwig Wittgenstein's terms: the world where being signifies identity in the form of immutable self-sameness or self-coincidence) against a world of interior consciousness that is characterized by *imagination* or by the possibility of thinking oneself as other than one actually is. In his formulation, acting in history is essentially trying to set up conditions where the world of imagination impinges on the world of exterior nature; and the desired result is a change that must, of necessity, be at best a change in the *relation* between interiority and exteriority, and a change, therefore, in the self or subject (working at 'not being' what we are).

The two realms are distinct, distinguished by this power of simultaneously seeing things 'as they are' and also 'as they might otherwise be'. Exteriority, in this, is fundamentally immune to consciousness; and, consequently, any change that occurs is fundamentally a change in consciousness and thus a change or difference that is now constitutive, paradoxically, of the identity of the subject. It is the 'I' of consciousness, and not the world of which the 'I' is conscious, that is the locus of change. In simple terms, we usually just call this something like reflecting on the world or thinking about one's place in history. This neo-Romantic structure, however, is not straightforward; and it essentially gives us the predicament that we usually call 'modernity' – as we will see in what follows.

In the logic advanced by Descombes, 'The historical protagonist *is* insofar as he acts, and he acts insofar as he is always *being different*.'[2] Consequently, we have an ostensibly counter-intuitive understanding of identity, as a sameness predicated on a difference, or as difference camouflaged under the sign of self-coinciding. Lurking behind this is the rather simple fact that there is a potential contradiction within the very concept of identity. On one hand, it must be defined in terms precisely of this 'self-sameness' or the coinciding of two (or more) instantiations of 'I'; on the other hand, the mere fact that there *are* two (or more) such instantiations – Virginia Woolf called them 'moments of being' – indicates that the 'I' exists in time.[3]

Therefore, identity considered as a characterization of an 'I' that exists in time – a historical or secular subject, then – *must* acknowledge that such coincidence is simply impossible: by definition, the 'I' in history, the 'I' as a material 'somewhat', enters into the realm of self-differing. 'Self-sameness' in the secular realm is anathema. The prevailing neo-Romantic sensibility, as revealed by Descombes, construes the relation of self to history in *spatial* terms (interiority of self set against an exteriority of world); but we should rather see that what is primarily at stake here is the *temporality* of identity. It is temporality that causes the problem and, in revealing the paradoxical and problematic nature of the mode of thought in question here, Descombes construes that problem essentially as one grounded in identity as the locus of a necessary deconstruction.[4]

Here is our conundrum, as expressed in terms of formal logic, by Descombes:

> there is identity not only, as formal logic would have it, between identity and identity, but between difference and difference; there is a certain *being* in *not-being*. Now, is there the slightest difference between the identity of identity with identity, and the identity of difference with difference? Certainly not. For there is no more *identity* between identity and identity than there is between difference and difference. And there is no more *difference* between difference and difference than there is between identity and identity. And yet identity and difference are clearly different types of relation. Yes, certainly. So the *identity* between, on the one hand, the identity of identity and identity, and on the other, the identity of difference and difference, is the very factor of *difference* between identity and difference.[5]

This linguistic wrestling is the attempt to grapple with identity as a historical – and thus temporally mutable – concept. Yet it also implies much more. If, for example, one considers identity as having some relation to the narrative of a life, then, of logical necessity, one has to consider the intimate relation of identity to *autonomy*, to the possibility that a human agent acts in history, and is neither simply a product nor merely an effect of that history: there is at least a dialectical relation between consciousness and exteriority. Against this, however, is the observation that we usually consider that it is precisely a pre-existing identity of consciousness that grounds the specific action that an agent undertakes in bringing about the state of affairs constitutive of exteriority at any given time: the imagination working on nature, as it were. I act as I do, we say, because of who I am (and we call that 'authenticity', as opposed to hypocrisy); and I am as and who I am because of the very actions that define me. The issue lying behind this is one that is fundamental to any theory of identity that sees identity as being in any way related to the social at all: it is the question of the possibility of *change*. Is change possible and, if so, how is it effected?

The suggestion that I am making here is that, in our current prevailing modes of critical thought, our identities, far from being autonomously determined, are, in fact, typically *given to* us, and that they are given to us as a means of officially delimiting and regulating our possible behaviours. Our identity is, as it were, 'official', given to us as a matter of office and limiting our possibilities precisely to the circumscriptions delineated by that office. It follows from this, further, that any genuinely historical act that we would commit is necessarily clandestine, a breaking with or a nonconformity with our office.

To put this another way, we are actually being denied the possibility of acting as autonomous historical agents precisely, and paradoxically, by being ascribed an 'official identity', an identity that precludes the possibility of our having the narrative of a life, and thus also precludes the possibility of our acting as autonomous historical agents, precisely at the moment when our alleged identity is being confirmed by our actions.

The tongue-twisting formulation of Descombes is one that enacts a tenet of deconstruction; but what it shows here, most importantly, is that, in our prevailing modes of thought – caught up in the modernity that has its roots in a certain Romantic sensibility – identity is itself identified as a form of self-sameness, or that identity can be described properly as *conformity to a rule*. Identity is established as this conformity to a rule – even if one identifies oneself as difference or as constantly self-differentiating: even in that extreme case, as Descombes helps show, constantly self-differing would itself become the very rule to which the self conforms. The important thing is the *rule*: identity is a matter for *regulation*. As Hamlet can show us, there is a certain determinacy in indeterminacy. In philosophical terms, Søren Kierkegaard shows the same thing when he points out that to defer a decision is in itself the very enacting and carrying out of a decision; or as Lyotard would have it, the decision to remain silent in the face of history is itself constitutive of a historical act: even a silence is a mode of *enchaînement*[6] or linking with what has gone before, with what has been given to us as our present historical condition.

There is, then, a 'law of identity'; and, as we know, identity is first and foremost a matter of legal substance and importance. The demand for identity is a demand for one's papers; and these *formal* and *official* papers have an enormous power and, more importantly, an authority and standing that is abstract and determining. The paper, in its very formal substance, is more important than the historical individual carrying it, at least in terms of what we can call the *verification* and authentication of identity; and the entitlement to an identity is, in fact, always something that is to be authenticated rather than something that is to be understood. I'll return to this question of the relative importance of verification in relation to authenticity later. The passport – the abstract and 'official' identity – as it were, *is* the identity, even when the passage of time and experience means that one no longer looks like the face pictured on it. Official identity operates at a remove from actuality, from an experience that is now relegated to the realm of the clandestine. This is the condition that is now eminently recognizable in our fully bureaucratized societies, wherein so-called 'modernization' – and modernity itself – becomes constituted precisely by abstract bureaucratization and 'management' of everyday life.

This present argument, however, is determinedly on the side of the *sans papiers*, as it were, the untitled, those who are 'not entitled' or who have no identity, no passport or papers.[7] Another way of putting this, and in some ways more importantly (at least as far as literary or aesthetic criticism is concerned) the argument that I will advance here is on the side of literary *experience*.[8] In the first section, I explore what is at stake in the relation between identity and experience. In this, we will see that, in shorthand terms, identity *is* form and that *formal* identities have little time for any specific or actual *content*. To gain access to such content, my next section will show that we need to find a way of describing the priority of our 'becoming' over our 'being'. Following from this, I will contend that the expression of an identity – our making it available as a public and social entity – depends upon a fundamental act of confession. In this, we will see the importance of identity as something constituted by forms of change; or, perhaps better, we will see the identity of the self as something necessarily predicated not just on self-criticism but upon a form of confession that is intrinsically tied to the kinds of conversion discussed in my opening chapter. In the final section, I will explore the stakes of this for a politics, and especially for the political dimensions of our predominant forms of literary or cultural criticism.

Experience

In his great essay, 'De l'expérience', the thirteenth essay in Book 3 of his great and constantly evolving and mutating work of *Essais*, Montaigne starts his exploration by stating, first of all, that 'There is no desire more natural than the desire for knowledge'; and that, when reason fails to give us such knowledge, we turn to empirical evidence, or experience, 'which is a feebler and less worthy means' of gaining that knowledge than is given to us by the operations of reason. In line with classical modes of rhetoric, he reaches immediately for an example.[9] He turns to an explicit address to the law and gives us the example of the French legal process in his day. France, he says, has more laws than the rest of the world put together; and yet, no matter how many laws we have, we can never really encapsulate the infinite variety of possible legal cases. That is to say, no matter how many laws we bring about, we can never hope to cover the potentially infinite variety of possible cases or historical events.

What he is getting at is that the judge, in every new case, will have to exercise a judgement which, at least in some particulars, will need to be made without recourse to previous laws, and that will therefore radically implicate the judge in the very act of judging, 'here-now' as it were.[10] This, however, leads to a potential series of predicaments regarding judgement and justice; and he turns to the possibility of what we would nowadays call a 'miscarriage of justice'. Here, he says, is one case from his own time:

> Certain men are condemned to death for a murder; their sentence, being agreed upon and determined, though not pronounced. At this point the judges are informed by the officers of an inferior court in the neighbourhood that they are holding some prisoners who openly confess to this murder, and throw unquestionable light upon the whole affair. And yet these judges deliberate whether they ought to interrupt or defer the execution of the sentence passed upon the first prisoners. They discuss the unusualness of the case, and the precedent it may set up for the reversal of judgements; for the sentence being juridically correct, the judges have no reason to change their minds. In short, these poor devils are sacrificed to the forms of justice.[11]

The particularity – the historical or material *actuality* – of individual humans is to be ignored in order to preserve the *form* of justice, not its content. In this case, we have a situation where the judgement is made; and what is at stake is not so much the identity of a murderer as the identity of the law: as Descombes might have it, the necessarily 'natural-seeming' or self-evidentiary naturalness of the law itself: the identity of the law with the law. When experience in the form of real history calls the judgement into question, by providing the *content* of a countervailing or critical experience, then that experience has to be discounted in the interests of conformity to a rule: in this case, preserving the *office* of the law, and perhaps yet more importantly that of the *officer of the law*.

This, then, is my first example of an 'official identity': the identity of an officer of the law. It is an identity that is established by the silencing of experience, by the placing of experience into the area of the clandestine, the underground, the invisible or illegitimate. The identity of the judge triumphs over the facts of experience or of history, truth and reality. In what way can this identity be 'true', or 'real', or materially historical, therefore? In what way can it be a *substantive* identity or an identity based upon the material facts of historical agency or existence?

By extension, I want to argue that the same thing happens in literary and cultural criticism: the identity of Montaigne's judge maps directly on to the identity of the contemporary critic (my second example: the official identity of the critic). This is, of course, what we have learned to call the form of criticism that is shaped by identity-politics; and it helps explain the triumph of what we can call, after Philippe Lejeune, an 'autobiographical pact' in criticism. The consequence of this pact is that criticism becomes an act of signing one's name.[12] It is a matter of style, of the reduction of the self as a location of experience to the pure emptiness of style, or to my 'office' as (say) Irish or working-class or specifically sexed and so on. In these, I am no longer simply

Irish, but I am instead 'an Irishman'; nor am I sexed in terms of my behaviour in life, but rather I become the sign that represents 'the gay' or 'the straight'; nor am I an electrician, but rather a representative of working-class interests in general, and so on. In short, not even my proper autobiography is told in this, for I become not an individual but the *sign* of an individual, a generalized representative of an office. Putting matters bluntly, we are all bureaucrats now, in this form of criticism.[13]

In short, the attention to an identity-politics, paradoxically, reduces experience to what I can now call my 'official' identity: an identity that is focused on the priority of being over becoming; and an identity, therefore, that is devoid of historical substance – perhaps even when the identity is given precisely as political, as in the case of an identity characterized or described in terms of social class.

In the middle of the last century, Leslie A. Fiedler pondered something similar in relation to abstract art, considered then as an art that was at a remove from material historical realities, or at least at a tangent to the idea that art might offer any function of representation. In an article called 'Archetype and signature', he argued that: 'The abstract painter, for instance, does not, as he sometimes claims really "paint paint," but signs his name. So-called abstract art is the ultimate expression of personality.'[14]

In this, Fiedler was perplexed by what was going on especially in the visual arts, and especially in so-called abstract expressionism. His point was that the artist, by endlessly repeating the same configurations on the canvas, was essentially making themselves 'recognizable' immediately. If you walk into an art gallery and see a painting that consists of large vertical lines of irregular width, joined together by irregularly placed ovals set in between the lines and touching them, then you know that you are looking at a 'Robert Motherwell' – or at least at a 'fake Robert Motherwell' – for all of Motherwell's paintings in this period are essentially revisitings of this configuration. Rectangles of colour with rough edges mean 'Mark Rothko'; or parallel lines successively moving towards the centre of the canvas but always following the shape of the canvas mean 'Frank Stella'.

For Fiedler, this explains abstract art in some ways: the painter paints a signature, and we are edging towards Andy Warhol as a kind of 'normative' art or art-value. It is perhaps, then, less of a surprise that a critical attitude in the years after this – broadly during the 1960s – witnesses essays of one kind or another charting the alleged 'death' of the author: if the prevailing mood is one that sees art as the celebration of the very being of an author, in the expressing of their name and identity, then it is not surprising that criticism – especially a criticism that sees itself as 'oppositional' – will want to call that identity – or more precisely that *being* – into question.[15]

Fiedler was writing predominantly about abstract visual art, of course. Yet the same can be said of any art that lends itself to repetition and thus to parody. Consider the stylistic trope of the short sentence in Ernest Hemingway, or the extended sub-clauses in a Proustian sentence, or the circumlocutions of Henry James. It is important that these styles are in some way unique, however. We might think of Dashiell Hammett or Raymond Chandler 'learning' from Hemingway; but, despite the preference for the short sentence, there is no way that they could be mistaken one for the other: each 'signs' their style. Likewise, although Claude Simon has sentences that, like some of Proust's, traverse page after page punctuated only by commas, with an endless proliferation of sub-clauses, the two writers are clearly distinct one from the other: their 'signatures' differ, and they constitute different events, so to speak.[16]

In all cases, what is at stake is the triumph of a style over a substance (and, later, we will start to consider more fully the nature of these 'substances'). In the terms of the present argument, what is at stake is the triumph of form over content to the extent that the content can be evacuated of primary significance. It is the *form* of the work that gives it an identity, and that even constitutes identity for its author and its reader. This last point is important: the allegedly stable identity of an author, standing over their stylized text or signature, also serves the function of imputing to the reader an ostensibly stable identity as well. The reader, receiving the autograph of the writer, knows where they stand in relation to the writer, takes their bearings from that stability, and finds their own name thereby: a different inflection of Lyotard's *Signé Malraux*,[17] as it were.

Perhaps one further observation worth adding here is that such a view narrows and delimits the possibilities for the artist. Her or his biography can no longer recognize other and disparate experiences that would result in different types of work. It is as if a biography is being reduced to a persona or personality. This, of course, is one way of describing what is probably the single most dominant form in contemporary popular culture: the identity that is given in the form of 'celebrity'. In this, an *ethos* or disposition, with all its mutable content and responsibility for decision-making or judgement, is reduced to the merest identity-image. At this level, identity is entirely consistent with a capitalist ethos that thrives on 'branding', the marking of ownership and servitude on one's skin. I will address the politics of this in the final section of this present chapter.

Now, one way of describing this prevailing state of affairs – that is, the condition of criticism in which identity and identity-politics become a grounding for value or truth or significance – would be to say that, in a modernity that has favoured abstraction over experience as a means of verifying truth, the *forms* of the law of identity are more important than the *content* of that law. For Jürgen Habermas, this is characterized as a kind of legitimation crisis: a state of affairs in which 'the belief in legitimacy shrinks to a belief in legality; the appeal to the legal manner in which a decision comes about suffices'.[18]

In such a modernity, legitimacy shrinks to the point where it becomes mere legalism, the proper and decorous observation of the offices. It is, in its purest form, the triumph of that form of bureaucracy that sees identity as something to be *managed* rather than to be represented or lived. And, by working within the rules like this, we lose our *ethos* and, with that, we also lose any ethical prerogative that might shape the possibilities of our being together or recognizing each other's identities in a commonality of experience.

If we can now say that identity is a matter of conformity, and if we can also add that this conformity is (as the word suggests) not only conformity to a rule but also conformity to a formal practice (especially to a formal *legal* practice), then we can conclude at this stage of the argument that there is indeed an intimate relationship between form and identity. Identity, in short, is a formal matter: identity *is* form; or, alternatively put, form is that which gives identity its specifics. Further, we might also say that identity, as we currently construe it – that is, as a neo-Romantic negotiation of the exteriority of a material world by the interiority of consciousness – is intrinsically *unethical* or at least that identitarianism is inimical to any ethical position or philosophy. This is all the more true precisely when we confound ethics with morality.

It is all forms of individual particularity – the very stuff that should be constitutive of identity – that get lost in all of this. I am not the 'real' Andy Warhol, so to speak; rather I am 'Andy Warhol', or *the* Andy Warhol (the definite article gives the game away), essentially a mythic creature and thus one doomed forever to repeat the 'same' aspects of existence. In short, such a creature is doomed to be expelled from historical existence, never allowed to 'become' anything and reduced to the status of 'merely' being. Specificity, which is precisely that which would counter mythology, is erased in these formulations. Yet more precisely, the specific material and historical events of experience are exactly what are occluded in this. Experience is reduced to nothing, evacuated of substantive content.

Becoming

Against all of the foregoing, we might begin by making a simple observation: the identity of an entity that acts in history is complex and requires an unusual ontology. Fundamentally, the attempt to grasp an identity-in-history – the identity of a living individual – is conditioned by the fact that such an identity is of necessity elusive. It is never a *being*, always a *becoming*; and, accordingly, if we are to grasp it, we need some understanding of an ontology that is grounded in becoming rather than in being. Deleuze offers us something of the required vocabulary here; and, in this section, I will argue for a criticism that takes seriously the issue of becoming, considered in terms of material or historical *force*.

In 1963, while reviewing Jean Rosset's structuralist work, *Forme et signification*, Derrida realized that the great strength of the structuralism of the epoch was that it dealt expertly with matters precisely of form. In his review, 'Force et signification' – incidentally one of the great founding documents of poststructuralism – Derrida did not oppose form to content, but rather he set form against force. He contended that, as he put it, '*Form* fascinates when one no longer has the force to understand force from within itself. That is, to create. This is why literary criticism is structuralist in every age, in its essence and destiny.'[19] Put succinctly, structuralism (and we can now say all forms of identitarian critique, critique that prioritizes form-as-identity) triumphs when one reduces the material realities of force to the merest *significations* of force, to stable representations or images of force. Here, 'force' is Derrida's term for what I have been calling the material contents of history or of experience.

Gilles Deleuze was also interested in force. With a brevity that is perhaps overly crude or simplistic, one might say that Deleuze saw history and material realities precisely as the play of forces, as in physics, forces that lead to *arrangements* of *events*: *des agencements* that are constitutive of *les événements*. For Deleuze, the concept of the event is absolutely central to an ontology of becoming, and thus to any ontology that is aware of the actual facts of material history, the grounding *conditions* or even *preconditions* and thus determinants of the possibilities of our being.

It is important to be precise here, on two counts at least. Firstly, we might say that 'becoming precedes being', so to speak: it is not the case that we *are* something and only then become something else; rather, the change that we call 'becoming' is the very condition of the possibility of our being at all. Secondly, the event here, in Deleuze, is not a definite something that is occasioned or brought about in a world of supposed 'exteriority' by an 'interiority' of consciousness that can determine material conditions in the world. The world of an alleged exteriority 'as such' does not in fact exist; rather, perhaps better, it exists only as an aspect of the arrangement or *agencement* of forces that are episodic and radically singular.

The point of these observations requires some further explanation. Deleuze takes a good deal of his philosophy from Henri Bergson and Baruch Spinoza. From Bergson, he derives the importance of *time* and of *movement*. Yet he does not remain satisfied simply to rehearse the Bergsonian notion of *durée*, duration, but prefers to give it a specific inflection. Duration, he says, 'is a becoming that endures, a change that is substance itself'.[20] This is already a major step. He then takes from Spinoza a very particular sense of *difference* and of *singularity*. The 'scandal' of Spinoza, as Deleuze sees it, is the scandal of dismissing any idea of the world as a duality at all, especially and above all a duality between a world of interiority and one of exteriority. 'According to the *Ethics* … what is an action in the mind is necessarily an action in the body as well, and what is a passion in the body is necessarily a passion in the mind. There is no primacy of one series over the other.'[21] Deleuze's ontology is entirely an ontology of becoming rather than of being.

Spinoza began his *Ethics* with a meditation on the identity of God and, as Deleuze indicates, he is especially engaged by the question of the substantiality of God. It is right at this early point in Spinoza that Deleuze finds a notion of what we might call absolute or primary difference: not difference that defines itself in opposition to something else, something 'self-same' or self-identical; but difference, rather, as an absolute condition of the very possibility of identity, so to speak. Spinoza's case, at the opening of his *Ethics*, is that God is at once infinite (and thus containing an infinity of possible attributes) while at the same time unique (and thus not amenable to re-presentation). As Michael Hardt puts it in his excellent book on Deleuze: 'God is both unique and absolute.'[22] For Deleuze, this offers a consistency with his reading of time and movement in Bergson, for it offers a version of substance that is *intrinsically different*: not 'different *from*' something else, for there *is no* something else (God is infinite), and not differing from itself in time (God is one thing). Rather, this is pure difference as constitutive of the substance of being.

The result, for Deleuze, once the theological issue is removed from the equation, is that one is never in a state of being (a being that would allow me to give an account of 'my identity'), but only becoming (in which 'I' never quite coincide with myself, since my temporal condition precludes any such possibility, and since the 'I' is a product of the movement or arrangement of forces). 'Being' would equate with death and is negative; 'becoming' is equivalent to living and is affirmative, joyful. Moreover, becoming is thus also the matter of material history itself: living.

This means, though, that all things are necessarily always in flux. In fact, it is even more radical than that: anything that we might want to identify as a specific 'somewhat' (or some 'thing') is nothing more than a pure instantiation of a play of forces that makes the somewhat *as it 'is'* an interruption in the otherwise continuous flow of becomings (the *is* constituted by the very *is-not* that is an elemental basis of differential identity); yet more, the perceiver of this 'somewhat' is themselves but an accident of the play of forces that phenomenologically brings the perception into line, however momentarily, with the perceived. To perceive is momentarily to arrest the flow of becomings, the play of forces that constitutes history, as it were. Within this, therefore, any 'event' – like the event of perception – is itself what we might call an 'accidental condition' of history.

There is, thus, no 'I' other than the play of forces that allows me, at whatever moment, to pretend to arrest the flow of becoming. This has a massive effect on the notion of agency (including, primarily, confessional agency) and, beyond that, of freedom. This is a way of describing how Deleuze thinks of 'events'. At one level, events are what constitute history; but, according to Deleuze, we must be careful to distinguish events from spectacle. The event takes place in what he thinks of as '*le temps mort*':

the event is inseparable from dead time. It's not even that there is dead time before and after the event, rather that dead time is in the event, for example the instant of the most brutal accident confounds itself with the immensity of empty time in which you see it arriving, as a spectator of that which has not yet happened, in a long suspense … Groethuysen said that every event was, as it were, in the time when nothing happens.[23]

Now, the event, therefore, is not something that is determined or even predetermined by a consciousness; rather, the emergence of the consciousness is that which comes about precisely as a result of the encounter that *is* the event itself, the play of forces that constitutes this 'dead time', a time that is taken out of formal narrative but that allows for the constitution of a subject.

In many other philosophies or social theories, especially those based either upon forms of psychoanalysis or upon forms of 'identity-politics', the subject is often typically characterized and described by their desire. For Deleuze, such desire is not a matter of exerting a will upon exteriority, much less a matter of 'choice', either consumerist or existentialist – in short, the desire does not 'bring something about'. Again, the desire is that which is produced through the encounter that, in the first place, is constitutive of both subject and object, and constitutive of them *as* subject and object. What Deleuze is trying to do is to find a way of addressing *movement* as the fundamental form of ontology, but ontology considered as the conditions of our becoming rather than as being.

The result is the production of what we can call the accidental conditions of consciousness or of desire. It is important to note that we are not here talking of desire as a set of 'wants' or 'choices' based on lack or need or wish. Rather, this desire is a way of describing the product of force; and it is akin also to the kinds of unwanted desires that worried Augustine, those moments when he feared that he 'sinned' but only 'accidentally', as it were. The play of forces or the arrangement of forces that constitutes becomings-in-time is something that is itself in constant flux; and it thus produces desire simply as the condition of producing yet more arrangements, more becoming. In this way, desire can be thought of as a pure 'affirmation', the affirming of positive becoming; and the significance of this is that it flies directly in the face of most radical 'critical' thinking that derives from Hegel or from any notion of criticism as negation. Desire, here, is what philosophy – and, by extension, radical social theory – should be about: it is about the production of more becoming, more *concepts*. This – the 'production of concepts' – is indeed Deleuze's answer to the great question, 'what is philosophy?'[24]

Insofar as this desire is, then, the very production of an affirmation that constitutes the momentary instantiation of a subject, we can name it more conventionally as a mode of 'confession' or revelation. The confession in question, though, is here not the revelation of something that was occluded prior to its being narrated; rather, the confessing is the very elaboration of forces that constitute that subjectivity in the first place. Augustine famously asks '*cur confiteor?*' – why do I confess? Why indeed, given that God, by definition, already knows the contents of my consciousness and the history of my deeds. The Deleuzian reply might be something along the lines of *Confiteor ergo sumus*, meaning by this that I confess as a very condition of the possibility of my being at all, and any such being is always already situated in relation to other potential subjects or 'confessors'. It is to this that we can now turn more explicitly.

Confessional communications

My presupposition here is that – in some at least minimal fashion – the literary text is essentially an act of confession, that it is founded in a confession or revelation or 'expressing' of identity. Put more dramatically, we might say that every literary act is an act of nomination. That is where Montaigne starts in his advice '*au lecteur*' at the start of the *Essais*: 'I want my portrait here to be drawn after how I actually am, simple, natural and ordinary, without research or artifice: for it is I that I am painting. My faults will be clearly discernible, as will my unvarnished form, or at least to the extent that public reverence can accept these things.'[25]

It is also where Rousseau starts in his great text of self-identification, the *Confessions*: 'I have resolved on an enterprise which has no precedent, and which, once complete, will have no imitator. My purpose is to display to my kind a portrait in every way true to nature, and the man I shall portray will be myself.'[26]

It is what we find in more recent times in a poet such as Lowell, when he transcribes letters written by his intimate others, and puts them, with line-breaks, into *History* and, perhaps more troublingly, in *The Dolphin*:

Sometime I must try to write the truth,
but almost everything has fallen away
lost in passage when we said goodbye in Rome.
Even the licence of my mind rebels,
and can find no lodging for my two lives ...[27]

Is my doubt, last flicker of the fading thing,
an honorable subject for conversation?
Do you know how you have changed from the true you?
I would change my trueself if I could:
I am doubtful ...[28]

Texts such as these – and perhaps Lowell is a kind of extreme test case here, for it is here that we see the explicit introduction of real names, of real signatures, of people other than the writer himself, from the ends of private letters, brought into the text – are fundamentally dramatizing the predicament laid out for us back where we started the present meditation, in Descombes: how do we reconcile the identity of our being with the historical fact of our becoming? How can our experience (the realm of becoming) be constitutive of our proper identity (the stable and solid being, the proper name, on which we hang those experiences)? Yet this seems to be working also on the assumption that these texts explore specific and particular experiences.

Long before all this, in Augustine, we find the philosophical delineation of the predicament. Augustine begins his own *Confessions* with what is essentially a philosophical meditation on experience, considered in terms of an inner and outer space of the self. In Book 1, Chapter 2, Augustine tries to establish the proper relation between himself and God. Here is how he tries to wrestle with the idea of the spatial relation between himself and God:

> How shall I call upon my God for aid, when the call I make is for my Lord and my God to come into myself? What place is there in me to which my God can come, what place that can receive the God who made heaven and earth? Does this then mean, O Lord my God, that there is in me something fit to contain you? ... Or is it rather that I should not exist, unless I existed in you? For *all things find in you their origin, their impulse, the centre of their being.* This, Lord, is the true answer to my question. But if I exist in you, how can I call upon you to come to me?[29]

In passing, of course, we might see here the perfect illustration of what Karl Marx will eventually call 'alienation', that process worked out in *The German Ideology* and in some of his early philosophical papers, whereby the human individual creates something within themselves, and then expresses it as a really existing power outside of the self, and a power that now has to be obeyed. In all such cases, however, we are seeing that 'modern' framework whereby the question of identity is being construed essentially as a spatial question concerning the relations of interiority and exteriority, and how we regulate the competing claims to power and supremacy of each. For my own later purposes, yet more importantly we see the question of how the self is always alien to itself, always governed through alterity.

Fundamentally, the question for Augustine, as he begins his confessional text, is whether God exists within Augustine or whether Augustine exists within God: is God within or outside the self; and is the self outside of God or somehow held within God? Clearly, this affects the whole question of identity, of Augustine's identity. The *Confessions* is at once an exercise in distinguishing Augustine from God while at the same time identifying Augustine with God. It is for this reason that it *has* to be a '*conversion*' text, charting the distance travelled in moving from distinction to intimacy; and it is for this reason, further, that it is the original *Bildungsroman*. It is a conversion text because it must chart the movement in Augustine from a position of being distanced from God to one where he is intimate with God; and it is a *Bildungsroman* because it sees the narrative of this movement as a process of learning or development, *formation* as the French has it, coming towards truth from falsehood or deception.

As such a text, it must focus on a delineation of the self that is fundamentally shaped by two things: a) experience within the self; and b) the expression – the putting outside of the self – of a version of that experience. It is structured around the necessity of confession as revelation of an obscured interiority; and it helps start the process, in one reading, whereby that interiority is characterized as selfhood.

At the opening of this section, I suggested that every literary act is in some minimal sense an act of nomination. We can now clarify this further. An act of nomination essentially requires a scene of recognition, in which there are at least two subject positions or two positions that have the potential for subjectivity, for pronouncing the deictic 'I'. This, however, is essentially a confessional scene: a scene in which an 'I' presents itself or reveals itself before some other 'I': 'Call me Ishmael,' perhaps, would be the fundamental American version of this, as in Herman Melville.[30] In this, 'I' present myself *as if* something interior is 'ex-pressing' itself to an exteriority. However, we have already argued that such a spatialized version of this state of affairs is essentially limited and circumscribed by a 'modern' mentality, a mentality that leads to a construction of selfhood in which identity is set up in a contest between the human consciousness and a world of nature.

Hence, if we look more carefully at this state of affairs, we now see that a better way of thinking about it is to see that the 'I' in question is always already in a scene of recognition, but one where it is recognizing *itself*, and doing so *in time* and as a substantive differing, as Deleuze would have it. In short, the I recognizes itself as a name, as an identity, if and only if it constructs a *narrative* scene in which recognition (and misrecognition of itself) is possible. The self is that which confesses itself to itself; and this is why, in the case of Augustine, the question of who is inside whom (God within Augustine or vice versa) is resolved eventually as it is, as a question of *time* and not of space.

Early on in the text, Augustine ponders the fact of his infancy, which is now over, and so 'My infancy is long since dead', as he puts it, 'yet I am still alive.'[31] How can these two things be reconciled, he wonders, and finds the answer in the odd temporality of God:

> you are infinite and never change. In you 'today' never comes to an end; and yet our 'today' does come to an end in you, because time, as well as everything else, exists in you. If it did not, it would have no means of passing. And since your years never come to an end, for you they are simply 'today'. The countless days of our lives and of our forefathers' lives have passed by within your 'today'. From it they have received their due measure of duration and their very existence. And so it will be with all the other days which are still to come. But you yourself are eternally the same. In your 'today' you will make all that is to exist tomorrow and thereafter, and in your 'today' you have made all that existed yesterday and for ever before.[32]

That is how Augustine phrases things at the start. However, the entire point of the text of the *Confessions* is to find an intimacy with God, to come to a position now where God knows Augustine (for Augustine acknowledges that, as God knows everything, he already knows Augustine entirely), but rather to a position where Augustine knows and can name God, and, in so naming, find and name himself.

It is at the end of the text that we see the final recognition scene in Augustine. He has argued that much remains mysterious about the relation between himself and God; but in the very final paragraph, he presents himself as a man knocking at God's door, when 'Only then shall we receive what we ask and find what we seek; only then will the door be opened to us.'[33] The final meeting, then, is presaged at the end, but presaged as a narrative possibility in and through which the I finds itself as a subject in time; but also as a subject of a conversion, a change.

By this stage in the text, a significant change has taken place in Augustine. At the start, he had pondered the question of whether he was in God or God in him. Now, at the end, he sees things differently. Instead of there being a dialectic, as it were, between interiority and exteriority, Augustine sees the relation of himself to the world as one that is essentially *mediated* by the odd temporality of God's existence. In Book XIII, Chapter 38, he writes that, 'We see the things which you have made, because they exist. But they only exist because you see them'; so who is actually seeing these things? The answer comes: 'Outside ourselves we see that they exist, and in our inner selves we see that they are good. But when you saw that it was right that they should be made, in the same act you saw them made.'[34]

In this, an important distinction is being made. On one hand, there is God, for whom there is an intimacy between *logos* and *ergon*, such that the thinking of something *immediately* brings it about. Such an intimacy is identified with God for whom all time is eternally present: God has no *Bildung*, as it were: by definition, this intimacy, constitutive of the being of God, is itself a state of 'truth': God's word cannot lie, its 'confession' or expression *is* the creation of the real ('You are Goodness itself,' he writes in this same chapter). On the other hand, there is the human 'being' (actually now a human becoming), for whom there remains a distinction between the realm of value ('we see that they are good') and the realm of fact ('we see that they exist'). Crucially, in explanation, Augustine explains that 'It was only *after a lapse of time* that we were impelled to do good' (emphasis added). This temporality, our condition of *becoming* on the way to *being*, is the story of a confessing, the story of how Augustine comes to take his stand, an 'I' before the door of God.[35]

Politics

In his 'Foreword' to the English translation of Jean-Luc Nancy's *The Experience of Freedom*, Peter Fenves makes an extremely interesting series of observations, partly on the differences between 'Continental' and 'Anglo-American' philosophy, but also simply on the relation between ideas of experience and facts of freedom: 'Empiricism, as a doctrine of experience, and civil liberties, as the political content of freedom, are united [in Anglo-American thought] in their effort to remove unjustified authorities.'[36] For Nancy, freedom is in some moments a matter of surprise, or even, in Woolfian terms, freedom is *the* 'moment' not of 'being' but rather of 'surprising': it is related to the concept of the event, or that which cannot be preprogrammed, that which opens us up precisely to the temporality of history whose opposite is Augustine's God. Augustine's God, being beyond history, being beyond becoming, is, of necessity, the eschewing of politics as such; and thus, this God is also the site where freedom is denied, replaced by an idea – a tragic Hegelian-Marxian idea – of history-as-necessity, *Ananke*.

Can experience be tied at all to political freedom; and can this have a bearing on the philosophy and practices of literary and cultural criticism? As critics influenced in recent times by various strands within Continental philosophy, we have in general been schooled to mistrust experience as a category, identifying it all-too-readily with ideology. Catherine Belsey prefaces her work on *Desire* with the exhortation: what will this book be about, and answers: 'Experience? Perish the thought.'[37] Giorgio Agamben puts it more philosophically: 'It is the character of the present time that all authority is founded on what cannot be experienced, and nobody would be inclined to accept the validity of an authority whose sole claim to legitimation was experience.'[38]

We mistrust experience initially because we see it as subjective, and therefore not only unscientific or not based in objective truth but also because, as a matter of subjective life, it is prone to ideological distortion. Experience, in fact, is almost aligned with ideology purely and simply; and this explains the mistrust of a critic such as Belsey towards it. And yet, at another level, what is history if not the summation of actual undergone experiences? Without this, we are in the realms of the absolutes and abstractions of theology (as in Augustine's God); or, at the least, we open ourselves to the dangerous possibility of the reduction of history to myth or abstraction and of identity to 'office', to the formal and official 'being' that constitutes my function in an organization or whole.

Behind this lies the question of the relation of form and identity to questions of autonomy: how does a subject distinguish and identify itself in relation to the authority of tradition, so to speak? In other terms, how does the I make a difference or 'emerge' from a weight of history that gives the I an already-given identity? It is the question that Marx raised at the start of the *Eighteenth Brumaire*; and it is a question of how one 'authorizes' oneself as a historical entity. If one simply conforms to that which one has been given, then one becomes simply a medium for the ghosts and spirits of the past, invoked by

Marx, who now speak through the present subject. Yet the question remains: how can one 'begin' oneself or have an identity that is *not* already given as a matter of formal being?

Arendt is helpful on this. In her essay 'On violence', she considers how it is possible for us to intervene historically in the world, and she writes that 'What makes man a political being is his faculty of action'; and, further, more suggestively for our present argument, that 'To act and to begin are not the same, but they are closely interrelated.'[39] What she is getting at in this is her own version of *events*, which, for her, 'are occurrences that interrupt routine processes and routine procedures'.[40] She argues that we have a tendency to ignore events, especially those events whose *actual* happening threatens the sanctity of our reasoned theory or expectation or prediction of what the theory says *should* take place in any given situation. The parallel, for my own argument, is with formal and official identity: we tend to ignore any act of actual becoming that has the potential to contradict the sanctity of our office, our being, our 'identity'. The price we pay for such ignoring, according to Arendt, is that we remove the theory 'further and further from reality'.[41] Likewise, our formal identity is what removes us from the possibilities of reality or of experience: identity such as this – identity-politics in criticism – paradoxically is the very thing that *distances* us from history.

Like Agamben much later, Arendt also saw a problem concerning authority, and especially the formal authority of what we are calling tradition, the weight and burden of the past that seems to condition our present. In a prefiguring of Agamben's actual phrasing, she writes that:

> authority has vanished from the modern world. Since we can no longer fall back upon authentic and undisputable experiences common to all, the very term has become clouded by controversy and confusion ... a constant, ever-widening and deepening crisis of authority has accompanied the development of the modern world in our [twentieth] century.[42]

The thing about authority, here – the authority that we have been systematically losing – is that it is akin both to religious thought and to an ontology of being:

> Authority, resting on a foundation in the past as its unshaken cornerstone, gave the world the permanence and durability which human beings need precisely because they are mortals ... Its loss is tantamount to the loss of the groundwork of the world, which indeed since then has begun to shift, to change and transform itself with ever-increasing rapidity from one shape into another, as though we were living and struggling with a Protean universe where everything at any moment can become almost anything else.[43]

This is the crux of our issue: does our identity conform to that which we are given by the authority of another (the past); or do we adopt the troubling condition of protean instability which, for all its vexations to us, nonetheless offers the possibility of change, of events, of action (and thus of political life)? Arendt herself is relatively clear here:

> the loss of worldly permanence and reliability – which politically is identical with the loss of authority – does not entail, at least not necessarily, the loss of the human capacity for building, preserving, and caring for a world that can survive us and remain a place fit to live in for those who come after us.[44]

It follows from this that, if we are to have a political living at all, then we need to accept the vexing problems of instability – and above all, of instability in what we call our own identity. Like Proteus, we are historical beings only to the extent that we change, that we become other than what we were. All else belongs, as in Augustine, to God and to other forms of absolute – and essentially therefore mythic, non-historical – form, or office.

In that mode of absolutist thinking – the thinking of official identity – we open ourselves to the dangerous possibility that large terms like 'Holocaust', in the wrong hands, are presented not just as myth but also as lie. My tendentious claim is that 'the wrong hands' are the hands of those who consider that we need to 'verify' or validate an identity in relation to such events. What we are saying, of course, is not that we should avoid the term 'Holocaust', but rather that we should realize that the Holocaust is not one simple or single identifiable thing: it is many experiences (between six and nine million at least), it is Primo Levi, it is Elie Wiesel, it is all the many stories of Claude Lanzmann's *Shoah*, it is Christian Boltanski's *Dead Swiss*. In short, it has no identity – and to give it an identity is to reduce it to form, to evacuate it of content, to hand it over to the right-wing for reduction to myth.

We have a modern example of a fictional character who is caught in the Augustinian trap, pondering the location of a selfhood in terms of the relation of interiority and external history: Beckett's Unnamable. Consider this self-identification:

> perhaps that's what I feel, an outside and an inside and me in the middle, perhaps that's what I am, the thing that divides the world in two, on the one side the outside, on the other the inside, that can be as thin as foil, I'm neither one side nor the other, I'm in the middle, I'm the partition, I've two surfaces and no thickness, perhaps that's what I feel, myself vibrating, I'm the tympanum, on the one hand the mind, on the other the world, I don't belong to either, it's not to me they're talking, it's not of me they're talking, no, that's not it, I feel nothing of all that, try something else, herd of shites, say something else[45]

The identity here becomes unnamable, 'improper'. It is as if the self is reduced to a kind of 'bare life' as in some of Agamben; but in Beckett this is formulated as if the Unnamable's self is pure skin, the site of a feeling or of a visceral experience: 'I don't know what I feel, tell me what I feel and I'll tell you who I am'. This skin, however is, in Beckett, the site of a writing or of a representation; and we can see the terrifying logic here, as the formally identifiable body becomes the site of a tattoo, and thus also for a taboo.[46] The body here is a site on which a number, say, can be tattooed. This is an effect of the prioritization of official identity, of identity-politics.

In more precise political thinking, this in turn is fully shaped by the aporia of Auschwitz. Here is Agamben from the preface to *Remnants of Auschwitz*: 'Some want to understand too much and too quickly; they have explanations for everything. Others refuse to understand; they offer only cheap mystifications. The only way forward lies in the space between these two options.'[47] And this is important, because Agamben sees what he calls 'the aporia of Auschwitz' as something profoundly philosophical. Auschwitz is characterized by a situation where its survivors are witness to 'the only true thing' and, at the same time, this truth is 'irreducible to the real elements that constitute it', and so we face 'a reality that necessarily exceeds its factual elements'. And so, as he puts it, 'The aporia of Auschwitz is, indeed, the very aporia of historical knowledge: a non-coincidence between facts and truth, between verification and comprehension.'[48] Fact need not be truth, in this. There is a non-coincidence between fact and truth; and this would be important if we are to counter Augustine's conception of God, for whom fact and value are one, unified or identified with each other through the power of God's word-as-deed, word-made-flesh, as John has it in his Revelations or 'confessional' Gospel.

Now, however, let us place this insight from Agamben in the context of the legalism that we saw in Montaigne. The result will be that we have, in criticism, actually prioritized verification over comprehension by our prioritizing of identity and its forms. We thus understand or comprehend nothing. To comprehend, in this case, will mean to explore that space between the options of explanation and mystification of which Agamben writes as he tries to find a new ethics of criticism.

In these terms, formal identity is that which effaces historical experience, which must now become clandestine if it is to exist at all. Formal or official identity – and identitarian politics with its preference for verification over comprehension – is that which operates and becomes valued when our society has become fully 'bureaucratized'. Identity-politics in criticism might present itself as radical and critical; yet, as the foregoing shows, it is entirely complicit with the very conservatism of the social formation that it pretends to oppose. Bureaucracy in governance and bureaucratic government exist in order to manage behaviour in predictable fashion, and thus to preclude the very possibility of there ever being an action or an event at all. As Arendt argued, 'It is the function ... of all action, as distinct from mere behavior, to interrupt what otherwise would have proceeded automatically and predictably.'[49] Official identity – and a criticism based on 'who I am' rather than on 'how we change' – is anathema to historical materialism, and to the necessary 'witnessing' of literature that calls us into becoming and into political activity.

To be a 'witness' to literature will mean opening ourselves to the fact of the clandestine experience, the experience that can have no formal presentation because it cannot be verified. And yet, at the same time, this is an experience that is not itself constitutive of identity. Yes, we can experience, we must acknowledge experience; but we can now do so only in a clandestine fashion, perhaps even a covert or occluded, 'private' fashion. Our experience cannot be officially acknowledged; for we live in a critical age of official identity, bureaucratic identity. This is what has shaped the criticism based on identity-politics which, while assuming itself to be radical, is in fact entirely in conformity with the law of the bureaucracy that demands one's papers. The more radical move – indeed the move that is more radical precisely because it acknowledges limitations and strives for comprehension – is the move that abandons the ID card and steps firmly on to the side of the *sans papiers*.

My next chapter has its source in an original man *sans papiers*, Shakespeare's Caliban.

3

This Thing of Darkness
I Acknowledge Mine

Mien, tien.
Ce chien est à moi, disaient ces pauvres enfants. C'est là ma
place au soleil. Voilà le commencement et l'image de
l'usurpation de toute la terre.

Mine, yours.
This dog is mine, said these poor children. That there is my
place in the sun. Thus the start of and the image
of the usurpation of the entire world.
Blaise Pascal, *Pensées*[1]

Roseau pensant.
Ce n'est point de l'espace que je dois chercher ma dignité, mais
c'est du règlement de ma pensée. Je n'aurai point d'avantage en
possédant des terres. Par l'espace l'univers me comprend et
m'engloutit comme un point: par la pensée je le comprends.

Thinking reed.
It is not at all in space that I should search for my worth, but rather
by the accounts of my thought. Ownership of lands will be of
absolutely no use to me. In space the universe contains me and
swallows me up like a speck: but in thought, I contain it.
Blaise Pascal, *Pensées*[2]

Introduction: intimate things

In the previous chapters on the 'now' and on a confessional identity, I addressed the issue of what it is that constitutes the contemporary, considered purely in terms of its temporality. In this chapter, I will build on that, specifically in relation to what I will call 'thisness', a form of intimacy with alterity. We can think of the contemporary, as we have seen, as a kind of intimacy of presence; but that also includes, as well as a reflection on the 'now', a further consideration of that which is most close to me, the 'here' as it were. If we are able to add the question of spatial proximity to the temporal question that we have already considered, we will eventually be able to arrive at a consideration of what Duns Scotus once thought of as *haecceitas*, a 'thisness' that marks the very singularity of any entity. One way of putting it would be to say that, in this chapter, my quarry is 'this thing of darkness [that] I acknowledge mine',[3] Prospero's description of Caliban.

I want, then, to address the issue of specificity: of 'thisness'; and we can begin with a consideration of 'this thing'. At the start of his meditation on 'The Thing', Martin Heidegger thinks of the thing in terms of technological issues of intimacy. Modern technology, he says, has effectively reduced all space and time, shrinking history into a kind of now, and also shrinking geography into a 'nearness' as he calls it. 'The thing', he then says, is what is specific to the here as well as to the now: it is what is 'near' me, as it were.

We see a similar motif in fiction, and specifically in Georges Perec's 1965 novel, *Les choses*. There, Jérôme and Sylvie are presented as a young couple surrounded by a world of modernity in which modern things equate somehow with a happiness that seems forever to elude them. Their life is not only precarious (dependent on things holding together in the world around them), it is also quietly desperate, in a manner seen in American fiction with the case of the young couple in Richard Yates's *Revolutionary Road*. In Perec, '*Il suffisait que quelque chose craque, un jour ... pour que tout s'écroule. Ils n'avaient rien devant eux, rien derrière eux*' ('It was enough that something should crack, one day ... for everything to fall apart. They had nothing before or behind them.'[4] Their situation brings them into a present that isolates them from all else, makes them intimate purely with each other.

For Jérôme and Sylvie, a fixation on the things of modernity and on their presence with each other in the plenitude of an intense here-now, as they sit in a restaurant, brings them to a supreme moment of ecstatic pleasure, however briefly:

le bonheur était en eux. Ils étaient assis l'un en face de l'autre, ils allaient manger après avoir eu faim, et toutes ces choses – la nappe blanche de grosse toile, la tache bleue d'un paquet de gitanes, les assiettes de faïence, les couverts un peu lourds, les verres à pied, la corbeille d'osier pleine de pain frais – composaient le cadre toujours neuf d'un plaisir presque viscéral, à la limite de l'engourdissement: l'impression, presque exactement contraire et presque exactement semblable à celle que procure la vitesse, d'une formidable stabilité, d'une formidable plénitude. A partir de cette table servie, ils avaient l'impression d'une synchronie parfait: ils étaient à l'unisson du monde.

happiness lay within them. They were seated face-to-face, they were about to eat, having felt hungry, and every thing – the white rough linen tablecloth, the blue mark of a packet of Gitanes, the china plates, the slightly heavy cutlery, the stem glasses, the wicker-basket full of fresh bread – all this always newly encapsulated the framework of a nearly visceral pleasure, at the edge of a dullness: the impression, almost exactly contrary to and almost exactly same as that which you get from speed, a feeling of a formidable stability, or of a formidable completeness. Starting with this set table, they had the impression of a perfect synchrony: they were at one with the world.[5]

When we turn to the philosophical explication of these matters, as opposed to these fictional treatments, we see in Heidegger, for example (and, perhaps, of course, it being Heidegger), that this kind of situation assumes a characteristically odd set of tongue-twisting linguistic formulations. The thing, he argues, is essentially that which brings together, in a kind of intrinsic unity, what he calls the 'fourfold' of earth, sky, divinities and mortals. What he means, essentially, is that the thing – as opposed to the object – is that which draws itself into itself as a specific manifestation of the world's presence. At the core of the argument, though, is the establishment of an intimacy between the subject and the thing, an intimacy that Heidegger calls 'nearness'. We will make more of this below, in what follows.

It is important to note as we advance the argument here that, for Heidegger, a thing is not necessarily an object. The object, by contrast with the thing, would be that which, in the thing, is there *for* a subject of consciousness, that which is available, so to speak, to an I that becomes the subject of perception or cognition. In other words, a Heideggerian object can be appropriated, owned; but a thing – which he elsewhere in the essay describes as a 'gathering' – is itself, separate, other than a subject and not immediately accessible to a subject. This thing, then, is, in many ways, a 'thing of darkness', its intrinsic condition of a radical otherness making it certainly dark, obscure. Perhaps by definition, we might say that a 'thing' is that which is not available to a consciousness as such: as Kant has it (though with a much more sophisticated argument and corollary), the thing-as-such or *Ding-an-sich* is not there 'for' me. The error made by Jérôme and Sylvie is that they cannot appreciate this distinction; and, good consumers as they become, they see a world of objects, not of things.

At stake in this, for present purposes, is the question of the substantiality or otherwise of the subject, the I that we have been assuming to be here, now, in the confessional mode: what is this thing that I acknowledge as being *so* intimate with me that I acknowledge it mine own, my *self*; and behind this (via Shakespeare's Prospero and Caliban) what is the very nature of property and propriety, the status of *le propre* with respect to confessing or expressing or revealing the status and being of the subject? Another way of putting this would be to ask the question concerning responsibility: can I 'own' my actions in the world, or are they beyond me, as it were? We can certainly interpret the world; but can we change it? More pressing still, can we be answerable for any action in the world, including an action that either interpret or changes that world, claiming it as a 'property' of the self or of 'my' identity?

The answers to these questions are fundamental to any philosophy that tries to consider the ethical or political conditions that attend the roles played by human agents in the determination of freedoms. In his *Conditions of Freedom* lectures, John Macmurray indicates the stakes of the argument. Firstly, he takes it that whatever the self might be, it is first and foremost to be characterized in terms of its practical agency or actions, rather than in terms of its theoretical self-imaginings. Then, he equates action with freedom: 'To act is to be free,' he writes.[6] However, to state things like this is too bald, too abstract and theoretical. In refining the position, he points to the paradox of what he calls 'the relativity of freedom'. Unlike other animate beings, humans cannot grasp their own nature: 'There is a gap between the reality of our being and its empirical expression,' and so, 'We are and yet we are not ourselves: *and in this is our freedom*.'[7] It would follow from this that 'my' self has a relation to 'my' actions, certainly; but the question to be explored here is whether that relation is one of identity, with the consequence in which 'I' can be expressed by the things that I determine as 'mine', including those things that are my actions, my bodily extension into space, my relations of 'nearness' with others or with the things of the world and of history.

The crisis of intimacy

The question of the contemporary is, almost by definition as we saw in my previous chapter, a problem of representation. A presentation of the present must always involve a re-presenting, which has the effect of marking the present moment with the passage of time, making it not self-identical or introducing difference into the deictic 'now'.[8] The contemporary – the 'with-time ness' of the present moment – thus has the effect of introducing an element of heterogeneity and difference into what is or should be regarded intuitively as homogeneous, self-identical, the self-present as such. This, as we now know, is actually more complicated than it appears.

There is, however, a second very obvious complication to the contemporary. The term, operating as a deictic, shifts its sense depending on where and when it is spoken. It therefore requires a subject of consciousness, an I, in relation to which something can be proposed precisely as the contemporary of the I. Perhaps yet more specifically, it requires *this* I, *hic ego* as it were, the I in all its own intrinsic specificity and singular identity; and that I needs, in turn, something close to it or at least deictically noted by it. It is perhaps better to start to think of the contemporary not in terms of a noun, but rather in terms of a verb. Contemporaneity is *what happens* when an I is produced as a subject sharing a time – even a transitory moment – with an event, and producing in that relation a specific solace, the solace of identification and of identity, the comfort of knowing this thing, even 'this thing of darkness', as mine own, as it were. Contemporaneity in this state of affairs or in these circumstances produces a fiction of the self as an entity that persists in time and across the various events which make up that self's history or biography, the 'self-life-writing', as it were, that allows the I to be stated or to exist.[9]

Contemporaneity, in these terms, would be the drive to turn the Heideggerian 'thing' into an 'object', to appropriate a moment in history; and, simultaneously, thereby to identify the subject in relation to their objects, through their others. It is no doubt within the necessary intimacies of the confessional text, as our most deictic of literary forms, that we will find this most clearly at work. When Erich Auerbach considered the problem of representation in *Mimesis*,[10] he turned for a telling example to Augustine, whose *Confessions* is a text in which, necessarily almost, the subject of the discourse appears to be present 'here, now'. Augustine, as we have already seen, is at many times at pains to indicate the presence of himself in and through the text, however problematic it may be. In Book 10, Chapter 3, Augustine writes:

> What does it profit me, then, O Lord ... I ask, also to make known to me in your sight, through this book, not what I once was, but what I am now? I know what profit I gain by confessing my past, and this I have declared. But many people who know me, and others who do not know me but have heard of me or read my books, wish to hear what I am now, at this moment, as I set down my confessions.[11]

In passing, we should note here that the question that will arise for us, following this, is the bleak one of whether and in what possible manner one can 'survive' confession. What, indeed, would survival mean, in this context? Can the I persist after the confessional act; or, otherwise expressed, what is at stake in *bearing witness*? Is the I transformed or transfigured by confession; and, if so, what is it that 'survives' the act of confessing? For one such as Albert Camus – for whom 'a guilty conscience needs to confess. A work of art is a confession' – this would be a question about the survival (as opposed to the death) of the author. Remaining for the moment more closely with the Augustinian text and Auerbach's response to it, we see that Auerbach notes in this text a new attitude to time, an attitude which we can see clearly replicated at the beginning of an emergent modernity in the eighteenth-century novel in England, a novel whose concerns were marked by a desire to be 'writing to the minute', to 'this' minute, a journalistic identification with and description of present or modern times.[12]

First, Auerbach indicates the key stylistic break that Augustine makes from his erstwhile normative classical traditions, a stylistic break into a modernity of sorts. Considering a passage from Book 6, Chapter 8, of *Confessions* (in which Augustine describes his young former pupil and friend, Alypius, as a man who all but loses his humanity in his obsessions with the brutal fighting in the gladiatorial arena in Rome), Auerbach notes the prevalence of what he characterizes as a specifically 'Christian' style of parataxis, that linking of narrated events by 'and then ... and then ...', the very condition that E.M. Forster would much later describe as the absence of plot. Here is Auerbach:

> Instead of the causal or at least temporal hypotaxis which we should expect in classical Latin ... [we get] a parataxis with *et* [*and*]; and this procedure, far from weakening the interdependence of the two events, brings it out more

emphatically: just as in English it is more dramatically effective to say: He opened his eyes and was struck … than: When he opened his eyes, or: Upon opening his eyes, he was struck.[13]

This part of *Confessions* is one where Augustine describes in some detail his relation to Alypius, who in some ways is Augustine's own version of a thing of darkness that he has to acknowledge. Alypius has been a friend and student of Augustine; but, as we find out in Book 6, their relation has become somewhat distanced. Alypius is tempted by the 'easy morals' at Carthage; and, though he and Augustine clearly like each other, a dispute between Augustine and the father of Alypius has driven a wedge between them, so that Alypius is no longer technically Augustine's pupil (though Augustine reveals that Alypius does attend at least some of Augustine's lectures). Things get worse still when Alypius goes to Rome, where he becomes totally caught up in the brutal savagery of the gladiatorial arena and its spectacles of blood and frenzy.

But Book 6 has started, not with Alypius at all, but rather with what is essentially a further description of a critical period when Augustine himself converts. He has been struck, he tells us, by the behaviour of his mother, Monica, who unquestioningly obeys the bishop Ambrose,[14] and he is very aware of his mother's belief that he, Augustine, will change. Augustine, with the benefit of hindsight as he writes, now, is able to state that he was about to pass through 'that which doctors call the crisis'.[15] This crisis involves an attitude to God that can only be described as a *crisis of intimacy*, a crisis pertaining to space and to the occupation of space.

We can recall that Augustine began his *Confessions* with the question of whether God was in him or he in God; and that spatial thinking (who 'contains' whom?) persists in Book 6, especially in Chapters 3 and 4. There, he describes the role that Ambrose plays in the conversion. Sitting listening to the preaching of Ambrose, Augustine understands that 'I learned that your spiritual children … do not understand the words *God made man in his own image* to mean that you are limited by the shape of a human body.'[16] From this, Augustine then again ponders the relation of God to spatial extension, and, crucially, he begins the transition whereby he moves from thinking in spatial terms towards thinking in terms of what we can call that crisis of *representational* intimacy, in the form of a nearness: the likeness that is constitutive of metaphor or simile, as it is also of the representations that shape democracy.

Here is what he writes:

O God, you who are so high above us and yet so close, hidden and yet always present, you have not parts, some greater and some smaller. You are everywhere, and everywhere you are entire. Nowhere are you limited by space. You have not the shape of a body like ours.[17]

This is how Chapter 3 ends; and then he starts, in Chapter 4, to consider the nature of this likeness. Essentially, when Augustine speaks of likeness here, he is indicating the start of his conversion (and, of course, in Chapter 5, he points out explicitly that 'From now on I began to prefer the Catholic teaching').[18] The conversion requires a change of thought; and one in which he turns not simply to faith (for he still indicates the potency of reason here), but rather to a mode of resolving his *spatial* conundrum from the very start of the text.

In brief, what he does here is to resolve the question of spatial perspective by thinking not just of bodies 'approaching' each other, but instead in terms of an essential intimacy, which he calls 'likeness'. He acknowledges himself as a thing of darkness, so to speak, that has now come into an assimilation with God. God acknowledges him, as Prospero does Augustine's fellow African, Caliban. It is as if God is using the very words that Shakespeare will give to Prospero; and it is in this way that Augustine realizes – makes real – his essential intimacy with God, appropriated, as it were, by God. Appropriation here, of course, does not mean simple ownership; rather, it is the 'making proper' of Augustine, or Augustine coming to be or *becoming* what he now is, eternally converting in the text.[19]

This assimilation is central to the conversion. From here, Augustine is God's. And, in the same way as God acknowledges Augustine as God's own thing, so now (in likeness to God) Augustine will acknowledge Alypius as his, as Augustine's. A key passage here is at the very end of Book 6, Chapter 8. We have been expecting to hear about some possible reconciliation between Alypius and Augustine; but instead, Augustine disappoints us and defers the telling of any such reconciliation. At the end of the chapter, he describes Alypius almost as a lost cause, a man characterized by 'a diseased mind', obsessed as he has become with the gladiatorial contests in Rome. Then Augustine addresses God: 'Yet you stretched out your almighty, ever merciful hand, O God, and rescued him from this madness. You taught him to trust in you, not in himself. But this was much later.'[20]

In this, Augustine does several things. Firstly, he defers the story's ending, projecting the temporality of the text forwards in time such that the now of writing is projected to futurity. At the same time, he already reveals the content of that futurity, bringing the future into a direct alignment with the present (Auerbach's 'figural' time, as we will see in a moment). Next, and more importantly, he indicates that God, not Augustine, saves Alypius. However, the chapter has demonstrated such an intimacy between God and Augustine that, essentially, when God saves Alypius he can do so through the mediating body of Augustine himself. It is thus that Augustine 'claims' Alypius, essentially, as a thing of darkness (the diseased mind) that can be acknowledged as 'mine'. That which was other becomes *propre*.

When Auerbach writes about this, considering primarily the style of writing and the prevalence of parataxis, he is essentially concerned with a style whose function is to replace time by space. The modernizing style of allegedly Christian parataxis produces a new and different conception of time, argues

Auerbach. It necessitates what he calls 'figural' interpretation, in which events are seen to be linked not by cause and effect and not even in a necessarily linear chronology. Events in figural time are connected when 'occurrences are vertically linked to Divine Providence, which alone is able to devise such a plan of history and supply the key to its understanding'.[21] That is to say, in this figural time, events are linked by dint of the fact that their significance always depends upon a single referent (in Auerbach's case a transcendental one called Divine Providence) which acts as their self-evident and single horizon of interpretation. The secular version of this would be that which assigns the place of Divine Providence to the self: character. In my next section, I shall consider a text that does just this, in a narrative move that refers everything back to the intimacy of the subject.

The emergence of character as the constitution of modernity

We might see the *crisis of intimacy*, as I have called it, in terms of the relations between characters, in terms of the fundamentals of ethics: love (and, behind that, beauty). What Augustine is describing in Book 6 essentially has to do with the movement and power of likeness or becoming-intimate as a founding condition for the possibility of love – in that book, love of God, love of the mother, and love between Alypius and Augustine. We can turn to a later, equally 'confessional' text, to get a fuller grasp of this, as a founding condition of the attitudes to time and historical becoming that shape our modernity. The intimacy in question, if we look at a wider range of textual materials, is an intimacy between the I and the things of the world: it is an intimacy that allows us to trace the foundation of what will be the great cornerstone of fiction within modernity, the establishment of character as 'point-of-view', of character as *position* or as 'that which is posited' and that can 'acknowledge' the things of its world.

When René Descartes made his *Méditations*, he also decided that his readers would benefit from a shorter explanation of his text, explicitly one that will outline the theory that governs those meditations. In the 1630s, he set himself the task of writing what is essentially a confessional text, the *Discours de la méthode*, published in 1637. In exactly the same way that Descartes ushers in a modern age of philosophy, so he also ushers in a certain normative mode of thought, and one that becomes foundational to the modern novel and its obsession with – or, if that is felt to be too strong, its grounding in – character.

In the *Discours*, Descartes presents himself as a modestly heroic figure. He begins by indicating that he is rather unexceptional: not only is '*le bon sens ... la chose du monde la mieux partagée*' but also, '*Pour moi, je n'ai jamais présumé que mon esprit fût en rien plus parfait que ceux du commun*' ('good sense [is] the most widely shared thing in the world … For my part, I have never presumed that my mind would be in any way more perfect than everyone else's').[22] He goes on to say that, notwithstanding his unexceptional status, a number of very specific things have happened to him, things that make him what he is as a unique individual. He might be the victim of all sorts of deception in terms of what he thinks about the world and reality; but he wants to submit himself for judgement, in a phrase that is unquestionably part of the confessional lexicon:

> *je serais bien aisé de faire voir, en ce discours, quels sont les chemins que j'ai suivis, et d'y représenter ma vie comme en un tableau, afin que chacun puisse juger.*

> I would be very comfortable in revealing, through this discourse, which roads I have taken, and to show my life as in a painting, so that anyone might judge.[23]

Fairly quickly, however, we will see him adopt a tone that is closer to the mode and mood of the later Rousseau in his great confessional text, when he indicates more fully the nature of his uniqueness. Having made the decision to doubt and to search for truth within himself, he is quick to point out that this is a dangerous path, and not one to be recommended to everyone:

> *La seule résolution de se défaire de toutes les opinions qu'on a reçues auparavant en sa créance, n'est pas un exemple que chacun doive suivre … Mais, comme un homme qui marche seul et dans les ténèbres, je me résolus d'aller.*

> The sole resolve – to rid oneself of all the opinions that one has received beforehand as beliefs – is not an example that each and everyone should follow … But, like a man who walks alone and through darkness, I resolved that I would go forward.[24]

In this last analysis, therefore, Descartes does eventually present himself as unique, a very specific thing, a 'thing that thinks' a thinking substance, as it is reported in the lengthier and more substantial *Méditations*.

This thing-that-thinks is characterized as a man who, though fully aware of what we would now call cultural relativism, nonetheless believes that there are some fundamental truths available to him, and that he will find them by examining his own experience and thought, rather like examining his own conscience. What he realizes, aware as he is of how truths seem to vary depending on one's culture (he gives the examples of how different the world will look if one is Persian or Chinese, for instance), is that he can come to know his *inner* world of thought. Very importantly, he argues that he cannot know with any certainty at all the world of exteriority. Our thoughts are at our disposal, so to speak, and available to us in ways that the exterior world and its happenstances are not:

> *il n'y a rien qui soit entièrement en notre pouvoir, que nos pensées, en sorte qu'après que nous avons fait notre mieux, touchant les choses qui nous sont extérieures, tout ce qui manque de nous réussir est, au regard de nous, absolument impossible.*

there is nothing that lies entirely in our power, other than our thoughts, so that after we have done our best, with regard to exterior things, all that fails to remain is, with respect to us, absolutely impossible.[25]

Given this, he can turn inwards and produce the famous *je pense, donc je suis*, as his first principle of philosophy or metaphysics. In Part 4 of the *Discours*, he turns explicitly to the order of his metaphysics, and comes to the general conclusion that what he can know is, fundamentally, the laws of geometry. These laws are fundamentally laws of space and of proportion. He can prove things about a triangle, say, without the necessity of there actually being any material triangle in existence. This is to say, having started out by claiming that his project is fully *empirical*, he ends up by suggesting that what he experiences is always in the world of his own inner mind, and therefore that he is simply examining the content of his own mind, a mind that, he says, is explicitly divorced from the body and from exteriority as such. His is what we have termed in earlier chapters a purely *formal* knowledge.

The 'confession' of Descartes, then, is one where, actually, he cannot be held accountable for anything historical, for anything that actually happens in a material realm of exteriority. This, I contend, is why he begins the text by claiming his likeness to others, but ends it by stressing his singularity, his unlikeness. For him, then, there is no crisis of intimacy with other human beings, no Augustinian *conversion*; instead, only a 'spirit of geometry' that tells him how the world *ought* to be, not how it is.

Some years later, another French thinker – almost certainly Blaise Pascal – wrote another brief text, a *Discours sur les passions de l'amour*. Pascal (assuming his authorship) makes a distinction in this discourse between '*deux sortes d'esprit: l'un géometrique et l'autre qu'on peut appeler de finesse*' ('two kinds of mind: the one geometric and the other what one might call a spirit of finesse').[26] The first of these – the geometric spirit – is characterized by solidity and inflexibility: certainty, in short, the certainty that one has with what Descartes had called clear and distinct ideas. The second, however, has a suppleness of thought that allows for the subject to perceive the world of exteriority and to have a relation with it. As he writes it:

L'esprit de finesse ... a une souplesse de pensées qui l'applique en même temps aux diverses parties aimables de ce qu'il aime : des yeux il va jusqu'au cœur et par le mouvement du dehors il connaît ce qui se passe au-dedans.

The spirit of finesse ... has a suppleness of thought that can apply it simultaneously to likeable parties that are different from those that one loves: from the eyes, it proceeds to the heart, and it is able to understand what is going on in the inner world from looking at external gestures.[27]

With this kind of spirit, love becomes possible, in short. We have the possibility of the crisis of intimacy that Augustine described, a state of affairs in which it becomes possible to engage with another human being, and acknowledge them in their separate uniqueness, a uniqueness that is modified by likeness, the nearness that makes them a 'thing', as it were, as opposed to being an object (which would solidify the identity of the subject perceiving them).

Pascal also wrote explicitly 'Sur la conversion du pécheur' – 'On the conversion of the sinner' – probably around 1653. That text seems to extend the question of love, and takes it more fully into a consideration of what happens when a sinner converts or turns to God. Pascal describes the movement as one where the sinner becomes less fixated on the things of the world or exteriority that have previously been her or his solace. There is a radical disturbance in the sinner's mind or soul, leading to a radical uncertainty:

> *D'une part, la présence des objets visibles la touche plus que l'espérance des invisibles, et de l'autre la solidité des invisibles la touche plus que la vanité des visibles. Et ainsi la présence des uns et la solidité des autres disputent son affection.*

> On one hand, the presence of visible objects touches it [the sinner's soul] more than the hopes placed in those that are invisible, and on the other hand the solidity of those invisible touches it more than the vanity of those things that are seen. And thus the presence of the one and the solidity of the other fight for its affections.[28]

Importantly, the question now becomes one of establishing not only intimacy with God but actual assimilation to God, appropriation of the sinner by God, as it were: the acknowledging by God of this thing of darkness, the sinner. The sinner comes to realize the transitoriness of all that has given them pleasure; but realizes equally, and by contrast, the essentially non-temporal nature of God. Things that one loves become less innately lovable if they are transitory, argues Pascal; and thus, by contrast, God becomes the most obvious site for a more fulfilling happiness:

> *Sa raison [la raison du pécheur] aidée des lumières de la grâce lui fait connaître qu'il n'y a rien de plus aimable que Dieu et qu'il ne peut être ôté qu'à ceux qui le rejettent, puisque c'est le posséder que de le désirer, et que le refuser, c'est le perdre.*

> His reasoning [the reasoning of the sinner] helped by the light of grace makes him realize that there is nothing more lovable than God and that he can only be taken away from those that reject him, since *to desire him is to possess him*, and to refuse him is to lose him [emphasis added][29]

Here, love is characterized in terms of a possession; and, importantly, this possession depends upon the sinner realizing what Auerbach calls 'figural' time: that is, the sinner has to eschew their historical being and attachment to the things of the world, realizing the world's temporal nature and thus its transitoriness. This takes us back into Augustine territory and back directly into the question of this figural time.

In its literary manifestations, figural time constructs the position of an omniscient narrator whose single point of view on the ostensibly divergent elements of the narrative guarantees the univocal meaning of the entire story. 'Figural time' is essentially the phrase that Auerbach uses to characterize the position of God, as that which unifies what are ostensibly 'fragments' of time that have no immediate or unmediated apparent intrinsic link: it is the time that unifies all world history. This can become, in fiction, either the position of an omniscient narrator or, more usually in fact, simply what we call 'character' in terms of point of view. The point of view gives the figure, or the ethos, in relation to which diverse happenings in the story can be unified or in relation to which they can make coherent sense.

To put it in the terms I have used above, in this figural time, events are linked by the fact that the subject position that marks their temporality is that of a transcendent God, who sees all 'contemporaneously'. The result, as Auerbach points out, is the *homogenization* of time and, as a corollary, the production of what becomes known as a 'Universal History', a history in which each and every event or happening is fundamentally a part of the same single story, interlinked in a way that produces a *spatialized* pattern or geometric image. In fiction, the homogenization is that which apparently makes the character self-identical, that which gives them a local habitation and a name.

Thus, in this state of affairs, we can prioritize 'point of view' in narrative: point of view becomes important – as the relativizing term that it is intended to be – if and only if we have or if we can infer a universalizing and homogenizing viewpoint that transcends all others: a plenitudinous eye or God. In such a history, of course, there can actually be no 'event' as such: such a history precludes the possibility of change in time, and that would be the very substance of an event or of a becoming.

The question of capital is also involved in this. In the case of Jérôme and Sylvie, in Perec's *Les choses*, we can trace a clear trajectory to their lives. When they first start to have money, very early in the novel, the things of their world all become as new: '*Ils changeaient, ils devenaient autres ... Tout était nouveau*' ('They were changing, they were becoming different people ... Everything was new').[30] Towards the end of the novel, 'exiled' in Tunisia, they find themselves in an Arab market, where they buy nothing: '*Ils passaient, amusés ou indifférents, mais tout ce qu'ils voyaient demeurait étranger, appartenait à un autre monde, ne les concernait pas*' ('They would pass by, amused or indifferent, but everything they looked at remained foreign, belonged to another world, had nothing to say to them'):[31] their whole world at this point goes hollow. The novel traces the typical bourgeois existence in which people 'discover' or reveal themselves in and through 'their' objects, only to find later that this is a vacuous 'exoticism' – what Marx would have called alienation – that deprives them of any historical existence.

Modernity as a mood and as a mode

It is perhaps for these reasons that Lyotard took a particular interest in Augustine, claiming him as a paradigmatic example of a certain version of modernity. Like Auerbach, Lyotard considers 'the modern' to be a matter of mood or of attitude (a matter, if you will, of the 'subject-position', the ethos of an I) rather than as a simple indicator of temporality, or of modernity construed in terms of before-or-after-ness or mere chronology. For him, the modern is very definitely not to be understood simplistically as a period (and thus, by logical extension, the postmodern cannot be thought of simply as that which comes 'after' the modern). In short, we might say that 'the modern' or even, more controversially, cultural modernity itself, is a matter of the establishment and legitimation of a subject position that replaces a mystical God with an implied totalizing 'point of view', an *implied* if not ever actually existing or actually graspable omniscience.

There have been various versions of this, of course; but my contention here is that they are all simply variants on this theme of the legitimation of an implied transcendent point of view or ethos. We might think, for example, of Hegel's conception of *Geist*, and that great *Geistesgeschichte* in which 'Spirit' progressively approaches the condition of 'Absolute Knowing'. Hegel, of course, was Christian; but, for more obviously secular versions of this, we might think of the growth of the European academies and their drive to become some kind of repository of total knowledge. At what might seem a more workaday level, we can think of Samuel Johnson's great *Dictionary of the English Language* project, the establishment of a kind of 'ur-text' that contains the possibility of all that can be said or meant. More ambitious still is the *Encyclopédie* of Denis Diderot, for example; and, alongside this, we can see that rival project, written about extensively by Alasdair MacIntyre, of the construction of the ninth edition of the *Encyclopaedia Britannica*.[32]

In all of this, what we see is the development in the grand philosophical style of something that happens at a micro-level in literature, with the development of European fiction in particular. In fiction, especially in the novel, we see the gradual normativity of the text being established around competing points of view, competing characters or *ethoi*, each complete in themselves, but each having only a relative knowledge. Behind them all lie what we have long since learned to call implied authors, such as a Gustave Flaubert or a James Joyce, ironizing and distanced; and, in that establishment of a distance, authors forging precisely the very opposite of what Augustine finds in his relation to Alypius.

What happens here is that the text proposes a number of specific or relativized points of view, which we call characters; and the relativism proposes, without necessarily realizing it, an implicit totalizing point of view, a point of omniscience that is offered as possibility or as potential. One way of putting this would be to say that the God is still there, but has re-established a distance, and thus hands over the intimacy to the relation between characters and reader: in the secular novel, we are tempted by the possibility of an absolute knowing – that is what writers like Joyce or Flaubert offer – without ever actually grasping it. They are trying to reopen time. The omniscient point of view – that which is proper to the realization of a figural time – proposes only homogeneous time, a time that 'takes no time' to fulfil itself, so to speak. Homogeneous time knows no history. In fictions where the writer establishes a distance from such a point of view, rather than an intimacy with it, what we witness is the attempt to reinstate the very possibility of history, of a time that knows no fulfilment and that remains open to futurity.

These characters in modern fiction are rather like those Persians and Chinese described by Descartes in his *Discours*. There, we recall, Descartes begins by acknowledging his own historical position: he is aware of the great tradition of knowing that precedes him, the tradition of knowledge as encompassed in the great books. He argues that, though it is important to read and know those books, one must remember that they are effectively set in the past; and we need instead to be alert to what is happening in the present moment. The danger, as he sees it, is that '*lorsqu'on est trop curieux des choses qui se pratiquaient aux siècles passés, on demeure ordinairement fort ignorant de celles qui se pratiquent en celui-ci*' ('since one is too curious about things that went on in centuries past, one remains ordinarily extremely ignorant of what's going on in the present one').[33] So, he will concentrate on 'looking within', as Virginia Woolf would much later put it in her famous essay on 'Modern Fiction'.

In doing this, though, he is aware that what he is essentially doing is removing any underpinning of his own thought. He compares his work to the rebuilding of a house, when one has knocked down the previous abode. In this state, one needs a *provisional* place to be; and he argues that, even though Persians and Chinese might have many better thoughts than those of which he will be capable, nonetheless he thinks it wiser to take as normative the values and customs of those among whom he has to live. Here, what is happening is that he is accepting pragmatically what we will later call ideology: accepting unquestioningly the underlying norms and values of his peers. Thus, while we can 'visit' the views of others, nonetheless, Descartes will always eventually find a philosophy that is consistent with what is taken for knowledge in the totality of his contemporary world. That becomes his normative horizon. This is what makes the *Discours* not only a confessional text, but also a proto-*Bildungsroman*.

In the modern European novel, we become equally aware of such relativism; but the novel proposes the placing of the reader in the implied point of view of total knowledge. In short, we might say that the project of modernity – in literature at least – is to make the reader into a substitute for a lost or absent God. This is a variant on the position described by Jean-Paul Sartre, when he wrote that 'the best way to conceive of the fundamental project of human reality is to say that man is the being whose project is to be God ... To be man means to reach toward being God. Or if you prefer, man fundamentally is the desire to be God.'[34] The novel is the modern European form that gives a secular substitute for such a desire.

Lyotard adds to the discussion of Augustinian temporality a further specifically 'modern' element, derived from the philosophy of what we now usually call the early modern period. He adds the subject-position in our other great confessional text, Descartes's *Discours de la méthode*. That subject-position ascribes to itself precisely the mastery implicit in the Augustinian notion of Divine Providence, and enables thereby the production of the specific literary form of omniscient, plot-dominated narrative, such as we have it developed and extended in the novel at least from the European eighteenth century onwards. The culmination of this combination of temporal attitude (temper) and masterful subject upon whom the meanings of history itself are seen to depend is in the production of the *Bildungsroman*, a form in which the horizon of interpretation, and thus the ultimate referent, is not a form of Divine Providence but rather the secularized version of this: a unified, if fictional, human self, a human subject thought to persist across a period of time: a locus, therefore, of stability amidst change, or a locus whose very identity as stability allows us to perceive change at all, from a 'point of view'. That is to say, of course, that this produces the human subject in the form of a transcendent monotheistic – indeed Christian – God. The trick of the novel as a form is to deny the actual existence of a God, while producing the sense of an 'absolute knowing' that characterizes the reader. Instead of there being an intimacy between God and human, there is a kind of total identification of the 'God-project' in the place of the reader, who assumes that transcendent position or spatial point of view of omniscience, however deferred that omniscience may be by the plot. The foundation for all such modern fiction is Descartes, in whose work we see the 'secularization' of God in the form of an intimacy with human character, the 'Self'.

In this, the reader 'arrests' the flow of time, or rather they are the locus for that arrest; but in being so, they also arrest their own possibility of engaging with history or with events. The task for the Benjaminian historical materialist is to make the activity of reading properly historical, to make it an event.

Auerbach indicates quite clearly what happens in this state of affairs to the notion of the contemporary, or the now: 'the here and now is no longer a mere link in an earthly chain of events, it is simultaneously something which has always been and which will be fulfilled in the future ... This conception of history is magnificent in its homogeneity.'[35]

We might set alongside this passage an interesting comment from Lyotard's essay on 'Time Today', in which he addresses Leibniz's *Monadology*. From this text, Lyotard points out that:

> God is the ultimate monad to the extent that he conserves in complete retention the totality of information constituting the world. And if divine retention is to be complete, it must also include those pieces of information not yet presented to the incomplete monads, such as our minds, and which remain to come in what we call the future. In this perspective, the 'not yet' is due only to the limit on the faculty of synthesis available to the intermediary monads. For the absolute memory of God, the future is always already given. We can thus conceive, for the temporal condition, an upper limit determined by a perfect recording or archival capacity. As consummate archivist, God is outside time.[36]

The function fulfilled in relation to time by God for Augustine is analogous to the function fulfilled by forms of information technology today: it is the very eradication of historicity as such. Lyotard goes on:

> Complete information means neutralizing more events. What is already known cannot, in principle, be experienced as an event. Consequently, if one wants to control a process, the best way of doing so is to subordinate the present to what is (still) called the 'future', since in these conditions the 'future' will be completely predetermined and the present itself will cease opening on to an uncertain and contingent 'afterwards'. Better: what comes 'after' the 'now' will have to come 'before' it.[37]

Perec's *Les choses* dramatizes this, as Perec points out that, in twentieth-century France, a young man, having done his studies and his military service, effectively has his life before him, but a life already lived, in which there will be no new events no matter how much may 'happen' to him:

> il sait avec certitude qu'un jour viendra où il aura son appartement, sa maison de campagne, sa voiture, sa chaîne haute-fidélité. Il se trouve pourtant que ces exaltantes promesses se font toujours fâcheusement attendre: elles appartiennent ... à un processus dont relèvent également ... le mariage, la naissance des enfants, l'évolution des valeurs morales, des attitudes sociales et des comportements humains.

> he knows with certainty that a day will come when he will have his apartment, his house in the country, his car, his hi-fi. He nonetheless finds that, irritatingly, these great promises make him wait: they belong ... to a process out of which come also marriage, the birth of children, the development of moral values, social attitudes and human behaviours.[38]

In this state of affairs, as Jérôme and Sylvie believe, impatience becomes the twentieth-century virtue. Seeing the future already in store, as it were, they know they can wait; but they want the future to always already have arrived: '*C'est en cela sans doute qu'ils étaient ce qu'il est convenu d'appeler des intellectuels*' ('It's no doubt this that makes them what we have come to call intellectuals').[39] They find fault in everything because the world fails, in the present moment, to live up to their abstract idea of it, an idea whose realization lies in the future. They cannot open themselves to time, and to the event which would mean that the future might actually remain unknown, or, better, heterogeneous with respect to the presence of the subject here-now. That is to say, they cannot see that the things of the world may *not* exist simply and purely *for them* or for appropriation by them and their consciousness. Like intellectuals, they feel they need to *understand*, almost as a privilege.

My collocation of Auerbach and Lyotard helps strengthen the claim that a Universal History is, paradoxically, peculiarly devoid of historicity. In its homogeneity and implicit simultaneity, its time is oddly 'empty', emptied of events; and, in its 'magnificent homogeneity', its time is also extraordinarily anti-social or at least non-social, non-communal: it is a time that cannot be lived 'together' and is thus 'non-contemporary', anathema to any now-time or *Jetztzeit*. If the ultimate referent of the now is always the transcendental, be it God or a fictionalized transcendental subject, then the now as experienced by specific human agents is always entirely isolated from the temporal existence of all other human agents. Emmanuel Levinas indicates the contradiction implicit in this conception of temporality when he shows, in *Le temps et l'autre*, that 'time is not something made by a singular and isolated subject ... rather it is the very relation of a subject with others'.[40]

In what remains of this present chapter, I shall indicate, firstly, the contradictory philosophy of identity at work in the prevalent conception of homogeneous time; and, secondly, I shall advance the case for a different order of temporality, one that is capable of attending to the specificity of 'the thing here', and also to the possibilities of experience of 'thisness'.

Time under arrest

Aesthetic modernism, by which I mean here that explosion of aesthetic experimentation across Europe from 1848 to 1939, infiltrating the United States at the turn of the century, advances a specifically new conception of the human subject of consciousness. As Virginia Woolf famously put it, 'on or about December 1910 human character changed'.[41] In some ways, the conception of this new subject is extremely optimistic, in the weak sense (the non-philosophical sense) of that term: the subject's individuality, considered as something pre-existing its historical construction or enactments, is seen as a bolster for the emergent modern democracy in which an individuated autonomy is the condition of social existence.[42] Yet it is exactly such an autonomy which – in its deviation into the validation of individualism and of the priority of the subject over the objects of a supposedly exterior or externalized world – eradicates historicity (that exterior world) precisely at the moment when it appears most fully to be internalizing the movement of history itself.

Put more bluntly: the human subject is no longer seen in this as simply the victim of a history to which it is subjected, as an emergent bourgeois democracy claims the principle of subjective autonomy and the possibility of active intervention and determination of history by the individuated subject of consciousness. 'I' am/is free precisely to the extent that I am 'I', or, axiomatically, the modern subject is free to shape and determine its own history. Yet this, while seeming to offer the subject the possibility of internalizing the movement of history (and thus controlling it, subduing it to the identity of the self), does so at the cost of that very heterogeneity which is of the essence of historical change. Instead of history as event (in the Lyotardian sense of the event as the non-predetermined), we have history as narrative, in which the identification of the subject of the narrative is of paramount importance and in which such an identification makes the subject omniscient, transcendent and therefore expelled from the movement of history itself: in short, the subject as Descartes, so to speak. Modernism, in this Cartesian mode and manner, claims and denies history simultaneously: it generates the 'scandal' or threat of human diversity in order to forestall the possibilities of genuine, fundamental historical change or in order to forestall events.

This is clear in the thinking of a writer such as T.S. Eliot. Like Augustine, he too pondered the question of time, both in his poetry and in his criticism. While in *Four Quartets* he appeared to be able to conceptualize a present moment which is rendered non-self-identical through the irruption into the present of time past and of time future, in his criticism such a state of affairs seems to elude him. The most obvious theoretical site for discussion here is his essay on 'Tradition and the Individual Talent' in which he argues – seemingly at one with the thought of the later *Four Quartets* – for the necessity of acquiring 'tradition', an acquisition that requires a specific critical mood or attitude. It is part of the work of a critic, argues Eliot, to see literature whole, rather akin to the way in which history might appear to Divine Providence in Auerbach's description of 'figural' interpretation; and, writes Eliot, 'this is eminently to see it not as consecrated by time, but to see it beyond time; to see the best work of our time and the best work of twenty-five hundred years ago with the same eyes'.[43]

Yet this tradition, like the historical sense which Eliot claims is so crucial to it, is not inert. He writes that:

> The historical sense involves a perception, not only of the pastness of the past, but of its presence ... The historical sense, which is a sense of the timeless as well as of the temporal and of the timeless and the temporal together, is what makes a writer traditional. And it is at the same time what makes a writer most acutely conscious of his place in time, of his contemporaneity.[44]

For Eliot, of course, the point of acquiring such tradition is in order to facilitate the becoming of the 'individual talent', a talent marked by a specific *identifiable* consciousness whose validation or legitimation lies not (as Eliot indicates at length himself) in personality, but rather in the subject as the *medium* for poetry and for the tradition itself. In this arrangement, history (or the tradition) becomes dependent for its articulation (or its narration) on the identity of the subject of consciousness in whose grasp (or voice) it is recorded or archivally maintained. Eliot, thus, sees tradition as instrumental in the construction of a philosophy not of personality but of identity; and such a philosophy is inimical to temporality itself. It is for this reason that Eliot can comfortably claim in his poetry that easy intimacy among past, present, future: all three are dependent upon the logical priority of the subject who narrates – in 'figural' fashion – their interrelations or their fundamental identification with each other. Identity – and this is the meaning of Levinas – is the counter to history; and the formulation, thus, of a history based upon the priority of the modern autonomous subject is inherently anti-historical or non-historical. I do not claim that this state of affairs is anything other than paradoxical, even counter-intuitive.

Walter Benjamin would seem to be, at first glance, an ally in countering the figural or sacred interpretation of history implicit in Eliot's position. In his 'Theses on the Philosophy of History', he consistently distinguishes historical materialism (which is good) from historicism (which is bad). He writes that, 'Historicism rightly culminates in universal history', and goes on to argue that 'Universal history has no theoretical armature. Its method is additive; it musters a mass of data to fill the homogeneous, empty time'.[45] That additive principle, essentially the very parataxis ('and then … and then …') adverted to by Auerbach, reappears here with its concomitant product: homogeneous, empty time. For Benjamin – more restless, less optimistic, than Auerbach in these matters – such a time is not yet and cannot yet be history: 'Materialist historiography, on the other hand, is based on a constructive [i.e. geometric rather than additive] principle. Thinking involves not only the flow of thoughts, but their arrest as well.'[46]

It is such an 'arrest' that is to be taken up in later philosophy as the attitude of time required for the 'event': that eruption into a theoretically comprehensible schema or order of things of some unforeseeable item which demands, but which cannot have, its recuperation into the predetermining theory which has produced its possibility in the first place. This 'arrest-event' is that which makes no sense according to the terms, conditions and norms of the very theory of history that has produced it for our inspection. 'Auschwitz' has become a classic example of this for some postmodern thinkers in that Auschwitz ostensibly cannot be 'explained' by the terms of modernity and enlightenment, even if it has been produced in terms recognizable to the very same reason that shapes enlightened modernity as such.[47] The eruption of the event is thus the interruption of our norms by something rather 'singular' (idiosyncratic, *purely* and literally 'autonomous', giving itself its own laws); and, insofar as it is singular in these terms, this event is the introduction of – or, better, *presentation* of – that which was not promised or foreseen, and thus of that which was not always already *represented*, always already a matter of representations.[48]

The idea of a 'contemporary' which would be a 'real presence' – not implicitly subject to representation – is important to Benjamin. He argues, as we have seen, for the importance of the *Jetztzeit*, a 'now-time' in Thesis 14, claiming there that 'History is the subject of a structure whose site is not homogeneous, empty time, but time filled by the presence of the now.'[49] So far, this appears to be the demand for a different order of time from that enjoyed by Eliot. Benjamin appears to criticize historicism on the grounds not only that it represents history as seen from the point of view of the victors in those struggles that are constitutive of history itself, but also – and more fundamentally – on the grounds that it *represents* at all, and especially from a *point of view*, a term whose very semantics stress the idea of a spatialized homogeneous time. The *Jetztzeit* in its full 'nowness' is inimical to the Eliotic principle that time past is contained in time future, or that past, present and future all commingle under some sacred sign or horizon of interpretation. And yet, in Appendix A to his 'Theses', Benjamin comes so close to Eliot as to be almost indistinguishable from him. It is in this appendix that he argues for a complexity in the notion of historical cause and effect. He rejects simple linearity, describing that as a way of telling history that is like telling rosary beads (in 'Christian' fashion), and argues instead that the historian must 'grasp the constellation which his own era has formed with a definite earlier one. Thus he establishes a conception of the present as the "time of the now" which is shot through with chips of Messianic time'.[50]

This ostensible indecision between two contrasting notions of time is perhaps resolved slightly more clearly in Thesis 16. There, Benjamin argues for the indispensability of a concept of the now which is not merely a transition, a now in which time has, as it were, stopped. In the argument, we get an especially vigorous metaphor, which is all the more striking or eventful and arresting for the fact that nothing elsewhere in the 'Theses' prepares the reader – or indeed Benjamin – for it:

> Historicism gives the 'eternal' image of the past; historical materialism supplies a unique experience with the past. The historical materialist leaves it to others to be drained by the whore called 'Once upon a time' in historicism's bordello. He remains in control of his powers, man enough to blast open the continuum of history.[51]

The first sentence here is unsurprising, and strengthens the claim that there are two competing conceptions of history in contest: the universal and homogenizing set against the discrete, particular and heterogeneous. But from where does the metaphor which suddenly follows this sentence emerge? What we have here is not an argument as much as a characterization of the historical materialist: a fictional self or subject in a narrative situation. Benjamin produces, through the metaphor, a construction of the historical materialist as a character in a tale; he is identified as the austere and manly master of the self or of his own subjectivity, the autonomous ruler of his own body. He is the autonomous subject, unthreatened, unseduced by any dissolution of his material corporeal self, a self dedicated to itself, determined to open a future rather than dwell in the arms of a female past of 'Once upon a time'. Yet the effect is, nonetheless, that of the narrative which begins 'Once upon a time, there was a historical materialist who, though tempted by the seductions of the world, yet remained above them, the austere subject of a consciousness in control of his objects or those others against who he defined himself and maintained himself in readiness for worldly actions.' This self-dramatizing is a re-run of Descartes, the modern philosopher doubting the external world and then refiguring it entirely based upon his own *dubio* and *cogito*. It is Augustine, the paratactician, who wanted to resist the seductions of the world – but 'not yet'; it is Eliot, the sacred critic, austerely denying personality (and thereby indirectly gaining it).

What remains constant throughout these examples is the construction of a philosophy of identity (or more precisely a philosophy of subjectivity) which, as I have indicated, is not only modernist but also non-secular (Christian, messianic, sacred) and hence profoundly anti-historical or non-historical. The 'now' of modernity does not – cannot – exist as such. It can only exist as a transitional and asymptotic moment between a past and a future. The function of history in these terms is to bolster the illusion or fiction of the self, a self which had been threatened by temporality itself right from the moment in Enlightenment when Hume argued against any philosophy based on the foundational principle of a stable selfhood. For the remainder of this present chapter, I shall look at a counter-position to what I have described here as the denial of history that we usually call 'modernity', the modern or (in management-speak) modernization.

The escape from intimacy; confession as the failure of *Selbstdarstellung*

For Levinas, time is the condition of our relation with alterity as such. That is to say: time is the condition of our being and of our sociality. The 'other' that conditions the self is a temporal and not a spatial other. I want to extend this slightly and to make the case that the now – or contemporaneity – can occur as a historical event if and only if it is marked by an intrinsic heterogeneity: now cannot happen now, so to speak.

In the 'figural' view of the now as described above, history is homogenized: the singularity of the historical event is lost under the sign of representation as the historian, ideally omniscient, constructs a universal history in which the single event makes sense as the representation of another event in relation to which it constructs its horizon of interpretability, or in which semiotic constellations are constructed, to be mastered by the individual consciousness of the subject of history, the human and individually identified agent.

I propose here instead a different notion of contemporaneity, one which demands the necessity of precisely attending to singularity and to the heterogeneity of the events constitutive of historical activity, agency and being. The philosophy which will help us to lay this most bare is perhaps that of Clément Rosset. Across a series of books, Rosset argues that the real is real if and only if it cannot be duplicated, and hence that an event is real (or 'historical' to put it in the terms of my argument) if and only if it is inimical to a primary representation, if and only if it is conditioned by its idiosyncrasy and its unimaginability.[52]

While the source of an offensive modernity such as that described earlier might be found in Augustine's Christian parataxis, we might find an alternative – I am tempted to say postmodern – attitude or mood in the thinking of Duns Scotus. I do not propose here an in-depth engagement with Scotist philosophy; rather, all I wish to retain from his thinking is the familiar importance of *haecceitas* or 'thisness': that attention to specificity which is recapitulated not only in the philosophy of Rosset but also in that of Deleuze, Agamben and other recent 'anatheoretical' thinkers.[53] Instead of prioritizing the individuality of the subject (as in the modern), Scotus prioritizes the individuality of the object of cognition, in an uncanny prefiguration of the 'fatal strategies' that we find in the much more recent, and often avowedly 'postmodern', thinking of Jean Baudrillard.[54] For Scotus, the world consists of singularities; and, for the poet who was most directly and overtly influenced by Scotist philosophy, Gerard Manley Hopkins, such an attitude resulted in a peculiar warping of language. There is no prevalence of parataxis in Hopkins's poetry, but rather the attempt to render everything in an object at once: its presence or nowness.

The peculiarity of Hopkins's language is increasingly revisited and made apparent in some more recent writing. There is a stylistic feature developing, influenced if not by Hopkins then by poets of a high modernity such as William Carlos Williams and Wallace Stevens. In this style, we find increasing attention to what we can see as 'not ideas about the thing but the thing itself' (as in the Stevens poem of that title) and an increasing belief in a specific materialism or empiricism that suggests that there are 'no ideas but in things' (as Williams reiterates in *Paterson*). We have seen the same in the French *nouveau roman*, whose early critics, struggling to find a way of describing these odd novels, coined the term '*chosiste*' to try to encapsulate what they held in common. There is a post-Heideggerian poetry of 'The Thing' itself; and this, this thing that I acknowledge mine, while at one level simply a matter of style, carries with it a philosophy as well.[55]

Some examples of the style can be found in the later poetry of Seamus Heaney, most obviously in the collection called *Seeing Things*, where we read, for instance, of 'The deep, still, *seeable-down-into* water' (emphasis added) in a seemingly deliberately clumsy phrase clearly reminiscent of Hopkins. What the phrase means is 'still water, deep down into which you can see'; but in Heaney's phrasing, the emphasis is on the water *as object*, and the subject ('you' or 'one') *has disappeared*. Or consider, for another paradigmatic example from this same collection, lines such as:

Willed down, waited for, in place at last and for good.
Trunk-hasped, cart-heavy, painted in ignorant brown,
And pew-strait, bin-deep, standing four-square as an ark

   ... cargoed with
Its own dumb, tongue-and-groove worthiness
And un-get-roundable weight[56]

In all these examples, as with Perec, we witness a renewed attention to the material otherness of a real and historical world. The importance for these writers, conditioned as they are by this new empiricism in writing, is no longer in the exploration of the subject's consciousness, but rather in the exploration of the material sensuality or sensuousness of the object itself in all its resistant and recalcitrant materiality, a materialism deemed to be unamenable to representation or even to consciousness at all. It is as if we begin the twentieth century with Virginia Woolf's famous call to 'look within', only to end it with a writing that determinedly looks outward, in puzzlement, concerned for this objective reality that we call worldliness.

Contemporary literature is playing out one of Baudrillard's fatal strategies, going over to the world of the object in the interests not of preserving some philosophical principle of reality but rather in the interests of finding out what might be the real in all its heterogeneity, in all its unavailability for human consciousness or for the subject. Further, this 'reality' is unavailable not because of its distance in space from the subject (not because it is 'outside' of consciousness), but because its perception depends upon a *temporal* difference that allows the subject to exist in time, to 'become' across time, as it were.

A similar thing had been attempted before in some European cinema, in which the vision of alterity began to supersede the exploration of the 'point of view' itself. It is clear in *L'année dernière à Marienbad* by Alain Resnais, for instance, where narrative gives way to the fixed stare of the camera on things, even to the point of offering the human characters to us as if they themselves were mere objects. We find such priorities also in the cinema of Robert Bresson, where an attention to the ostensibly trivial object defuses the characterological or subjectivist interest of the film, and stresses instead what it might mean actually to 'see' an object. For Bresson and some of his contemporaries, such seeing must be of the nature of an event: that is to say, the object of sight resists comprehension as a semiotic counter in some grander 'vision' that the subject may have (or even a vision that renders the subject up to us as such). In other words, the thinginess of the world resists theorization.

This is a cinema not of seeing so much as of witnessing. In witnessing, some of the fundamental aspects of cinema are subverted. Ostensibly, cinema is, above all, a visual artform. However, at least since the advent of talkie cinema, there has been a steady tendency to circumvent the sensuality (or sensibilities) of the visual with the sense-making (and rationalities) of dialogue.[57] This becomes evident in a certain strain in cinema, such as that of Barry Levinson, wherein dialogue and the possibilities of communication are paramount. It is central to a film such as Francis Ford Coppola's *The Conversation* of 1974; and it has a much more recent directness in a film such as Tom Hooper's *The King's Speech* (2010). In films such as these, we are encouraged to turn the sensuality of the image into the abstraction of reason through the primacy of a dialogical impulse. In short, what is said is more important than what is seen, for what is said makes sense, whereas what is seen demands a visceral response that may defy signification.

A cinema of witness, however, is one that tends to reverse those priorities. Thus, for example, Bresson opens *Une femme douce* with a sequence in which the camera is focused on the handle of a door. A woman enters the frame and opens the door, and we hear the noise of something falling. The camera advances through the now open door, and we see a table and flower-pot falling on the veranda. Beyond this, there is a further noise, that of a car screeching to a halt on the road below. The camera cuts to a shot, taken from ground-level, of a white scarf falling through the air. At no point, yet, have we seen a human face; every body in the frame appears without a headshot of any kind. It is only after we have seen the falling of the table and pot, and the falling of the scarf, that we then see also a body, face down, on the ground. Our inference, at this point, that a woman has jumped from the balcony (that is, our 'making sense' of the scene) happens only long after we have been required to attend to the visual aspects of the scene, denied any human point of view. In this way, we become not voyeurs of the suicidal jump, but witnesses. We are forced to have a kind of sensual response to an act that we do not directly see; and that response is shaped and informed by the upturned life on the table (the broken flower-pot as it falls to the floor of the veranda) and, above all, by the white scarf falling gracefully and slowly towards us on the ground. We *make sense* of what we see; we *feel* and thus know, as from the inside, what we witness.[58]

The philosophical stakes of this are perhaps best revealed, not entirely surprisingly, in a literary as opposed to an abstract philosophical text. Ian McEwan's *The Child in Time*, though perhaps romanticizing to some extent the notion of an infantile attitude to the world, nonetheless hits on the effect which I am aiming to describe in this alternative contemporaneity. At one key moment in the text, Stephen, the father of the disappeared child, Kate, imagines in her absence how she might see the world before him:

> It needed a child, Stephen thought, succumbing to the inevitable. Kate would not be aware of the car half a mile behind, or of the wood's perimeters and all that lay, beyond them, roads, opinions, Government. The wood, this spider rotating on its thread, this beetle lumbering over blades of grass, would be all, the moment would be everything. He needed her good influence, her lessons in celebrating the specific, how to fill the present and be filled by it to the point where identity faded to nothing. He was always partly somewhere else.[59]

What Stephen appreciates is a seduction of the subject by the objects that constitute the subject as a consciousness at all. The result is the loss of a sense of progressive linear time, and its replacement by a now, a *Jetztzeit* that is not part of a larger schema of history at all, a now that in fact cannot be narrated, since it does not consist in a moment of transition between past and future. It is instead a now which, in all its attention to alterity and heterogeneity, allows the very possibility of the experience of an event in time at all.

The modern, by contrast, is that world inhabited by Stephen who is 'partly somewhere else', whose now is always a transitory movement; but this is Stephen, now and here, Stephen who has lost identity to become this, an event in which he is a constituent part but which he does not control in an act of subjective appropriation of the world or of history.

The now, the here, the *this* are all deictics that depend for their significance, value or meaning on the subject in relation to which they are spoken or to which they owe their existence. The modern – let us call it 'figural' – attitude to this is the attitude that breeds a philosophy of identity in which the now, the here, the this are thought to exist *for* the subject of consciousness; and as such, therefore, they have no existence in their own right.

In philosophy, as I have argued above, we have seen this expressed most fully in Descartes; and Cartesian philosophy is what grounds this entire project, this modernity that places the subject at the centre of meaning. Further, Cartesian philosophy deploys a concept of God to guarantee the being of the objects, the thisness of the world; a being that is now itself, in fact, dependent upon the subject – for the being here is dependent on its meaning in the whole schema. This, therefore, is actually pre-Copernican.

These objects, existing *for* the subject of consciousness, the Cartesian I, find themselves in a position where their *haecceitas* is stripped from them as they are reduced to the status of being but an element in the constitution of a specific subject who enjoys, courtesy of the reification of the now, here and this as commodities, the solace (actually a fiction) of identity and mastery. The non-figural attitude is one which, by contrast, returns to the deictic its own specificity, even to the point of endangering that 'solace of good form' – that identity – of the subject of consciousness.[60] It is in this latter state that contemporaneity can take place, can 'happen'. Paradoxically, the modern, then, knows no contemporaneity: it is only what we might now more comfortably call the postmodern, in its openness to the undetermined, that can make the contemporary happen or become an event.

Yet we must also recall that the postmodern is but a mood or an attitude and not something that is of necessary recent date. The mood in question here is one that is shaped by an attention to the alterity of the world, an alterity that means that the world is not there *for* a subject of consciousness, and a world therefore whose meaning does not depend upon the identification of a stable point-of-view (character or ethos) from which it is viewed. Such a mood is one that may be rather anguished, for it is a mood that acknowledges that the subject, always *now* in history, must fill that now with the exercising of a judgement; but this judgement must be made *without criteria*, and most especially without the solace of a criterion that is grounded in the identity of the self. The counter to such a mood is that which says, 'I judge this as an x, y, or z', where x, y, or z is an official identity (working-class female; Muslim; gay man; Arab, etc.). There *is* no such identity; or rather, better, in a properly confessional mode, identity both *is* and *is not* at once. Identity depends upon alterity.

Thus it is that, at an earlier historical moment, Prospero comes to acknowledge himself in his other, 'this thing I acknowledge mine', this Caliban, in *The Tempest*. It is in the intimacy with his other that Prospero can actually 'confess' himself; but that intimacy gives him (and Caliban) a problem with language. 'I gave you language', Prospero famously tells Caliban; and Prospero, expecting thanks for this, gets only curses. His error is to believe that, in giving Caliban language, Caliban will want to speak that same language: his error is to believe that Caliban can be Prospero's intimate 'likeness'. What the play shows, instead, is the spatial distance between them. It shows that the existence of both characters depends upon a kind of absolute distance that allows them to remain as 'things' – a thing of darkness – and, as things and not objects, they do not exist *for* each other. They simply cannot comprehend each other.

The final paradox, then, is that, for a confession to be genuine and a matter of real historical experience – for it to be an event – it cannot be comprehended as something that is amenable to a 'me, here'. If you confess to me, the confession is only genuine if I cannot understand it (though I may yet witness it). This way, not only can you and I undergo confession as an experience that has a real historical substance and content, but also we refuse the solace in which confession allows for that mode of 'forgiveness' in which we forget the distance that separates us, or that allows us to 'identify' with each other in a fallacious intimacy that is sometimes called 'reconciliation'. Confession is much more serious than that: it potentially shatters the world, breaking the here into distinct and fragmented parts, and shattering the now into historical becoming. That is confession as event; and as an event in which we can finally properly acknowledge the things of darkness that are never ours alone.

PART TWO

4

Dilatory Time

Or, The Necessity of Slowing Down

Conversation and the silent witness

In the central part of his great 1936 film, *Modern Times*, Charlie Chaplin – playing the role of a worker in a self-consciously high-performance and technologically advanced factory – finds himself in the midst of a great industrial experiment. As part of a process and technique of so-called economic modernization, now recognizable explicitly in terms of Taylorist efficiency or productivity, it has been calculated that the worker could save his employer a great deal of time and could be more productive if his lunch-break could become as mechanized as the rest of his day. Chaplin, as the crash-test-dummy for the demonstration, finds himself seated in an odd contraption of a chair. This chair, into which he is strapped tightly, is reminiscent of both an infant high-chair and a threatening electric chair. Chaplin thus finds himself positioned between the beginning and end of a life, between birth and death, and thus caught in the very midst of life itself, as one hovering between innocent infant helplessness and criminal culpability; and this, in fact, is the characterization of the worker in the eyes of the employer. Moreover, symbolically, 'all human life' is contained, as it were, in this motif: we are witnessing, in political terms, the speeding-up of Chaplin's life (proposed as an economic necessity) to the moment where it passes as in an instant or as in an instantaneous now, a *Jetztzeit*. In this construction, he becomes as instantly disposable as the very commodities that he is employed in making; and the question arises for the viewer: what is the worth or value of a life and especially of a life caught in the midst of the now-time?

The meal begins. The problem for the capitalists is that Chaplin's body is – almost instinctively or involuntarily – the site of a resistance not only to the capitalist characterization of the worker-figure, but also (and yet more fundamentally) it is the site of a resistance to a specific conception of the economies of time. It has difficulty in conforming to this economic necessity of speeding-up production. No wonder, of course, in that, as one seated in a proto-electric chair, it realizes that its own very extinction is at stake. In this scene, his body cannot keep up with the regularized tempo of the machine; and, in a kind of exemplification of Bergson's theory of comedy with its struggle for supremacy between the animate and the inanimate worlds, we get the predictably comic and chaotic results, though with highly serious intent. Chaplin is more or less assaulted by the machine, unable to live up to its mechanical 'efficiencies'; as a result, he ends up unfed. For the bosses, of course, the problem is located not in the machinery but rather in the body of Chaplin; for Chaplin, and for the audience, it is the other way round. In these modern times, Chaplin's body is explicitly politicized (we have entered the realm of the bio-political); and the body is threatened with a starvation because of its failures to fit in, temporally, with the modern environment (its *Jetztzeit* is disruptive to the economy).

This fits in with an entire tradition of satire that goes back at least as far as Jonathan Swift, who also brilliantly satirized the attitude of the British to a victimized and starving Irish population and workforce, in his 'Modest Proposal'. One of the key elements in Swift's satirical writing, a writing that often punctured the self-important arrogance of those who believed they were in control of history, was the way in which he demonstrated a rift between the body and its machineries on one hand, and the mind on the other. Swift took delight in noting that, no matter how elevated the mind of the socially pretentious individual, his body still farted, say, despite the best endeavours of a presiding consciousness to ignore the fact or to control such involuntary necessity. We find a similar thing outside of satire, in Montaigne, for example, when he writes in 'On the power of the imagination' of sexual stirrings that happen 'despite' himself:

> We have reason to remark the untractable liberties taken by this member, which intrudes so tiresomely when we do not require it and fails us so annoyingly when we need it most, imperiously pitting its authority against that of the will, and most proudly and obstinately refusing our solicitations both mental and manual.

From this, Montaigne derives the observation that, often, our bodies give away what is going on in our thoughts.[1] In yet more recent times, we find the same thing happening in Beckett, whose tramps especially find themselves or their bodies breaking with convention, and sometimes breaking wind as they do so. All through this satirical tradition, what is happening is the establishment of a discrepancy between a world of interiority and an external or public sphere. More pointedly for our purposes, what is happening is what we might call an *unintentional confession*, in which the body makes public that which the mind would have wanted to keep private. As Montaigne puts it in the essay, 'How often do the involuntary movements of our features reveal what we are secretly thinking and betray us to those about us!'[2]

Perhaps a more precise way of describing this is to suggest that the body enters into the realm of history, one of the first effects of which is to *establish* a separation between the public sphere and an interior realm of secrecy. Once the body acts, as it were, this very division or spatial conceptualisation of the world comes into being. Another way of putting all of this, of course, is to follow Jameson in saying that 'History is what hurts', though clearly this was not entirely what Fredric Jameson had in mind when he came up with that formulation.[3] We might even think of illness itself as the body's method of establishing a division between public and private space, and with it the idea that there is a presiding consciousness that inhabits a different order of being from the body.[4]

Film from the early silent era is especially pertinent here. The technology of cinema in those early days is such that the visual – and in Chaplin's case, specifically the body of the tramp-figure – has to do two things at once: it must be a part of the public realm, the world of exteriority or of nature and history, while simultaneously revealing the existence of a private realm, the world as seen from the point of view of Chaplin's characters themselves. The Chaplin example in *Modern Times* shows that, even in a part-talkie such as this, what is at stake is not just the comic Bergsonian relation between body and machine but, perhaps more fundamentally, the question of temporality itself.[5] What the modern world discovers or reveals, and what it also cannot easily bear, is that the ostensibly single and commonly shared space of the real can be lived at different times and at different speeds.[6]

Perhaps a yet more precise way of putting this might be to say that the temporal order of the private realm need not coincide with that of the public sphere. It is, in fact, the necessity of a discrepancy between these two orders of time that constitutes 'character' or, in more advanced terms, 'identity'. The *distance* or *décalage* between the public and private establishes the specific individuality of particular private orders of time, particular individuals. Individual characters are individuated precisely to the extent that they establish discrepancies between each other with respect to the relative speed at which they live history, and also in terms of their relations with what they perceive to be the more objective speed of the world of the public sphere. That is to say that the public sphere is not made up of individuals who all *simultaneously* reveal their inner conscience; rather, the public sphere is that arena in which power can be established through a play of forces in which individuals reveal or 'confess' themselves *but do so strategically*. The strategy in question relates to the time or moment in which a confession is made. This is nowhere clearer than in declarations of love or of violence.

If it is the case that the body helps to establish not only a distinction of inner and outer worlds, but also a potential discrepancy between them, then it follows that the way in which each body relates to the world need not entirely coincide: we experience or live the world at different paces, therefore. Capitalism, however, with its three eight-hour shifts proposed as a kind of advance on the monastic organization of the day marked by prayer, requires its subjects, its victims, its children, to live at a regularizable speed.[7] That is to say: capitalist society requires that we subscribe to the belief that our confessions can all be coincident with each other, that they are all made *as if at the same moment*. In this way, confessional culture begins its steady trajectory towards the positive validation and evaluations of an ideology of *transparency*.

Chaplin appears to be fully aware of these issues, and *Modern Times* marks an awareness of the possibility that the material body itself, with all its idiosyncratic particularity, might be the site of a resistance to such regularity, such regulation. The body, that is, might prove to be the site of opacity rather than of revelation; and it might thus start to become a bulwark against the *intrusions* of the public sphere. Crucially, of course, it is the recognizable body of Chaplin – the awkward gait, the moustache, the ill-fitting jacket, the boots – which constitutes his specific cinematic and visual identity; and the tenor of the film is that precisely this kind of personal identity – and the realm of interiority, the realm of a private life, even the realm of silent contemplation – is under threat in the mid-twentieth-century condition of capital. In this cinema, it is taken for granted that the saving of such identity is a good thing. Among many other things, *Modern Times* is about the determination to maintain the possibility of a private realm, of a world that is not always already 'owned' and controlled by the demands of the public sphere or of capitalist politics.

For the purposes of this present chapter, the single most significant aspect of this is the link between personal identity and temporality, and the link between these and *silence*. Subjectivity is constituted culturally upon the sense that each individuated subject's 'inner' temporality is the determining instance of identity as such, even when it may be at odds with the hypothetical 'outer' or social temporality of the world of objects. Much of the interest of modern and of modernist fiction lies precisely in this fact and in this constructed discrepancy between inner and outer times, as Virginia Woolf famously indicated[8]. Yet it would also be fair to claim that the tension between such a double order of temporality – inner versus outer, personal versus social – is the very condition of modern fictional narrative, especially as it is formulated in the novel from the eighteenth century to present times, as I have argued earlier in my description of the rise of character or of the self-as-point-of-view. In what conventionally constitutes both 'realism' and 'naturalism', the text finds ways of bringing together the two temporal orders in harmony, usually through the ostensible prioritization of an external temporality to which the central character must, in time, conform.

Yet, to drive a character to ensuring that their identity 'conforms' to the identity of a public sphere is, of course, itself tantamount to silencing the character. Against this, a positive silence can be a powerful means of retaining a private realm, even a private life. In religious terms, a confession is a way of saying something while simultaneously and paradoxically maintaining a silence about it. The confessor is there not to hear, but rather to be the earpiece of a god: that is, the confessor 'hears' what the confessant says; but does not hear it in the way of a standard conversation. The confessant knows that they can say anything safe in the knowledge that their saying it does not allow it to pass into the public sphere. The confessional is a site of an essential silence. That is to say: the confessional box represents a *reduction* of space and of time: it is a 'here-now' that cannot be represented (its words cannot be rehearsed again, for the confessor is sworn to silence), and it is thus a kind of space that is nowhere: a utopia.

A good example for discussion of the stakes here is Francis Ford Coppola's 1974 film, *The Conversation*. Ostensibly a film about surveillance, it becomes – explicitly at one point – a film about the act of confession and the issues of silence for the witness. The film opens with a long-distance aerial shot of a busy lunch-time scene in Union Square, San Francisco. We hear the fragments of conversation, the noise of musicians and the general hubbub of the square. Gradually, at the bottom left-hand corner of the square and of the screen, we see the figure of a street mime-artist. His mime involves the imitation of the walking style of passers-by, picking up their body movements and walking characteristics and following them. The imitation is amusing in itself, and it also serves to draw attention to the sensuality of the body. The mime artist is, as it were, the silent witness who, in following precisely the passers-by, gives them a 'character'. In the moments between his acts, when he is looking out for the next walk to imitate, he goes into a kind of default position of walking around in imitation of the famous gait of Charlie Chaplin.

It is this mime-artist who brings the film's central character, Harry Caul (Gene Hackman), into the film. As Caul enters the frame and the square, the mime follows him: it is as if Caul is being 'introduced' into the film itself by Chaplin. The plot of the film requires Caul to record a single conversation that is going on in the square. The couple talking together are randomly walking around ('in circles', as one of them repeatedly says), and so their voices are not only difficult to follow but at times also virtually inaudible under the general cacophony of the square's activities. Caul deploys sophisticated techniques, recording from multiple sources, and then, in the privacy of his editing-room, putting together a full conversation. The client who has hired him to do this is referred to simply as 'the Director'; and we, along with Caul, gradually discern that 'the Director' suspects his wife (one of the participants in the conversation) of infidelity.

Caul is haunted by a memory of an earlier surveillance job in which three people were killed; and, as he carries out this particular project, he begins to fear that the couple whom he has recorded are in similar danger. The question for him is one of responsibility: he repeatedly asserts that 'I don't care what they're talking about. I just want a nice fat recording'; and yet he gets insistently caught up in imagining the backdrop to the conversation. The couple make an assignation to meet in the Jack Tar Hotel, room 773; Caul takes the room next door and goes to work trying to bug the events in their room by listening through a device that he plants in the wall between the rooms. He recoils in horror as he hears the tape of the Union Square conversation being played; and imagining that 'the Director' is confronting the couple with their sexual betrayal of him, Caul visualizes the Director murdering the wife.

However, when he goes to confront the Director, it emerges that he has misconstrued the central action: the couple, in fact, have murdered the Director, with the assistance of the Director's assistant, Martin Stett (Harrison Ford); and Caul himself becomes the victim of surveillance, as he receives a phone call from Stett telling him that he is being watched all the time from now on, since he knows the secret of the murder.

At one level, then, this is a straightforward thriller plot. Yet it is also a good deal more than that; and it becomes a story explicitly about the relation between the examination of conscience and questions of surveillance, the relation of confession to conversation in a public square (a 'Union' square) and a culture of transparency. Caul is a Roman Catholic, upset at any hint of blasphemy. Throughout the film, he wears a plastic mac, regardless of the weather; but the striking thing about the mac is that it is transparent, and the lighting plays on that transparency throughout. The narrative is set around Christmas time, and we find out that this is also Caul's birthday. We thus have a quiet relation established between Caul and a Christ-figure of sorts. At the end of the film, when Caul effectively trashes his own apartment looking for the bugs that are keeping him under surveillance by Stett, he protects (until the very last moment) a small kitsch statue of the Virgin Mary. When he eventually smashes this too, he discovers that it is empty.

The essential thing about *transparency* is not just that it reveals the inside of something; rather, the essence of transparency is that it does this *immediately*. That is to say, transparency is related to the immediacy of the moment: it literally takes no time at all to see what is going on inside something or inside someone's head. However, as in Chaplin's *Modern Times*, Coppola's film here indicates that such revelations *take time*: it takes a long while, with much *stammering* and repetitions of parts of his three recordings, for Caul to reconstruct or to hear the conversation in the square. Further, the demand for transparency occurs when one feels that there is something being occluded, some obscure *mystery* that needs to be opened up. Such a mystery, within Catholicism, is that of a Virgin birth; but Caul discovers the vacuity of his statue: there is nothing inside, and the only individual whose birth is in question here is already outside, in the external world: Caul himself.

At a crucial moment in the film, Caul goes to confession. We see him in the tiny space of the confessional box, trying (and not quite managing) to confess to what is really on his mind, which is the question of his potential responsibility for the death of three people in the earlier job and the potential death of two more now. Crucially, as this scene flows, the camera focuses less and less on Caul's face and we start to see, emerging in the background, the woven net, the semi-transparent wall, that separates his mouth from the ear of the priest on the other side. As this comes more into focus, we also see the ear of the priest. Importantly, though, the priest remains in total silence. This is the silence of the witness.

This scene is 'matched' by that in which Caul eavesdrops on events in the Jack Tar Hotel room. When he hears his own tapes being played, he is in the position of the priest in the confessional; but, unlike the priest, he tries to drown out what he can hear. He determinedly plays the TV very loudly and buries his head under the bed-covers. As this scene closes, we overhear a news item on the TV: it is about President Nixon.[9] Yet more telling, however, is that in his efforts to overhear events next door, Caul has to get himself into the tiny space underneath the bathroom sink. There, he sits crouched in what is essentially a foetal position, overhearing an adult conversation outside of his body, but in a voice that he himself has already captured and whose words he has internalized, as if he himself could say them. It is this voice – essentially now his own voice – that he must stifle.

As the film closes, he realizes that he is himself forever under surveillance; and thus he can no longer speak at all. The closing scenes leave him, in his destroyed apartment, playing his sax while the camera swivels around, exactly like a street surveillance camera. He has been reduced to an essential silencing of his voice. He has become the mime-artist who introduced him to the film in the opening sequence. Instead of a voice that makes sense, we have a sax that plays sensuality. At this stage, the film becomes one less about conversation and more about the silence that constitutes witnessing; but, as with all witnessing, the witness who is reduced to silence nonetheless experiences the demand to speak. It is this tension that the film captures.

The silence of the witness is what allows a confession to take place; but the question is whether that conversation takes place in a crowded public sphere, a sphere governed by the temporality of a dilatory time in which things are not ever transparent, or whether it takes place under the sign of a non-secular 'eternity' in the confined space of the confessional, where the public is emptied of significance and emptied of time, and where the relation to a transcendent God-figure is determining.

Of wit, witchcraft and capital

This is not just a cinematic phenomenon, nor is it simply of recent date. At roughly the same time as when the modern novel formulates itself into a recognizable 'character-based' genre, philosophers such as Hume were pondering the temporal condition of personal identity. He contests those philosophers who make a foundational principle of the self, claiming instead that we are but a succession of perceptions:

> self or person is not any one impression, but that to which our several impressions and ideas are suppos'd to have a reference. If any impression gives rise to the idea of self, that impression must continue invariably the same, thro' the whole

course of our lives; since self is suppos'd to exist after that manner. But there is no impression constant and invariable. Pain and pleasure, grief and joy, passions and sensations succeed each other, and never all exist at the same time.[10]

Here, Hume asserts that the very condition of temporality, in the form of temporal succession, may constitute a narrative, but cannot found that narrative upon the supposed stability or identity of something called a permanency of self. Consequently, what he calls 'succession' shapes the very idea of selfhood: it can never be, in the terms I am using here, *immediate* or *transparent*. It is, if you will, a position that either retains such a stability and ascribes it to the condition that we conventionally call God, or that acknowledges that such a position simply does not exist. He goes on, in a fashion proleptic of Woolf and, later still, of Deleuze, to claim that 'I may venture to affirm to the rest of mankind, that they are nothing but a bundle or collection of different perceptions, which succeed each other with an inconceivable rapidity, and are in a perpetual flux and movement.'[11]

It is in the face of this scepticism that the *fiction* of a self must be constructed; and one might venture so far as to affirm that the novel exists in answer precisely to this difficulty of considering the self as a entity that is dissolved in or attacked by the fact of temporality. The novel is one of the first 'strategies of containment' in the face of an emergent sceptical and anti-foundationalist philosophy. What it 'contains' is the dissolution of identity through the strategy of insistence upon an essentially autobiographical fiction. In a deconstructive manoeuvre, the self – ostensibly threatened by the temporality of the narratives of successive experience which produces a personal history – becomes, in the novel, the condition of the possibility of narrative itself.

Such manoeuvring comes under further pressure in the twentieth century, when the temporal dimension of fiction is often thematized and foregrounded. Proust's great text, *A la recherche du temps perdu*, offers a time that overlaps with itself, giving us continuous present moments that act as a repository of the past while being simultaneously an enactment of the present. Joyce organizes *Ulysses* around a classical framework of twenty-four hours, simultaneously stressing the specificity of 16 June 1904 and aligning its every moment with a mythic classical precursor. Woolf repeatedly celebrates the transitory and evanescent series of fleeting moments that fail to amount to a chronology. The later *nouveau roman* in France, much influenced by these modernist writings (as we have already seen in the case of Perec), experiments with what Nathalie Sarraute described as temporal *Tropismes*, with repetitions and contradictions whose point is the rupturing of any kind of linear temporality, progress or developmental narrative. In mid-twentieth century Europe and the United States, theoretical feminism starts to argue against the construction of time as simply linear, claiming that such linearity is intimately associated with masculinism; and the effect of this theoretical move is to reassert the link between time and the (now gendered) body. No longer can time be construed in fiction as the expression of an immaterial subjectivity (*durée*) but rather as a corporeal experience, tied firmly to material history and especially to the materiality of that history as it is inscribed on the body.

This, I stress, is not a new issue; rather, it is the condition of the problem of narrative itself. For random examples, Samuel Richardson's *Clarissa* offers us a central character whose somatic experience is every bit as firmly tied to temporality – to delay and deferral – as Woolf's *Mrs Dalloway*. Henry Fielding's *Tom Jones* is as conditioned by contradictory time – if in different corporeal ways – as is Joseph Conrad's *Nostromo*. Yet, in every case, no matter the historical period, what is fundamentally at issue is the construction of a philosophy of identity; and what is engaged is the strategy of containment which cannot bear the anti-foundational impetus uncovered by Hume. The result is that narrative, paradoxically, while being conditioned necessarily by temporality ('what happens next?') is nonetheless also the site for the circumvention of temporality and of its effects. Narrative is thus a kind of 'scandal' which allows a culture to believe that it is fully facing up to the facts of temporality (i.e. fully facing up to the eventual fact of death), allowing it also to believe that it has countered the dangerous or menacing effects of time on personal identity, while actually being engaged in a project of denial of temporality as such.[12]

Nowhere is this more apparent than in the great modern form of the *Bildungsroman* where, as Franco Moretti has convincingly argued, the entire temporal dimension is always subservient to a spatial organization of the network of social relations.[13] The central characters of the *Bildungsroman* find themselves on the margins – or sometimes 'outside' – of their society or community. They lack authority or legitimacy, often by dint of the fact of their relative youth: typically, when we meet the character, they are at the early stage of maturity. Accordingly, lacking in recognition and legitimacy by the social formation, and feeling themselves to be on the outside of it, they must use their time in order to establish the proper relation or distance with regard to that community. Typically, then, the character undergoes what I have called the *crisis of intimacy*; and it is by finding an appropriate or 'proper' place in such a community, often through a marital or otherwise erotic engagement with one who is perceived to be already 'on the inside', that the character resolves their difficulties of identity and of legitimation.[14] This most temporal of narrative forms is actually a cover for the establishment of a kind of spatial consensus-formation, in which 'outsiders' can be accommodated; and the accommodation in question is one that gives them their identity – and with it their authority – explicitly as 'insiders', in agreement with the dominant norms of their social formation. In this, the outsider fundamentally has to ignore their own inner temporality (their youth, say), and to regulate themselves with respect to the social formation: they internalize its ideology, and thus become themselves internal to that ideology, accepted within the society. This is what we saw being deplored by Chaplin, and more specifically by Chaplin's body, of course, in *Modern Times*. It is that condition in which a Harry Caul tries to prioritize the non-secular relation established by confession-as-examination-of-conscience over the opacities of a public sphere in which dilatory time ensures that the private is not always immediately revealed or in which transparency becomes the poor substitute for truth.

The most successful explanation of these suppressed temporalities, and the philosophy which 'excuses' our ignoring the anti-foundational condition of the temporal or historical subject, is phenomenology. In the work of Georges Poulet, Jean Pouillon, Jean-Pierre Richard, A.A. Mendilow and, more recently, Paul Ricoeur, we see the explication of modern and modernist time in terms of the experience of temporality by a subject of consciousness which takes its identity in relation to whatever it construes as its objects: such an experience is always conditioned by the subject's 'point of view' upon an essentially stable order of objects in the world.[15] The experience of time has given way to an experience of distance or perspective upon the objects which are thought to constitute the real.[16] In such a manoeuvre, this historicity of both the real and of the subject can be evaded. The result is that time is homogenized in what is fundamentally that *theological* version of time that Auerbach characterized as 'figural' time.[17] How might we recuperate a heterogeneous time which lies repressed under the predilection for a spatial consciousness whose function appears to be the preservation of a philosophy of identity in the face of the anti-foundationalisms that, after postmodernism, we now know very well?

Michel Serres argues for a different and less homogeneous (or transparent) sense of the temporal. He indicates that the past is not necessarily always finished with, and that different levels of time can overlap with each other. He offers the simple example of the modern car which, though apparently merely a twentieth-century phenomenon, nonetheless is temporally much more complex:

> *elle forme un agrégat disparate de solutions scientifiques et techniques d'âges différents; on peut la dater pièce à pièce; tel organe fut inventé au début du siècle, l'autre il y a dix ans et le cycle de Carnot à presque deux cent ans. Sans compter que la roue remonte au néolithique*

> It forms a disparate agglomeration of scientific and technical solutions from different ages; you can date it bit by bit; such and such a component was invented at the start of the century, another piece ten years ago and the Carnot cycle nearly two hundred years back. Not to mention the wheel, which goes back to neolithic times.[18]

He corroborates a view that a linear conception of time marked under the sign of constant progress and 'modernization' is inherently theological.[19] He argues that this mode of thinking is that of 'breaks' or 'ruptures', progressive steps:

> *Entre l'Antiquité mythique et la science contemporaine, intervient une fracture qui rend à la fois le passé révolu et le présent véridique. Cette thèse m'a toujours*

paru de l'ordre de la réligion: entre un archaisme perdu et l'ère nouvelle, il y a un événement, la naissance d'un nouveau temps.

Between mythic Antiquity and contemporary science, we have the intervention of a break that both renders the past superseded and the present veracious. This thesis has always seemed to me to be of the order of religion: between a lost archaism and the new era, there is an event, the birth of a new time.[20]

The very notion of progress is one that produces an alleged or implied intimacy between the present moment and truth itself, such that to be in the 'now' is to be in the know as well. Such Optimism, in philosophical terms, is fundamentally religious, and also fundamentally non-historical, in a paradoxical sense. We have here, according to Serres, not time at all, but rather simply a form of *violence*:

Ce n'est pas là le temps, mais une simple ligne: ce n'est même pas une ligne, mais la trajectoire de la course à la première place, à l'école, aux Jeux Olympiques ou au prix Nobel. Ce n'est pas du temps, mais le simple jeu de la concurrence: encore la guerre ... Plus profondément: seul, en effet, le temps peut rendre compossibles deux choses contradictoires; exemple: je suis jeune et vieux; seule ma vie, son temps ou sa durée, peut rendre ces deux propositions cohérentes entre elles; l'erreur de Hegel fut de renverser cette évidence logique et de prétendre que la contradiction produit le temps, alors que l'inverse seulement est vrai, que le temps rend possible la contradiction. D'où toutes les absurdités racontées depuis lors sur la guerre, mère de l'histoire.

This isn't time, but a simple line: it's not even a line, but the trajectory of the race for first place, at school, at the Olympic Games, or for the Nobel Prize. It is not time, but the simple play of coincidence: war again ... More profoundly: in fact, only time can make two contradictory things able to coexist; for example: I am young and old; only my life, in its time or duration, can make these two propositions cohere with each other; Hegel's mistake was to overthrow this logical evidence and to pretend that contradiction produces time, when in fact only the inverse is true, that time makes contradiction possible. From this come all the absurdities recounted ever since about war as the mother of history.[21]

A different conception of time is implied by this Serresian logic. According to this, the present can never simply be the present in all its supposed transparent identity. As we have seen before, the present cannot coincide with itself: *now is always then.* The present is marked by the contradiction of difference; and, further, such contradiction is fundamentally the counter to a more primal violence or to a 'war-mentality' which more usually conditions our ideological formulations regarding temporality or progress or history as endless chronicle or 'annalistic' movement. For Serres, the presence of the past is as important as the presence of the present; and it follows from this that we might attend to our experience of time, time as it is lived, as being never constituted simply or purely by a present tense that is considered as some kind of advance on the past.[22] Every moment as it arises opens a new present or a new set of temporal possibilities, relations, intimacies; and, consequently, history 'eventuates' or actually happens – that is, takes place as an event – when we are made aware of the inter-relation between two or more temporalities. This is close to what André Gide might have meant when he described his ideal novel as one where the plot would not cohere, where '*l'action ne s'engagera pas*'. It is also closer to the notion of time that we see in some other great literary modernists, like the Eliot of the opening of *Four Quartets* or of Proust.

In *Le temps sensible*, her great study of Proust, Julia Kristeva proposes something similar to Serres when she asks:

> *En effet, dans quel temps vivez-vous? Dans quel temps parlez-vous? Un dictateur nationaliste, qui a vite fait de répandre l'intégrisme, vous rappelle un Moyen Age inquisitorial ... Nous vivons une chronologie disloquée qui n'a pas trouvé son concept.*
>
> In fact, in what time do you live? In what time do you speak? A nationalist dictator, who has quickly moved to spread integrationism, recalls for you an inquisitorial Middle Ages ... We inhabit a dislocated chronology that has not found its concept.[23]

Two competing notions of history are at work in these different conceptions of time. The first, marked by Optimism and contaminated by religion, is that accepted by many forms of leftist 'historicizing' criticisms. It reveals a narrative of history whose truth is fundamentally guaranteed by the fact that it is the latest version of events. This is the truth of the modernists, as satirized by Swift in *A Tale of a Tub*, when his author, the protagonist in another battle between times or between ancients and moderns, writes that 'I here think fit to lay hold on that great and honourable privilege of being the last writer. I claim an absolute authority in right, as the freshest modern, which gives me a despotic power over all authors before me.'[24] In this manner of thinking, time is *only ostensibly* heterogeneous, for the different times of the past are all guaranteed as fundamentally homogeneous by the *identity* of the subject who narrates them: by definition, 'I'. This is, as it were, the author as guarantor of Auerbach's figural time.

A surface level of difference, according to which we say that yesterday is different from tomorrow, is merely incidental to the identity formation of the subject in whose consciousness such differences are finally eradicated in the construction of an identity-position which makes a narrative sense of the world, and then claims this as the only – or totalizing – narrative sense of the world. Thus, the critical 'I' claims a truth grounded in that 'I', but a truth that is only a falsely constructed transparency. This critical 'I' confesses itself, reveals itself as the very substance of what it claims as history; but to do so it has to appeal to a now-time that is itself taken out of history and evacuated of content. This is the 'I' of Coppola's confessional box: an I that has divorced itself from the public square and that gains its identity by an appeal to a transcendent and non-historical transparency or immediacy.

The second understanding of history here is one that is less concerned with the construction of a 'coherent' identity for the subject of its narrative. In contradistinction to the first, this second history is 'dislocated', in Kristeva's terms. It is a time which, in the language of Serres, makes contradiction – and hence criticism – possible.[25] With regard to time in fiction, the effect of this is the production of different types of plot-structure. Kermode described plot in terms of the minimal, yet substantive, distinction between the 'tick' and the 'tock' of a clock as it marks the movement of time. However (as I have argued at length elsewhere),[26] this structure is by no means universally accepted, nor has it even really been a normative structure for the novel, as we have inherited that form from the late Renaissance to the present day. What Kermode described was plot as the difference between a beginning and an ending; yet it is still clear that there remains a philosophy of identity and of 'self-sameness' here, for the beginning and ending are the beginning and ending always of *the same thing*, such sameness being the very condition that permits the perception of difference in the first place.[27] But what if 'your' end is 'my' beginning, or vice versa? What if the beginnings and endings are not contained within the one whole or structure: that is, what if these are historical beginnings and endings that do not necessarily coincide in an alleged single universal history? In this, the critic's 'confession' is a gambit in a conversation held in the public sphere.

The 'tick-tock' model of fictional time is one where plot is homogenized into a single and univocal sense. It is thus the structure usually ascribed to a hypothetical 'classical realist novel'. However, what is much more important for the development of this present argument is the element of *speed* in this. As A.A. Mendilow indicated in his early study of time in the novel, the word 'speed' is intimately related to the word 'success' or, as I would prefer it, 'succession' and successive time.[28] For instance, the plot of classic detective fiction operates according to a certain dynamic of speed and logic of succession: it is the task of the reader in this fiction to get one step ahead of the detective, to hasten things towards a resolution in which the disparate elements of the narrative or plot can fall into their 'proper' or assigned and definitive steps, ranged and rearranged in order to construct one vision of a single homogeneous and plenitudinous time: all moments accounted for, and all in their 'proper' and defined place. The element of suspense usually associated with such fiction is itself directly related to speed and to this hastening towards a teleological thinking whose guiding principle remains that of philosophical Optimism, and whose driving force is that of an alleged historical progress under the sign of a homogeneous, univocal – or, as we have seen already in Auerbach's expression, 'figural' – narrative. The plot structure of 'success' and 'succession' is one that operates as a guarantor of truth in the epistemology of fiction, for it produces the identity of the reading subject, and legitimizes such identity through the identification of the reader's temporal solution of the text with that of its focalizing point of view in the detective.

Of course, fiction does not always conform to this theoretical model. It is my contention that, within every such temporality of succession, there lurks an impetus to arrest time, to slow things down and to deny thereby the optimism implicit in the idea of universal history, progress and the accords of a univocal view of what constitutes the truth of the things of the world. This is most obviously laid bare in a fiction such as *Tristram Shandy*, where Laurence Sterne explicitly describes his preferred organization of plot as one based not upon progress but upon digression and deviation, and in which there are found many examples of the refusal to accept speed as the condition of narrative. Yet more important is the refusal to accept speed as the condition of the eventual marrying or coinciding or *intimacy* between text and reader that allows the reader to subscribe to a belief in a single universal history in which we can all be located as coinciding with each other or as living the same moment. Interestingly, this textual example, ostensibly about the identity of Tristram, denies the solace of such a good formal identity: not only does the text not really get any further than the day of Tristram's birth, it also gives the character the 'wrong' name, poses problems about the genealogical heritage of the character, and reduces identity to – at best – the notion of the 'hobby-horsical' obsessions of one such as 'my Uncle Toby'.

Sterne's text initiates a tradition that acts as a counter to the philosophy of identity at work in the temporality of fiction. That tradition has come to appear more and more insistently in writing that figures under the sign of the so-called postmodern. Stevens, for example, in Kazuo Ishiguro's *The Remains of the Day*, undertakes a six-day trip whose temporal direction is consistently regressive; Tom Crick, in Graham Swift's *Waterland*, recounts a personal history whose roots lie in the ancient history of Fenland in a tale that is almost Faulknerian in its dilatory telling; Martin Amis, in *London Fields*, digresses in Dickensian serializing fashion, following that with a text whose temporal organization is explicitly backwards, *Time's Arrow*; and so on through many other less celebrated examples. In the latter part of this chapter, I will attend in some more detail to one paradigmatic text in this tradition, Ian McEwan's *The Child in Time*, in order to reveal more fully the stakes of this tendency to *slowing down*.

The Child in Time follows to some extent in a tradition associated with the postmodern in which the contemporary novel looks back to the great themes or forms of the past. While certainly not a novel in Linda Hutcheon's category of 'historiographic metafiction', nor Ackroydian *imitatio* such as *Hawksmoor*, nor yet a Barthian parody in the manner of *The Sot-Weed Factor*, it is nonetheless a text that tackles a great Victorian theme: the construction of childhood and the 'sentimental education' of one who thinks of himself as already sentimentally educated.

In some ways, the text is structured like a Victorian novel, though never quite as explicitly as in the case of Amis's *London Fields*, say. Where this latter almost revels in its Dickensian scope, McEwan's novel prefers a tight organization, in which Hardyesque scenes of déjà-vu overlap with events strongly linked by metaphorical coincidence or structural repetition. *The Child in Time* opens with the kind of random occurrence favoured by Woolf and theorized by Gide in his notebook for *Les faux-monnayeurs*, where he argued for the necessity of a plot in which '*l'action ne s'engagera pas*'.[29] In McEwan's case, the event is the disappearance of a child, which sets up the neo-Romantic quest structure that ghosts the novel; but, for McEwan's characters, such a structure is set up to engender not the keeping of an appointment or the establishment of a coinciding of the time of the child with that of her parents again, but rather a structure of *disappointment*. Kate, the child, is never seen again; and, to some extent, her disappearance is but the excuse for a narrative that does not concern her, that takes place as if in another time entirely.

McEwan, like some of his modernist precursors, is looking here for what is ostensibly a contradiction in terms: he seeks a plot that is 'un-preprogrammed' or *undetermined* while not yet being simply aleatory. This is a modification of conventional plotting, which we might think of as an organization of things based on the *magical* power that is metaphor. The time of metaphor is, of course, *immediacy*: metaphor brings together two ostensibly unrelated events or things and links them in a chronology that is instantaneous. Michel Butor explains something of what is at stake here in his *L'emploi du temps*, where his character George Burton outlines how detective fiction works:

> *tout roman policier est bâti sur deux meurtres dont le premier, commis par l'assassin, n'est que l'occasion du second dans lequel il est la victime du meurtrier pur et impunissable, du détective qui le met à mort... par l'explosion de la vérité ...*
>
> *Le détective est le fils du meurtrier, Oedipe ... parce qu'il tue celui à qui il doit son titre ... parce que ce meurtre lui a été prédit dès sa naissance, ou, si vous préférez, qu'il est inscrit dans sa nature.*

> every detective novel is built upon two murders of which the first, committed by the murderer, is but the occasion for the second in which he is the victim of the pure and unpunishable murderer, the detective who puts him to death ... by the explosion of truth ...
>
> The detective is the son of the murderer, Oedipus ... because he kills the person to whom he owes his identity ... because this murder has been predicted for him ever since his birth, or, if you prefer, it is inscribed in his very nature.[30]

The detective is immediately – metaphorically – linked to the criminal in a way that brings their temporal existence into immediate relation: they live the same moment, as it were, just like Oedipus and Laius. Further, this Oedipal structure is one where not only is there a kind of interchangeability between Oedipus and Laius, between criminal and detective, but also (and more pertinent to our present argument), *time itself is controlled*, and controlled in such a way as to *prevent* any kind of event: '*ce meurtre lui a été* prédit dès sa naissance' ('this murder has been *predicted for him ever since his birth*'). The character simply fulfils a pre-existing role, and realizes an essence that was always already there and latent; and this, of course, is anathema to action or event.

The temporal relation involved here is one that has been seen before, in the early modern period, for example. Shakespeare's *Macbeth* is built upon precisely this metaphorical 'magical' structure, in which 'tomorrow and tomorrow and tomorrow' is always already with us, as it were. The witches are there partly as a reminder that time itself is controlled; and, as they control it, urging it ever onwards to its predetermined fulfilment or resolution, so the future becomes the 'immediate', visible, here-and-now. The play is one in which there is no temporal dilation, no ability among any of the characters to slow things down such that they can be fully in their present tense. Always, the action is geared towards a future which insistently contaminates, infiltrates and, indeed, *informs* or gives an identity to the present moment.

This is the control of time and of speed; and there is a philosophy explicitly associated with such control; and that philosophy is capitalist through and through. Lyotard is interesting in this regard. Like the McEwan of *The Child in Time*, looking for the underdetermined event in his plot, Lyotard describes the 'event' of thinking – indeed, philosophy itself – as the unprogrammed, as the thought that answers to no predetermining theory or homogenizing force. Thinking, for Lyotard, aims not at the solace of the good form of consensus or of a truth that would not be subject to temporal difference, a truth that could be transparent, immediate and so self-evidencing that it means the end of persuasion; rather, it is always dissident precisely because, insofar as it is genuinely historical thinking, its content cannot have been entirely or purely predetermined by the circumstances that give it its occasion.

In his essay on 'Time Today', Lyotard argues against the Optimism and totalizing impetus of a Leibnizian monadology, claiming that the perfect monad (God) is an entity for whom time is an impossibility. For such an entity, as for the witches in *Macbeth*, all history is homogenized – *and thus cancelled* – under the sign of instantaneity. To think the world in the totalizing terms of Optimism or the monad or a single univocal and universal history – and, by analogy in passing, to think the novel in terms of predetermined 'Oedipal' plot – is to pretend or aspire to control the future, to deny its possibilities, and finally to foreclose the future to the extent that it actually comes 'before' the present. As he explains this, Lyotard is able to tie this attitude to temporality and the homogenization of history to a specific political or philosophical economy. Here is how he puts it:

> what comes 'after' the now will have to come 'before' it. In as much as a monad in thus saturating its memory is stocking the future, the present loses its privilege of being an ungraspable point [a point that asymptotically disappears 'between' a past and a future] ...

Now there is a model of such a temporal situation. It is offered by the daily practice of exchange. Someone (X) gives someone (Y) an object a at time t. This giving has as its condition that Y will give X an object b at time $t1$ ... the first phase of the exchange takes place if and only if the second is perfectly guaranteed, to the point that it can be considered to have already happened.[31]

The political dimension becomes clear and can be related directly back to the predicament in which we left Charlie Chaplin at the opening of this present chapter. If the future can be brought thus into strict intimacy with the present, we are in a situation governed by the excess of speed. Technological speed thus brings about the identification of times t and $t1$, to the point where they entirely coincide. At this point, if you will, Oedipus becomes his own father. Two consequences follow: first, the myth of the autonomy of the subject begins; secondly, history as such is eradicated. That is to say, the construction of the myth of modernity, characterized by the autonomy of the subject, finds that such autonomy is established at the cost of the possibility of historical agency. The modern malaise is that we become autonomous and free precisely at the point where we leave the arena in which such autonomy might count, in which we might actually do something.

Capital, whose value structures find their origins in the kind of exchange described by Lyotard, is thus complicit also with the eradication of history: paradoxically, this most energizing and mobile of political forms knows only the 'scandal' of time and permits only superficial historical change: indeed, as we already know, change at the level of the superstructure thrives on the monumental solidity and unchanging nature of the base. In these terms, capital is anathema to history for the simple reason that it cannot see the historical event in its singularity; capital requires the magic of metaphor, the programming of a future, the 'plotting' or spatialization of historical time if it is to survive.

At the opening to our cultural modernity, Shakespeare was already aware of something akin to this. In *Othello*, Iago knows well the political importance of time and speed. Having told Roderigo to put money in his purse – in passing, we should note the link to the economics of a situation – Iago urges patience in terms which make it clear that he knows the lessons that will soon be displayed in *Macbeth*, written and performed probably just a few years later. He tells Roderigo the difference between wit and witchcraft: the latter is immediate, rather like those Lyotardian exchanges or like metaphor; and thus, witchcraft is also like the operation of capital. The former, wit, depends however upon the dilations of time: 'Thou know'st we work by wit and not by witchcraft, / And wit depends on dilatory time.'

When the novel emerges as the dominant form of literary modernity, it emerges as a form that conventionally depends upon witchcraft, insofar as it depends upon the compression of time or speed: the reduction of the time of the plot into a single temporal moment, or into space. The novel conventionally works by producing sets of 'coincidences', and the entire impetus of the structure is geared towards a speed in which the reader attempts to forestall, to 'prevent', the text's resolutions through the witchcraft that we call prediction.

McEwan's *The Child in Time* adopts a contrary principle to this principle of coincidence. Like a number of newer fictions, especially those associated with an experimentalism admittedly far removed from McEwan, this novel adopts the principle of *disappointment*. Where Beckett's characters, Vladimir and Estragon, can console themselves in *Waiting for Godot* with the assurance that at least they keep their side of the appointment, here it is the failure to coincide that opens the text to temporality, playing its disappointments off against the more usual temporalities that we associated with modern narrative. *The Child in Time* is concerned with Iago's 'dilatory time', with a time that will allow for an attention to the specificity of the singular event without always requiring that such an event finds a metaphorical correlate elsewhere which will give it significance or value, or which will reduce it to an element of our 'understanding'. The novel is aware that there may be events that are simply not available for our understanding, or that are not there in order to be understood; rather, some events – insofar as they genuinely are historical events – are there to be undergone, experienced.

We have a number of examples of this dilation of time in McEwan's text. Consider, for instance, the road traffic accident in which Stephen is involved. When Stephen is driving to see Julie on one occasion, a truck in front of him overturns and blocks the road. As he travels inexorably towards the truck, Stephen experiences the event – according to the standard and apocryphal view of these things – as one in which time is felt to slow down. The text emphasizes this tardiness, this duration which, in objective terms, is but a matter of seconds but which is experienced entirely differently:

> In what followed, the rapidity of events was accompanied by the slowing of time ... Stephen headed into it [the truck] from a distance of less than a hundred feet and at a speed which he estimated, in a detached kind of way, to be forty-five miles an hour.
> Now, in this slowing of time, there was a sense of a fresh beginning ... He had removed his foot from the brakes, reasoning – and it was as if he had just completed a monograph on the subject – that they were pulling the car to one side ... The whole experience had lasted no longer than five seconds. Julie would have appreciated what had happened to time, how duration had shaped itself around the intensity of the event.[32]

Following this, Stephen helps the driver from the wrecked cabin of his truck. McEwan gives a lengthy description of how this is done, the effect of which is to increase the peculiarly realistic intensity of the event itself. Yet this is a scene that will later be realized as having been uncannily proleptic; but the important point for the present argument is that the prolepsis is unseen for the moment. At the time, it does not call out for any 'magical' or witchcraft-like metaphorical completion in any latter narreme which will 'resolve' its function in the text. Instead, it is read simply as an episode marked by verisimilitude and intensity.

Towards the end of the novel, Stephen – and McEwan – will recall it for the reader when Stephen is delivering the child to whom Julie gives birth. The child's head as it emerges is paralleled with the head of the truck-driver in the crash. There, in the crash, we have seen the truck-driver's cabin, upside-down, crushed into a small space; and the truck-driver's head sticks out, awaiting what we can now see as a 'delivery' at the hands of Stephen. The effect of this structure, however, is almost precisely a counter to the 'magic witchcraft' structure of the capitalism of which the novel's content is critical. Where the capitalist organization of time gives a present tense whose function is to control the future and homogenize time, here, in McEwan, the future sends us back once more to the singular intensity of the primary or original event. Importantly, further, the future event does not 'redeem' the past by making a sense of it: on the contrary, the later event serves to enhance the peculiar particularity of the former event.

The effect of this narrative organization is to slow the reader down, to send them backwards in time – and backwards in the text – in order to appreciate once more and more fully the singular and radically heterogeneous intensity of the event of the accident on the road. This can be seen to be 'wittily' linked to the birth of Julie's and Stephen's second child; but it cannot be assimilated fully to that birth. It most certainly neither foretells nor structurally 'demands' or requires it. Neither the birth nor the accident is the product of the control of time; rather, they are the effects of its uncontrollability and of its dilation.

This backwards motion, or temporal dilation, is reflected in the larger scale of things by the trajectory of the character of Charles Darke. Darke, who reverts to childhood in a very unsettling fashion in the text, is seen to play out his adult life in a series of intense experiences whose value is increased precisely because he takes – or recaptures – the time required to indulge them, his own version of an earlier Proustian 'lost time'. The loss with which this text concerns itself is not just that of a child; rather it is a novel focused on the loss of *time* itself, on the loss of the kind of temporality that we experience in childhood, an open temporality that is pure history in the sense that, in childhood, we lack the necessary ability to make sense of one thing in terms of another.

We have another series of circumstances in this text, directly involving Stephen and his own birth, which will help attest to just such a claim. When Stephen visits Julie in the country, he stops near a pub called the Bell. The Bell marks time in this text in a very specific way. Stephen feels drawn towards the pub and, looking in through the window in a somewhat disturbed state of mind, he sees his parents. Here, he is not looking across space and not across a distance; rather, he is looking across time, though he does not yet know it. The significance of this event is once again delayed or deferred, and is to be revealed only when his mother also looks across time, recapturing a lost moment when she informs Stephen that the matter of his own birth had been resolved when his parents sat in the Bell, and his mother 'saw' Stephen, not yet born, as she looked out through the pub's window. When the story is shared between them, much later in the text, Stephen's mother does not claim any kind of deep correspondence; rather, she contents herself by saying only that '"It almost connects up ... Almost."'[33]

It is with his mother that Stephen establishes a deep temporal relation. Before she was married, her name was Claire Temperly, already suggestive of some notion of a 'clear time'. She works in a department store where she is praised for her punctuality; and her meeting with Mr Lewis, Stephen's father, comes about when she is transferred to the clock department of the store. She is a kind of repository or archive of time itself; and, insofar as Stephen's detective-like Oedipal position is confirmed, it is confirmed precisely by a *dis*-identification with his father, and by a close intimacy with the womb of his mother.

It is this intimacy that is played out in the pregnancy of Julie, of course. When Stephen makes his first visit to Julie in the country, the visit that is punctuated by the stop at the Bell, they make love. He plans to return later but fails to do so, delayed as he is by the road traffic accident. It is on his third visit, some nine months later, that Julie and he will rediscover the possibility of their relation. Julie had become pregnant as a result of their sexual relation in that first visit, and she now gives birth to the child who will certainly not be a replacement for the lost Kate, who will not act as any kind of magical or metaphorical redoubling of her, who will not make her loss in any way understandable or bearable, but who will open Julie and Stephen to the possibility once more of a future, to the possibility of their having a historical life. It is at the end of the text that we can see it all to have been a kind of intensely delayed and experienced present tense, from the moment of the disappearance of Kate to the moment in which their child is born. The structure is a kind of reverse-chronology, making its way from the disappearance of a child back to the moment of a child's birth; but it is vital to stress that the children in the case are not interchangeable, one not a substitute or representation of the other. The second child does not redeem the loss of the first. We do not have here anything as simple as a kind of flashback structure; rather, we have a narrative structure in which the same (the child) turns out to be different (not Kate), and in which time's passage is so arrested, so dilated, that it appears to stall and go backwards.

Finally, it is clear that there is a philosophy associated with this temporal dilation. In the countryside, Stephen stands alone at one moment and ponders that the place where he stands 'needed a child'. He goes on:

> Kate would not be aware of the car half a mile behind, or of the wood's perimeters and all that lay, beyond them, roads, opinions, Government. The wood, this spider rotating on its thread, this beetle lumbering over blades of grass, would be

all, the moment would be everything. He needed her good influence, her lessons in celebrating the specific; how to fill the present and be filled by it to the point where identity faded to nothing.[34]

It is the celebration of the specific, the ability to experience time itself, that Stephen is after here. The consequence of such an experience is, paradoxically, the loss of an identity; after all, identity requires that there be a coinciding between the I and time t and the I and time $t1$; and an attention to the particularity of the present precludes such identity being established. It is, in short, a celebration not just of heterogeneity as such, but of the heterogeneity of time that is proper history, and also the heterogeneity of the I that is always *becoming*, always differing from itself, always, thus, historical. I am not claiming here the validity of a kind of 'intensity of the present', for the text as a whole demonstrates clearly the points made by Serres and reiterated by Kristeva that the present is itself always already contaminated by other times. The present is not the site of identity at all but rather of difference in a specific form. Such difference is associated with what Clément Rosset called a form of 'idiocy': a specificity which, insofar as it is real at all, is thereby inimical to duplication, to representation, to metaphor – and hence to capital. Dilatory time offers the wit necessary to outwit the politics of the kind of government (recognizably Conservative and capitalist) deplored in *The Child in Time*. It allows for an opposition to the time that is being imposed on Charlie Chaplin as he sits in his high-chair, a high-chair that is really an electric chair, in *Modern Times*.

It is for this reason that slowing down offers a narrative politics whose impetus, perhaps paradoxically, can be called 'progressive'. More importantly for the purposes of this book, it gives a historical dimension to any act of confession, making it an event in the public sphere.

5

Waste and the Ecology of Anguish

L'homme n'est qu'un roseau, le plus faible de la nature, mais c'est
un roseau pensant. Il ne faut pas que l'univers entier s'arme
pour l'écraser; une vapeur, une goutte d'eau suffit pour le
tuer. Mais quand l'univers l'écraserait, l'homme serait encore
plus noble que ce qui le tue, puisqu'il sait qu'il meurt et
l'avantage que l'univers a sur lui. L'univers n'en sait rien.

Toute notre dignité consiste donc en la pensée. C'est de là qu'il
nous faut relever et non de l'espace et de la durée, que
nous ne saurions remplir. Travaillons donc bien à penser:
voilà le principe de la morale.

Man is but a reed, the weakest such in nature, but he is a thinking
reed. The entire universe has no need of arming itself in order to
crush him; a vapour, a drop of water suffices to kill him.
But when the universe would crush him, man would be yet more
noble than that which kills him, because he knows that he
dies and he knows the advantage that the universe has over
him. The universe knows nothing of this.

All our worth consists therefore in thought. It's from there that we
need to set ourselves up and not from space or duration, which we
wouldn't know how to fill. Let's work hard therefore at thinking:
there is the principle of morality.
Blaise Pascal, *Pensées*[1]

Je plains le temps de ma jeunesse ...

I pity the days of my youth ...
François Villon, 'Le testament'[2]

In confessing, the self is faced with a specific set of issues that we might
now start to identify as the issue of reduction or kenosis. The self has to
evacuate from itself all that is extraneous to its intrinsic integrity and austere
purity, all that is not I-here-now, in order the better to be able to reveal, in
truth, the very constitution of the I-here-now itself. This is something that we
have seen, clearly, in Descartes, whose entire opening intellectual gambit in the
Meditations is precisely this anorexic reduction of the self.

Such a reduction to the bare self, however, is structurally modelled on another act of reduction that has its basis in religion. Specifically, in fact, it is the structure of the 'event' that is known within Christianity as the resurrection, that movement of a radical reduction of the self, even to the moment of death, before its resurgence. Descartes likewise reduces the self philosophically or in theory to a kind of threshold or liminal zero-point (doubting to the point of eradication the external world, then doubting likewise the body that mediates between external and internal worlds, and finally then doubting the substantive interiority that is the mind) before rebounding back, like sand in an hourglass, and reconstituting the very solidity that he had denied in the first place (the certainty of doubt, the certainty of being a thinking substance, the certainty that this thinking substance has a kind of access to the world, and thus the resulting certainty of the existence of the very world – but now transformed – that had been doubted in the first place).

The result, of course, is that, in the case of Descartes, what we call 'modernity' begins when the *meaning* of the world supplants in importance the *being* of the world, and where the meaning of the world depends on the I or is subtended by the I. In all acts of writing, in fact, we see something similar. The case is laid bare, as we have seen in earlier chapters, by the Robbe-Grillet of *Dans le labyrinthe*; but we can find it elsewhere as well, from Montaigne's reflections on the self or in Shakespeare's Hamlet or Lear, through an entire history of Romantic thought and on into the self-reflexivities of modernist literature. All acts of writing, as Maurice Blanchot would tell us, in some way depend on this structure of kenosis.

One response to this, the response favoured by Blaise Pascal among others, is to see the Cartesian worldview as not just solipsistic but also nihilistic. For Pascal, the rational secularism of the Cartesian view is one where the existence of anything outside I is ostensibly denied (thus solipsism), leading to a radical reduction of reality to a zero-point (thus nihilism). The response is the famous wager, the wager on the existence of something absolute and absolutizing beyond the self, God. Once God is in place, however unprovable and ineffable, we have a resulting awareness of a responsibility of sorts, a sense that there is something absolute against my zero-self to whom I must justify myself. Again, the logical structure of a confessional mentality becomes a necessity, this time marked by absolutist religion.

We can begin to explore this via Blanchot. He opens his *Faux pas* by noting that 'A writer who writes "I am alone" … can seem a little ludicrous'.[3] To write this phrase presupposes the existence of someone else to whom it is written, for whom it is written, against whose existence one defines one's solitude. It is a paradox, and, indeed, for Blanchot, the preliminary and fundamental or foundational paradox of literature itself. 'As soon as one utters it [the word 'alone'], one makes present everything that it excludes,' he writes.[4] Stronger than the word 'paradox', of course, is the word 'lying'. In writing this reduction of the self to its intrinsic solitude, the solitude that is necessary as a kenosis for confession to occur authentically, the writer is seemingly forced to lie, or at least to base the act of writing the confession upon a ground of inauthenticity. Yet, if confession is to be worth anything, it needs to be true.

Thus – and in this Blanchot is a precursor of Beckett in his *Three Dialogues with Georges Duthuit* – the writer 'finds himself in the increasingly ludicrous condition of having nothing to write, of having no means with which to write it, and of being constrained by the utter necessity of always writing it'.[5] The writer, in this condition of kenosis, a condition that is an absolutely necessary precondition of the possibility of confession, must somehow express this negation in its purest sense:

> And he himself is already reduced to nothing. Nothingness is his material. He rejects any forms in which it offers itself to him, since they are something. He wants to seize it not in an allusion but in its own actual truth. He is looking for a 'No' that is not 'No' to this, 'No' to that, 'No' to everything, but 'No' pure and simple … the 'I have nothing to say' of the writer, like that of the accused, encloses the whole secret of his solitary condition.[6]

This neatly brings the structure of confession – which, for Pascal, would have been marked by religion – into the realm of the legal as well. There is always, and necessarily, a suspicion regarding the validity of, or at least the trustworthiness of, a criminal confession; and here, we see the fundamental reason for it. It is, of course, exacerbated by factors such as torture or even the simple demand or request for confession; but, at base, even if a confession to a crime is simply proffered, it is of necessity suspect.

In some ways, we could see this kenosis as a kind of reduction of the self – the wasting away of the self – to the condition of total transparency. It is the moment when the I is able to reduce itself to being not really there at all, the moment when I becomes 'Not-I', as it were, or, to put it more bluntly, the moment of the disappearance of I, precisely and paradoxically as the mode of the assertion of the presence of I. The word that we use to describe this condition is death or dying. Confession, thus, is linked to a mode of literary suicide, metaphorical destruction of the very self that, in its destruction, necessarily reasserts itself. It is the Krapp of Beckett's *Krapp's Last Tape* or the speaker in his *Not I*; it is the necessity of suicide as 'the only serious philosophical question' in Camus. It is also what Simon Critchley describes as a condition of human being itself. Following Heidegger, Critchley writes succinctly that 'The human being is death in the process of becoming', itself a kind of modification of Montaigne and Cicero in saying that '*Philosopher ce n'est autre chose que s'aprester a la mort*', that is, that the study of philosophy is essentially a readying of oneself for death.[7]

In this present chapter, I want to explore more fully the importance of death as an element that shapes the confessional drive. In one of his essays,

Montaigne argues that we should not make judgements about our happiness or otherwise until the moment of our death.[8] Death is, as it were, the moment of a final confession, be it religious, juridical or purely secular. In earlier chapters, I have suggested that confession operates as a kind of apotropaic warding-off of death, that it is a way of surviving one's own death. It is this that now needs further exploration. The question relates to how we encounter what I will call 'the ecology of anguish'. Anguish here relates to the confessional demand that seems to be always incomplete: a confession unheard or unwitnessed, as in my previous chapter, becomes constitutive of anguish. It generates an ecology of abundance: the necessity to repeat the confessional discourse; and at the same time it is constituted by kenosis, a reduction of self.

We will look at the body, survival and the relation of both of these to the emergence of witnessing. If the confessant confesses in order to survive their own death, then what of the witness who, by definition, lives on. The chapter will of necessity look at the idea of bare life, and of how Agamben considers the position of the bare life in relation to the ongoing function of the camps that shape our contemporary moment.

In this present chapter, then, I will also start to explore more fully the nature of what I'll call the 'wasting' of the self, this anorexic movement in which the self is reduced to what Critchley refers to as 'very little, almost nothing'. I shall examine how it is that confession is seemingly moulded by a structure in which we go down to zero before re-emerging as one, as the only one, as the one and only. This looks forward to work on the relation of confession explicitly to democracy: a one that is *representative* of many, a confessing one that is reduced to zero and wasting away while at the same time being greater than itself and constitutive of a community as a whole.

Autonomy and responsibility

One key element that determines the shape of cultural modernity is the drive towards autonomy. Within this, there must be a definitive attempt to become responsible for one's own entire being: to give birth to the self, as it were. We have seen something of this in my discussion of Coppola's *The Conversation* in Chapter 4; but the more usual way we have described this is in terms of modernist literary self-reflexivity, whereby texts become seen as texts that somehow not only refer to themselves, but seem to be auto-generative. The *Kunstlerroman* (literally 'artist's novel') would be the classic form of this: a text that is about how the author came to be in a position to write the very text that one has just read.

The precursor to this might lie within a Romantic tradition, such as we see it in Samuel Taylor Coleridge's *Biographia Literaria* or, more obviously, in William Wordsworth's *The Prelude*, where we see the growth of the mind of the poet who becomes able, once that mind has grown and developed, to write the very poem that details and describes the growth, the coming-into-being of the poem itself. That poem, of course, itself grows organically through various rewritings; and that growth is part of its intrinsic logic. It demands its own re-reading, as it were; and this catches something of the sense of confession as marked by the stammering of a beginning, such as I described when discussing Heaney. One modernist text that makes this kind of expansiveness and necessary reiteration into a theme is Proust's ever-developing *A la recherche du temps perdu*.

When Robert David MacDonald decided, in 1979, to stage Proust's work at the Glasgow Citizens Theatre, he produced a translation of the excessively abundant novel, calling it *A Waste of Time*. He was playing on various senses of the term, obviously: waste here suggesting expanse;[9] but the phrase also suggests waste in the sense of loss: an unproductive loss of time.[10] This latter sense is interesting: it implies an expansion of time, but an evacuation of its content, a time that is both full and empty at once.[11] At more or less the same moment, Joyce in *Ulysses* and Woolf in *Mrs Dalloway* are 'reducing' great expanses of history into the schematic form of a single day. Eliot is writing *The Waste Land*, a poem that attends to the fact that the spaces of Europe have been laid waste after the First World War: its London Bridge crowded, but with the dead; its 'hooded hordes swarming' towards cities of the Unreal. The cities are there all right, but these too are now reduced purely to *formal* elements, their content at best shadowy, like the merest ghostly representations of a reality that has been lost, a proto-Hiroshima in which the body is but a burnt shadow on the earth. Indeed, one might even say that the very pilgrimage in question in this poem is a pilgrimage in search not of lost time and disappearing history, but rather in search of lost space and lost place.

Waste of time and waste of space: these key modernist texts are at the centre of the theme for this section of our question, in which I will be exploring the confessing of the self as a reduced entity, a transparent or bare self, as a prelude to a more full examination of the relation of representation to democracy within modernity.

That relation depends, to some extent, on the location of an individual within a community; and such a relation is a matter not just of their location in space, but also in time. In one sense – the ancient sense of the word – an 'individual' is one who is entirely representative in that they cannot be distinguished from – divided out from – the group that gives them an identity; yet, in another sense – and this has become the modern sense – an individual is individual precisely to the extent that each *is* distinguished from their community. The simplest way to consider such distinction is to think of the individual as being in some way out of place or out of time: the alienated youth of the *Bildungsroman*, say, who feels themselves to be adjacent to or even opposed to their community; or the avant-garde writer, who is already inhabiting a future aesthetic and awaiting the day when the rest of the community will catch up. For these, Hamlet-like, the time is always out of joint;[12] and we have learnt to think of this in terms that are given to us not simply by Hamlet himself, but, behind that, by Montaigne: how do we constitute ourselves as historical agents, with a sense of responsibility or answerability – literally a 'confession' – for any action that we might initiate? Further, how do we even consider the possibility of 'initiating' an action?[13]

In such cases, the question of that locatedness of an individual can be considered in terms of a question of what we can call the anguished economy of the self. In what follows, I shall explore this under the general terms of waste and abundance within the thinking that constitutes modernity.

Although they have been characterized above as dealing in waste, nonetheless both Eliot and Proust (and, in different ways, Joyce and Woolf) are writing texts that are grounded in a certain abundance or cornucopia as well. For Proust, the abundance lies partly, though not entirely, of course, in the sheer epic size of the task; and the novel, in its functioning as a comic and social satire, draws mocking attention to the riches and abundance of a certain high society whose self-definition rests on a notion of *grandeur*, a modern-day equivalent of Pierre Corneille's *gloire*. Excess is one of the key themes of the text; and excessive size – a sheer 'too-muchness' – is part of its point. Proust is a little like those burghers among the Dutch elite of the seventeenth century, flouting their wealth ostentatiously to the delight and irritation of the English traveller (as described by Simon Schama in *The Embarrassment of Riches*).[14]

Eliot's text, though relatively thin itself (and made more anorexic by Ezra Pound, of course, who took pleasure in trimming it back) is yet enriched by being a kind of nodal point around which the history of European literature is called up. Like a brash Walt Whitman, Eliot's text 'contains multitudes', but whereas Whitman's brashness is seen in his unrestrainable 'long line' sprawling itself across the page like a frontiersman edging across America, Eliot's 'containment' of the multitude that is European literature and culture is marked by restraint, by the short and sometimes abruptly cut or interrupted line, and by understatement. Yet in this text, what we have is not just the words of Eliot, but also that stammering thunder at the end of the poem, the 'Da' that tries to stutter out three Sanskrit words; and we have that prefaced essentially by an act of listening, but listening to the voices of the dead as they speak through the poem and its quoted allusions.

Both Proust and Eliot, then, give us expanses of time and of space. The staging of Proust's work in Glasgow in 1979–80 is also of symbolic significance. This is the beginning of a period that will see the flamboyant parading of wealth offered as a social norm, via a Thatcherite valorization of 'business' and of private gain. For Thatcher, 'there is no such thing as society'. It is in the face of this kind of attitude that the Glasgow Citizens Theatre staged Proust's great text, with direction by Giles Havergal and design by Philip Prowse. These two, with MacDonald, were a triumvirate who made this theatre into a major cultural venue. The location is important. At the time, the theatre sat in the middle of one of the most economically deprived areas of Britain: the Gorbals. However, the Gorbals was being steadily demolished, and the Citizens Theatre ended up as the sole remaining building in the middle of an enormous waste land. It became a focal point for a political and social demand: the demand for community. The area may have been deprived, and even deprived of its buildings; but a theatre remained, and in that space, we did not have a reflection of Glasgow but rather the exploration of a world beyond, a world of possibility. In this, the economic deprivations were countered by communication: by the professing, as it were, of an identity for the economically starved and marginalized, of a very specific polity. The theatre survived the devastation of all around, as the Gorbals eventually shrunk into the space occupied by the theatre; but it survived in that it became the source for a reasserted identity, and one that was transformed or redeemed in the rebuilt and now more bourgeois revived public space.

There is a particular relation here, to which I want to draw attention as our starting point. The relation is one explicitly between waste and abundance. The abundance of wealth is itself precisely wasted, wasteful: indeed, it is a pure version of waste. The terms are certainly not opposites; one need not be a deconstructor to see that waste is abundance and vice versa. Yet if I say that that which is superfluous is wasteful, what would we do with other kinds of superfluity, such as that discussed by Wordsworth in the Preface to the *Lyrical Ballads* where he describes poetry as a 'spontaneous overflow of powerful emotions'?[15] An overflowing is, by definition, literally a kind of superfluity; and, to that extent, an overflowing is something inessential and unnecessary – a waste. Or what if we simply describe that which is abundant as being 'redundant'; how might we feel about describing abundance as a form of redundancy, or even 'unemployment'?

I offer these two examples: Wordsworth and the unemployed – to give a sense that not only are we here talking about economic terms, but also that the economy in question has both an aesthetic and a political or social dimension. In summing up this theoretical preamble or framework, however, I also want briefly to return to the observation that I make about both Proust and Eliot. I suggested that they give us a way in to answering our predicaments in that their texts lay bare the possibility of our having the *forms* of space and of time without the space and time in question having any specific and material *content*. In this, I claim further evidence that they are indebted to a philosophy that derives from Augustine, and to an Augustinian form of thinking – the confessional impetus – that gains ground and legitimacy as part of the condition of our modernity itself.

Augustine famously pondered repetitively – indeed, abundantly – the question of time. In his greatest address to the topic, not in *Confessions* but in the waste land that is the *City of God*, Augustine relates time directly to the question of death. Explicitly there, he points out that to think the content of the temporal 'present' is akin to thinking the content of the word 'dying'. He argues that it is difficult to identify the moment when a person is dying or 'in death', not just in empirical terms but firstly in logical terms. There are, he says, three conditions: that which is 'before death' or living; that 'in death' or dying; and that 'after death' or dead. He rhetorically conjures away the middle ground, the moment of dying, by a philosophical reduction: one is either alive or dead, before death or after death; and, he argues, it is extremely difficult – if not strictly impossible – to identify a moment of transition, the moment 'in death' or the moment of dying.[16]

While dying certainly happens, the moment in which it happens is rhetorically reduced to a kind of inexistence: we have, as it were, the formal necessity of the moment's having taken place, but the content of the moment cannot be detected or experienced, given its status as pure transition, pure transitoriness. Augustine then makes his key connection between this and time. Exactly the same structure, he says, shapes our experience of time: the future mutates into the past 'without transition' as it were; and thus, the present moment is also now – like the moment 'in death' – emptied of content, while also being formally a necessity. Clearly, both the present moment and the moment of dying actually exist in some way, but as if in another order of existence; and, most simply put, they now have a purely formal existence, an existence without content. The present, therefore, is but one part of a formally necessary narrative structure that allows us to relate past to future in what we call a plot, say; but now, we have to effect that relation, that plot, in terms not of a presenting but of a *re-presentation*. The present – like death – can only exist in the form of its representations; and, moreover, it has only a formal being, with no actual content.

This is important for modernity and for modern narrative, as can be seen if we think of some emblematic moments: European romanticism would not have taken the shapes it did without its elegiac tone; to some extent Proust's great text is haunted by the death of the grandmother; Eliot is haunted by the Sybil, unable to die, and still, in 1922, by the dedicatee of his 1917 volume, Jean Verdenal, '*mort aux Dardanelles*' (dead in the Dardanelles, or Hellespont); a death in the waste land that is Venice for Thomas Mann; the wartime death of Percival and the post-war death of Septimus Warren Smith in an alienating London for Virginia Woolf; D.H. Lawrence's Gerald dying in the snow and ice of *Women in Love*; Michael Furey and his no longer to be heard 'very good voice' haunting Joyce and his characters in 'The Dead'; Faulkner in *As I Lay Dying*. Such emblematic moments continue all the way into contemporary literature (as in Gabriel García Márquez's *Chronicle of a Death Foretold*, of the work of Primo Levi, or Jim Crace's *Being Dead*, or Graham Swift's *Last Orders*, or Maggie Gee's *Dying, In Other Words*) and, of course, in theory (Blanchot, Derrida, Agamben, to list the most obvious). All this, of course, not to mention Beckett (of whom more later).

Modern narrative, we might say, is a structure that attempts the apotropaic warding off of death, a structure that tries to deal with the unbearableness of death – the unbearable lightness of being in a present moment which, if we are present to it, is a moment of death. It tries to deal with this unbearable moment by emptying it of content, precisely at the moment when it also renders the moment formally central to a narrative; and the result is a kind of celebration of the *representation* of death. Indeed, one might go so far as to say that it is a celebration of representation *as* death, and as a way of avoiding the content of death simultaneously.

The paradox to which I draw attention here is that the moment of death, in its identification as the moment of the present, becomes the ground of autonomy and of responsibility. It is from this moment that modernity draws a symbolic 'birthing' of the self, a giving birth to the self; or, more simply, it is in this moment of *crisis* that modernity finds the possibility of a self asserting responsibility for its own *beginning* of something, its initiation of itself and thus also its 'self-confessing'.

Of the embodied voice as witness

These, then, are essentially questions pertaining to what we might call 'the economies of the literary'.[17] In our time, we have seen this question assuming a great importance pedagogically. New media have generated a culture of immediacy, alongside which is an ideological assumption that 'transparency' should be a normative value; and we have seen consequently a corresponding reluctance to delay not only the 'consumption' of material goods, but also the processing of texts.[18] Anecdotally, but perhaps also empirically, it is thought that few students or readers have the time for the older 'big texts', or even for long poems; rather, we live in and through a culture of the anthology, the fragmented parts of texts: a whole ecology of sampling. This is itself akin to Eliot's method, of course; but for him, the anthology was not sufficient, and it was vital that, in hearing a line of Dante, we somehow were aware of the entirety of his work and able to conjure it up through one nodal citation; in opening *The Waste Land* proper with an echo of Geoffrey Chaucer, the reader is supposed to be able to summon up the entirety of the *Canterbury Tales*, and, indeed, part of the sense of the text as a pilgrimage-poem derives from our awareness of a geography that takes Eliot eastwards, way beyond Canterbury, to an endpoint that seems close to the Ganges where the thunder speaks in faltering and stammering Sanskrit.

Among the many things that this poem asks is a question that will become focal to what I am arguing here: what is the *proper* place of the human? What constitutes our *propre*, our 'property' or properties, that which is proper to our self? How do we assert our identity and the *limits* of that identity or selfhood; and in relation to what original sources or roots can I take my identity, again as something *propre* or without my identity spilling over into those places that are beyond the circumscribed life? Further, how do we assert our own voice, and thus claim the possibility of confessing authentically, if we speak in the voices of absent others, of the dead? What, in short, is the relation of witnessing to the dead when we rehearse their words, when we cite them in order to find our own confessing voice, as in Eliot?

This kind of question can only be asked once one is aware of the full significance of (for present exemplary purposes) Chaucer, say, acknowledging the totality of that identity as we find ourselves 'hearing' the whole of the *Tales* in Eliot's opening line. The allusions that punctuate Eliot's text draw attention to particular places and to a geo-politics that gives the text much of its meaning. These allusions are not simply economic, therefore (shorthand references, synecdoche, as it were), but are also *ecological*: they have to do with an environment, with how we as humans figure in the waste of space that is the waste and wasted land.

Let us develop our inquiry, then, from the question of economy and ecology and the relation of these to writing, and especially to modern and contemporary writing. Following from the Eliotic example, we can approach the issue of ecology and economy by thinking more about the place of the body in literature. How does the body relate to its environment? In Beckett's great narrative trilogy, we have a moment that seems to replicate Augustine. We have *Molloy* 'before death', *Malone Dies* 'in death', and *The Unnamable* in some other place or state. We have already seen, the condition of the Unnamable reduced to the transparency of the 'thing that divides the world in two', reduced, as it were, to the merest fold of skin: 'perhaps that's what I feel, an outside and an inside and me in the middle, perhaps that's what I am, the thing that divides the world in two, on the one side the outside, on the other the inside, that can be as thin as foil'.[19]

For Beckett here, the body can be reduced to essentially to the medium for the voice or for language itself. Beckett asks the same question as does Agamben, when in *Il linguaggio e la morte* he writes that '*Noi parliamo con la voce che non abbiamo, che non è mai state scritta … E il linguaggio è sempre "lettera morta"*' ('we speak in a language that we do not have, and that has never been written … and language is always "dead letter"').[20] In Beckett, as in this particular argument of Agamben, the body is reduced or reducible to an extremely bare form, not just to the medium through which the voice of the dead speaks, but also like the membranous form of the skin.[21] If that is also the site of a writing or of a representation, then we can immediately see the terrifying logic here: the body becomes the site of a tattoo, and thus also for a taboo.

In at least one waste land that haunts the modern world, the body becomes the site on which a number can be tattooed, a certain abundance of numbers, between six and nine million; and the existence of that number on the skin that is now the self is something that effects the reduction of the self to pure waste, to an *availability for death*, as it were.[22] The self is reduced, as in Primo Levi, as in William Styron's *Sophie's Choice*, to a number tattooed on the arm. The self, in this transparent condition, is prey to – indeed, is essential to – the bureaucratized condition of modern being where the human has been reduced to pure instrumentality, pure function. In this, confession becomes a matter of an allegedly transparent faith, a belief or ideology (one 'confesses' Jewishness, for example, in the way that one belong to a 'confession' or faith) that is so *immediately* transparent that it brooks no discussion and will result only in a silencing that brings a death from which there can be no ensuing transformation or autonomy.

For the moment, however, let us remain with the literary aspect of this, as opposed to the directly political. This excessively – abundantly – anorexic body of the Unnamable has its literary precursors. So let us look for a moment elsewhere, and at the literary body. There has been a long history of thinking the body in rather excessive terms. François Rabelais might appropriately start us off here, with Gargantua and Pantagruel, giant bodies whose sheer abundance of size allows Rabelais to make a series of comic observations about human wastefulness, and, indeed about human waste or excrement. The history can be traced through later medieval or early Renaissance allegories of the human body (Edmund Spenser's House of Alma, the lyric poems of Charles d'Orléans), and on into Swift, say, whose satirical explorations of perspective, with the giant Gulliver, lay open or transparently reveal what the anti-psychiatrist Norman O. Brown famously called his 'excremental vision'.[23] It continues to the present day in the work of a satirical allegorist such as Will Self, or even in that of J.K. Rowling, whose Hagrid owes something to the Falstaffian tradition of the naively roguish larger-than-life figure. As is well known, many critics have been content to allegorize the stage in Beckett's *Endgame* as the interiority of a human head, its high back windows proposed as eyes and so on. We can also think of a whole tradition of American poetry, with that Whitmanian 'long line' mentioned earlier travelled still in John Ashbery and the like. These lines transgress boundaries: they announce the ever-onward movement across the terrain of the page; they are as expansive as the spirit of Whitman himself.

At the core of this is an ecology of the human body; and we can possibly see this most clearly if we turn to look at two examples from the seventeenth century, at the very foundations of what we now recognize as our modernity: *King Lear* and Andrew Marvell. In *King Lear*, I want to draw attention to a moment when Lear is accused of a particular wastefulness in the abundance of his following courtiers, with all their rich accoutrements. This play is organized from the start around various questions of economy: indeed, it lays bare for us the very terms of the emergent management of space that accompanies a new economics of capitalism, where land and sex enter explicitly into measured exchange, thus allowing us to think even of sex and its associated rituals or activities as potentially wasteful in their potential abundance (that 'expense of spirit in a waist of shame'). How much land is worth how much love, asks Lear, for example; or what will Burgundy or France accept by way of a dowry with Cordelia? And, of course, what will she confess in the way of love, and how will her confession (as those of her sisters) be determined by the economy that shapes the play's governing and presiding idea of values and truth?

These issues set up a tone of measurement in which Lear, like some contemporary accountant or auditor, explores how we might quantify quality. The profligate France, of course, is the antithesis of this, seen as odd – or what we will later call 'sentimental' – in his willingness to think of love as being outside of the economy, not subject to rationed and rationalized measurement: wasteful, abundant and all the more 'un-English' for this dyseconomical profligacy and prodigality. Later, as we will see, such prodigality is the condition of a *grace* that serves a political purpose in its disturbing of an early capitalist economic structure.

Essentially, Lear starts by giving us an example of the very predicament regarding the relation of waste to abundance with which I began this present chapter. He gives up the *content* of kingship while determinedly trying to hold on to its *form*. That form is symbolized by the retinue of one hundred knights that he will retain, and that he expects to be entertained, month and month about, by Goneril and Regan. In the horrendous Act 2, Scene 4, with Lear's knights making excessive noise, their voices fully heard, Lear is told by Goneril that she will accept only half of his retinue – fifty knights and no more – at her house. He curses her. He then flies to Regan who, primed in this by her sister, halves the number again, reducing him to five-and-twenty. He is now near silenced. And then, in one of the play's most cruel moments, Goneril says: 'Hear me, my lord. / What need you five-and-twenty? Ten? Or five? / To follow in a house where twice so many / Have a command to tend you?' And, as if this is not enough, Regan then interjects with the final and fatal blow: 'What need one?' Lear's response is a plea for abundance: 'O reason not the need! Our basest beggars / Are in the poorest thing superfluous.' This, then, is Lear being stripped to the bare life, to the unaccommodated man that he sees himself reflected in eventually in the figure of Poor Tom, naked on the heath.

Later in that same century, Andrew Marvell writes a paean of praise to Fairfax, 'Upon Appleton House'. Interestingly, Marvell comments on what is essentially a modesty of sorts – a non-abundance, as it were – within this impressively large place. He compares the building of Appleton House with the brash and showy wasteful abundance of other stately homes. Here is what he writes:

> Why should of all things man unruled
> Such unproportioned dwellings build?
> The beasts are by their dens expressed:
> And birds contrive an equal nest;
> The low-roofed tortoises do dwell
> In cases fit of tortoise shell:
> No creature loves an empty space;
> Their bodies measure out their place.
>
> But he, superfluously spread,
> Demands more room alive than dead …[24]

Here, he notes the sheer size of the space, and comments explicitly on it; but comes round to thinking that there is really no need for such excess, such abundance. The human, at the limit or considered in terms of fundamentals, can be best identified not by the house and surroundings, but really rather by the bare life of the single body itself. It needs no more space to be itself that the space that can essentially be circumscribed as the space of the coffin.

In these pages, I have repeated the term 'bare life' to describe what is at stake in this stripping bare of the human being. The term, in my usage of it here, comes from Agamben who, following Michel Foucault, sees the politicization of biological existence as the decisive entry-point into our modernity: 'the entry of *zoē* into the sphere of the polis – the politicisation of bare life as such – constitutes the decisive event of modernity'.[25] The ancients made a distinction between *bios* and *zoē*. The latter is the crude fact of existence itself – bare life; while the former equates to a kind of mode of living – bare life as modified by its living, by experience. The bare life is at the root of this issue of waste for us; and we arrive at it here, now, in modernity, as a political situation in which the body as such has been politicized.

In a certain sense, we find ourselves reduced anorexically to the bare life, to the position of the Unnamable; and our only possible distinction is on the surface of the skin: no inside, no outside, pure surface – and whatever makes us distinct from someone else, in this situation, is operating structurally in exactly the same way as the tattooed number on the arm in the camps. The tattoo is, as it were, a writing on the body that not only politicizes the body itself but also politicizes it as the site of a *transparent confession*, an allegedly unmediated 'evidencing' of identity and meaning.

In this predicament, we are all bearing the tattoo of the camps, and the camps have become the inescapable and carceral condition of modernity. The contemporary world, politically, is precisely that domain in which we increasingly see the triumph of form over content – which is actually here another way of describing the politicization of bare life, the transmutation of *zoē* into *bios*. No one has a right to a private life anymore; for such privacy would mean a return to content, to the quality that makes us *propre*.

This was all prefigured for us by Walter Benjamin in his celebrated 'Work of art in the age of mechanical reproduction' essay.[26] In these pages, I want to address just one small aspect of that extremely complex and rich essay. Benjamin points out that, prior to the age of mechanical reproducibility, art is rather difficult to access in an odd but very precise way – given that there is but one singular work, typically it is geographically or geo-culturally distant. If we do manage to get into the presence of the single work, we become aware of its aura, that 'unique phenomenon of a distance' through which we become enabled to see the art as a product of struggle or even of violence. As he will put it in the 'Theses on the philosophy of history', we can see the barbarism that underpins and is the dark side of the culture. Thus, when I do go and see a work that has not been or that could not have been reproduced, I become aware of the work as the site of a 'contained' history: the work, in a quite literal sense, 'contains' the historical struggles and is filled with the substance of the history that made its very existence possible; and, in that containment or substantive filling, it simultaneously and paradoxically both makes those struggles availably apparent while yet occluding them under the ostensible subject matter and execution of the work itself. The work is, as it were, like the point in the middle of an hourglass: it sits isolated at the centre, containing or filtering a before and an after, the before being the historical struggle, and the after being our critical reception.

In the age of mechanical reproduction, by contrast, I lose the specificity of that 'contained' content, and see instead merely a beautiful picture: I see, as it were, those elements of the work that we have learnt precisely to call the *formal* elements in their aesthetic structuring, but I ignore the history and struggles that produced the very particularity of the image. For Benjamin, the distinction between these two modes of approach to a work of art is decisive, and has a political corollary.

For Benjamin, fascism is what happens when we find ourselves in the normative condition of evacuating historical content from art, and believing that form is the primary totality of that work. As he puts it in the odd afterword to the essay, the masses have a right to change property relations; and capital says in reply, 'let them express that right'. The content of the right is replaced by the poor substitute of a persuasive rhetorical but formal argument. This is extremely close to Agamben's claim, following the politicization of bare life – that biopolitics that constitutes modernity – that modern democracy is contaminated by the persistence of Nazism and fascism. 'Today,' writes Agamben, 'politics knows no value ... other than life, and until the contradictions that this fact implies are dissolved, Nazism and fascism – which transformed the decision on bare life into the supreme political principle – will remain stubbornly with us', leading to a state of affairs where there is 'an inner solidarity between democracy and totalitarianism'.[27]

Crucially for my present argument, it follows that representation *as such* is in some sense complicit with the active forgetting – the elision of content and its supervention by the diversion of form – that enables fascism to take root. In this state of affairs, my body is *not* my own, not *propre* or proper to me; rather, it is tattooed, its very skin marked, as a representation of (for example) a class, a gender, a sexual orientation, a colour. Inasmuch as it is thus representative, it is intrinsically doubled – excessive to itself, abundant with respect to itself; and the actual life – my bare life – is also therefore waste, potentially unnecessary. Fascism says that it is disposable; but, importantly, a certain form of democracy based upon bourgeois representation – as also a society of bureaucratized individuality – also structurally fundamentally echoes that same position.

Put simply, if I fail somehow adequately to represent my class, gender or whatever, then someone else will have to step in to do it better. I have no right to a private life, for there is no substance to a private – present – life. Not only have I earned what Blanchot called 'the right to death', I also am now identified entirely with the enacting of that right. Blanchot, haunted by the after-effect of the French Revolution, thinks of this as the Reign of Terror, which may still be with us:

> No one has a right to a private life any longer, everything is public ... And in the end no one has a right to his life any longer, to his actually separate and physical existence. This is the meaning of the Reign of Terror. Every citizen has a right to death, so to speak: death is not a sentence passed on him, it is his most essential right.[28]

Economies of representation

More importantly still, we can see in these examples a sense of an economy in literary representation of human being in which the self can become identified with the dead or dying self, the self 'in death'. That reduction to 'the thing itself' – the thing without waste, or without abundance, 'graceless' – is a reduction to the self at the point of death. A democracy based upon *formal* modes of representation is characterized therefore by our 'availability for death', we might say, or by the potential for sacrificing our bare life, or the *content* of a life. We may lay down our life for country or for friend, and may see in that the essence of a democratic polity or relatedness within the social or public sphere; and if so, we have just consented to a democracy being based upon the militarization of everyday life.[29]

And yet ... And yet dying is in fact a supremely private act in at least one sense. Derrida argued that death is the one event where representation cedes place to presentation: it is the one thing that no one else can do on my behalf. As he has it, in passages that are heavily influenced not just by Heidegger but also, and maybe more importantly, by Levinas:

> Death is very much that which nobody else can undergo or confront in my place. My irreplaceability is therefore conferred, delivered, "given," one can say, by death ... It is from the site of death as the place of my irreplaceability, that is, of my singularity, that I feel called to responsibility. In this sense, only a mortal can be responsible.[30]

Perhaps equally significantly, in this sense also, only one who is 'singular', not amenable to or given over to 're-presentation' and its (diplomatic or duplicitous) doublings, can be responsible.

Now why is this important for our purposes here? In short, the bare self, as the self-in-death, is equivalent to the end of representation of the self. We can invert this to suggest that representation might properly be thought of as the very embodiment of waste. Why do we need representation at all? Why do we have it? In extreme and fundamental form, the argument goes back to Plato's *Cratylus*, certainly; but perhaps the most important recent meditation on this is in the work of Clément Rosset. Rosset has examined what he calls 'the singular object'; and the logic of his argument indicates that a thing's material reality is determined precisely to the extent that it eschews representability. The thing itself – its bare life – is 'idiotic' and is real only to the extent that it is not doubled in representations. That is what gives it its Scotist *haecceitas* (its 'thisness'), its Aquinas-inflected *quidditas* (its essence, its 'whatness'), its *propre* (its property). It is what makes it what it is: its identity, now meaning a self-sameness that is so intrinsic that it cannot be represented – and, equally, cannot be representative, if we are to remain in the idiom of truth.

It follows, further, that the expression of our self or of our conscience in an act that constitutes a supposedly authentic 'confessing' of the self or of identity must be flawed. Indeed, it cannot constitute truth. And it follows from this that *either* a) confession must axiomatically be self-undoing in that it cannot tell the truth; *or* b) confession is not a matter of conscience at all, nor has it anything to do with a representation that would have positive and ethically progressive meaning in the political sphere.

If we were to take all this in a literal fashion, we might come up with an argument that says that those forms of political ideology – such as a bourgeois democracy, that are based on a notion of truthful or legitimate representation – work precisely to the extent that they de-realize the original person or voter who wishes to have herself represented, emptying her of her specific *content* and reducing her to the merest *form* of an individual. Our 'representatives' exist at the cost of our own specific reality; and, in the extreme limit, we die that they be given their 'democratic' legitimacy, or, to put it less bluntly, their legitimacy depends upon our availability for the sacrificing of our bare life. This is a problem.

Let us remain, for the moment, with the philosophical rather than the political aspect of the problem. Put very crudely, the hypothesis that we now need to consider, stated in its extreme form, is that representation as we usually consider it (both aesthetically and politically) is governed by a logic of waste. Further, 'waste' here implies the availability for wasting of the bare life of individual people, whose bare lives can be wasted precisely because they have no content and are to be viewed purely as formal abstraction (in modern employment terminology, 'human resource'). Their lives are intrinsically seen as 'not worth living' precisely because they are purely formal or bureaucratic entities: they are but branded tattoos, and can be removed when they start to embarrass the 'leaders' who design and write the tattoo or brand. Such wastefulness might be seen as symptomatic of a culture in decadence, a culture of decadent abundance.

Perhaps yet more importantly still, there now appears to be a fissure in the structure of representation. Representation can never do what it claims to do, in that – as in the *Cratylus*, as in Rosset – it can never genuinely or legitimately duplicate the thing that is its subject. Thus, while on the one hand, it ostensibly claims to allow me to be present where I am not (as in a bourgeois democratic parliament, say, where my representative will supposedly speak on my behalf), it actually curtails my 'excessiveness', my ability to exist somewhere else or beyond the confines of my material body here now. It cannot allow me to exist in some form *beyond* my bare self, in some metaphysical fashion. Its logic implies that any self that is beyond the bare self can have no reality, since it cannot be quantified in the economies of representation. In this way, the subject's *imagination* – that element of consciousness that allows us to identify our very self legitimately as a self elsewhere, in another world or in another time – is anathema to representation. This form of representation, we might say, cannot permit a *culture* of the individual, by which I mean to imply that it cannot abide the fact that the individual may grow, especially through some edifying encounter with the alterity that constitutes the literary experience.

In short, this kind of representation, based as it is upon vacuous formal entities, enters into precisely that kind of quantification of quality that caused Lear his problem. It is tied to a crude economy; and, more importantly for present purposes, an economy that cannot allow for anything 'extra'. It is the economy satirized by Dickens in *Hard Times* and *Great Expectations*, an economy that eschews the possibility of a pure giving, of what we might call *grace* (a word by which I mean, here, to imply no specific religious connotations). Grace, or 'gifting', is of the nature of an *event*, as that term has been used by Lyotard, Deleuze or Badiou in recent times: it is an act whose outcome could not have been prefigured from the state of affairs prior to its taking place; or an act that, once it has taken place, can be used to 'explain' or define the state of a relation between the before and the after of the giving itself. In this sense, grace is culture itself, and not merely one possible aspect of a cultured society.

Political grace

Let me try to sum up where we are, and to point towards some conclusion that will open a new question for us. The logic of the argument thus far suggests an intimacy between waste (and all that it entails in the way of redundancy) and the act of representation, with at least two possible consequences. I can lay them out here. In these paragraphs, I address the fundamental question of representation; but I consider the confessional drive – in its traditional sense as an expressing of the self – to be a paradigmatic example of this representation.

The first possibility is that we accept that representation is based upon a necessary act of 'de-realization' of an original material subject. In this view, only that which is singular – only that which eschews the possibility of representation – can be real, or can have any real content. In this view, representation becomes a kind of fiction; and any legitimacy that it may have (either with respect to truth, aesthetically speaking; or with respect to viability, politically speaking) is based upon our willingness to substitute a narrative for the material facts of history, and to subscribe to that narrative in a way that allows us to use it to set norms that can be communally shared. The result of this would be, for example, that we understand historical conflicts as essentially being contests over the legitimacy of competing narratives. In this view, 'democracy' eventually becomes a kind of rhetorical contest in which the more appealing tales (the tales that have most adherents) propose themselves as legislators for all. There is a clear question here about the legitimacy of any such polity, not to mention a question about the establishment of norms of aesthetic taste and value (or what we usually call 'criticism').

The second possibility is that we understand representation *as such* to be intrinsically flawed and antipathetic to any form of democracy. In this view, we accept that for representation to work at all, the subject that is to be represented must be evacuated of any specific content, and reduced instead to the merest form of that content. The material or historical specificity of the subject must be elided and occluded under a 'lowest common denominator' that will allow for the subject to be inserted into a narrative as a type of 'character'; and, in this, what typically will happen is an exercise in synecdoche in which one aspect of the subject's identity is taken as the driver for the entirety of the identity.

More importantly still, that aspect will be one that is shared with other 'characters': it may be a class, a gender, a sexual orientation or whatever. At that point, instead of a narrative being told about specific individuals, representation requires that we tell narratives about these purely formal 'qualities' (and thus tell the history of sexual preferences, or of class struggle and so on). It is not the case that these narratives lack legitimacy as such: indeed, they are important. However, they lack legitimacy in terms of their aspiration to *represent* specific individuals, for they require that the material singularity of each individual – their *content* as an individual – be ignored in the interests of the tale of the history of concepts that, in the end, are purely *formal*, not shaped by the particularity of specific experience. In this sense, confession as a revelation of one's conscience would be anathema to democracy, for it precludes the possibility of the public sphere having any material content, preferring it to be shaped by pure abstractions of 'character'.

It would follow from both of these positions that aesthetic and political representations *in which we make some claims upon truth or legitimacy* are, of necessity, self-contradictory: they de-legitimize themselves precisely in the moment of their claiming legitimacy.

In these terms, then, we reach the possibility of a conclusion and a question. The conclusion would go like this. Political representation is at once both necessary and problematic. It is *necessary* in that it is required if we are to counter the 'idiotic', and to allow for a general theory or even for a community to exist at all. Community as such requires that we identify points of contact and of identification among different specific individuals; and I take it as read that democracy requires some form of acknowledgement of community. Yet it is also *problematic* in that, precisely as it succeeds in establishing the identity of a community (by 'formalizing the specificities of content', as we might now put it), it necessarily *misrepresents* or presents its subjects not as specific subjects, but rather as empty and exchangeable counters in a formal narrative, pawns in a tale that is being told by someone else or by something else.

What happens to democracy in this state of affairs? Essentially, for it to have any currency, democracy must be seen as a fiction of sorts. It is a fiction not only in the weak sense that it pretends to do what it cannot do (that is, to represent adequately and with a serious legitimacy or truth-content its participants and subjects); but it is also a fiction in the stronger sense that its workings depend precisely upon what are essentially aesthetic questions concerning narrative, plot and characterization.

Proust, Joyce, Eliot, Woolf and many others knew this. They knew it when they produced their over-abundant texts, texts where the very fact of wastefulness becomes, finally, an issue in the starkest terms: the terms concerning the definition of the democratic human subject as one who is available for death within and on behalf of a community. In attending so centrally to the question of death – and even sometimes appearing to romanticize it – they have been taken as being sympathetic to certain right-wing fantasies; yet I think that it is important to see that in their writing, they are writing *against* death, and *for* the specificity of the particular, however complicated that is becoming in the mass cultures of modernity. In doing this, they are addressing the fraught issue of the wastefulness of human lives with their desire to give and to return content to the material subjects – Marcel, Leopold, Jean, Percival or Septimus – who haunt them – and who should haunt us in their absolute alterity, their *unavailability* for us.

And, for some thinking about a philosophy of the future? Perhaps democracy is better thought of not in terms of representation and its economies at all; rather, perhaps it is better to think our way through the considerable problems that democracy might bring us by placing it under the sign of the dyseconomies of grace, of giving, of offering. A grace such as this might be characterized as that which disrupts any economy, for it is a giving that does not foresee any return, cannot prefigure its own representation in a gift returned. Such grace makes of democracy a pure event: something that is yet to happen, but whose happening will be genuinely transformative, and never final. We can explore it further in my next chapter.

6

Confession and Democracy

Of Democracy and Grace: The Economy of Confession

For J. Hillis Miller

He was trying to overcome an immense obstacle in his mind,
which I suppose is what confession's all about
John Le Carré, *Our Kind of Traitor*[1]

The ground of friendship is ... the inevitable need we have to be
ourselves ... The basic condition of this is that we should enter
into fellowship, that we should love the other. So love may
be defined as the complete affirmation of the other by the self:
and since to be completely oneself is to be completely
free, fellowship is the basic condition of freedom.
John Macmurray, *Conditions of Freedom*[2]

Towards grace

In 1959, Robert Lowell published *Life Studies*, a collection that seemed to crystallize a specific tendency in mid-twentieth-century American poetry. That tendency became widely known, following M.L Rosenthal's review in the *Nation* that year, as 'confessional poetry'. Rosenthal himself tended later to downplay the sense that this was something new. He wrote that:

> The impulse to reveal and share things that everybody known but no one ordinarily talks about ... is one of the most human motives of lyric poetry. Before there was any large body of such poetry, in anything like the modern sense, poets were discovering and being guided by that confessional impulse.[3]

What is new at this moment, though, is a specific *attitude* regarding the importance of confessional poetry. For Rosenthal, it showed 'the chief link between poetry and the common life'.[4] The importance of the emergence or coming to prominence of such poetry, especially in the United States, relates to this desire to see poetry as being something of material substance for 'common life', and thus of importance for what we might more usually now call the 'public sphere'. Rosenthal's formulation of 'confessional poetry' is, in fact, itself catching up with a theoretical inquiry that has emerged steadily in many cultural practices and in European thought through the 1950s, in Roland Barthes and in Maurice Blanchot especially. That inquiry, we might say, comes to a specific kind of material and political culmination in the election of John F. Kennedy as US President in 1960.

At one level, the entire trajectory or inquiry in question is a clear echo of the shift noted in the Preface to the *Lyrical Ballads* as that point of entry into romanticism that is given by the use of a selection of the language of everyday life; and there is indeed a persistent neo-Romantic tendency in some of this modern American poetry.[5] Yet more significant, historically speaking, is the coincidence of confessional poetry with the ideological mood of Kennedy's America, an America that sees itself explicitly in terms of rebirth and renewal, a people making a clean breast of things and starting afresh.

In his inauguration speech, on 20 January 1961, Kennedy evoked the spirit that the literary world would have recognized from Eliot's 'Tradition and the individual talent' essay of 1919, a spirit bringing together in tense unity both the historical sense and a definite break with the past. Such a collocation of tradition and novelty was, and remains, a condition of 'modernity'; and, in his inauguration speech, Kennedy spoke directly of 'beginning anew', saying that the day marked a 'celebration of freedom … signifying renewal, as well as change'. It is this idea of 'renewal, as well as change' and its bond with a certain 'freedom' that links the speech to a specific literary and cultural modernity, the very cultural modernity that Eliot would have seen in the flourishing of individual talents who were firmly grounded in tradition and who carried it within their very bones. Famously, of course, Kennedy also closes the speech with the rousing challenge to each and every American individual to become an embodiment of the whole: 'ask not what your country can do for you – ask what you can do for your country'. This rhetorical trope of near-chiasmus is a precise linguistic formulation and inflection of the kind of democracy that Kennedy had in mind, a democracy in which there is an intimacy between the individual self and the national project, such that the one acts as a mirroring representative of the other. Crucial to the chiasmus is a questioning of the self, a kind of examination of conscience; but it is a conscience that is also the conscience of a country, a 'common life' of America.

To some extent, then, confessional poetry becomes important culturally, chiming concordantly with the political mood of the moment because it considers the poet as the one who is perhaps pre-eminently *representative* of modern common life. Through this, it sees poetry as being associated with a particular American version of democracy, specifically that Kennedian inflection of a mythic America as an optimistic if nonetheless cold-war democracy embattled and threatened by communism. This poetry was not removed from common life, but rather, in confessional mode, the poet found a way of acting as a representative of everybody, of a community, bringing her or his own personal life into line with a common life of the polity.

Interestingly, at the end of the decade, in another inauguration speech exactly eight years later, on 20 January 1969, Richard Nixon essentially repeats some of the Kennedy language. He argues that America is suffering a 'crisis of the spirit', the answer to which requires only that, this time like a modernist Virginia Woolf, we 'look within ourselves'. He asks that we 'lower our voices' because America has 'suffered from a fever of words', and says that 'We cannot learn from one another until we stop shouting at one another – until we speak quietly enough so that our words can be heard as well as our voices.'

There is, across the decade, a subtle shift in this political rhetoric; and it, too, is something that finds, in its appeal to an increasing silence, or reduction of the volume of the voice, its quiet echo in literature. I am not simply referring here to the importance of a writer such as Beckett or a composer such as John Cage (whose '4'33' was composed long before this, in 1952); rather, I will draw attention instead to a more general tendency of 'reduction', a kind of kenosis in which the human self looks for a 'zero degree' of being. (The musical equivalent might be found in a certain minimalism, such as that practised by Terry Riley, Steve Reich or Philip Glass, all of whom come to prominence during the 1960s, and all of whom bridge a divide between art-music and popular music, the music of common life, as it were.)[6]

In 1947, Barthes had come up with an idea about a certain kind of writing at 'degree zero', when he discussed Camus; and this becomes his 1953 book, *Le degré zero de l'écriture*. At the same time, Blanchot in particular is repeatedly looking for 'Man at point zero', as he calls it in his review of Lévi-Strauss's *Tristes Tropiques* in 1954. In what follows below, I shall be exploring the importance of this reduction to zero as a condition for confessional thinking or writing, for a whole confessional culture that will eventuate finally in the myth of anorexic transparency, the very disappearance of the subject as such.

It is as if we can trace a movement through the American 1960s from Eliot to Woolf, from a question of the individual expressing their Eliotic talent against the traditional backdrop to a very different question, characterized by a Woolfian desire to 'look within'. Of course, that introspection is what might be required for any idea of a confessional discourse that arises after the classic Catholic idea of the 'examination of conscience'.[7] However, it is also consistent with the growth of a culture of *surveillance*, of which Nixon's Watergate is but one very small (and actually atypical) example.

Additionally, this progressive inward look is one where the democratic subject is being asked to confront themselves in a kind of pure and naked form, all extraneous matter removed. We are arriving at the idea of a reduced subject, the subject who themselves approaches a kind of anorexic reduction to a bare or zero-point, a self that is so *transparent* as to be immaterial, in a very precise sense. This gives us the most obvious paradox that shapes confessional culture: the confession is, as it were, a confession that is made *without a subject*, for the subject is reduced to a zero-point.[8]

As a consequence, there must also be a problem for any kind of democratic culture that bases itself upon the idea of any form of 'communicative action', as Habermas would later call it. One dominant version of this cold-war democracy would be that which sees the democratic society as being grounded in 'deliberation', a kind of agora of diverse voices, all of them speaking what they see as the truth and revealing (or confessing) their innermost self in an effort to contribute equally to the whole. However, while this may be admirable in principle, it simply cannot happen in any meaningful way if the subject is so transparent as to disappear, effectively.

I have repeated the term 'cold-war democracy' here. There is a good reason for this. As we can see from the inauguration speeches (and perhaps that of Kennedy more clearly), a straightforward opposition is set up within the culture between, on the one hand, the 'common life' (which is valued and which the confessional poet represents) and 'communism' (which is characterized as the very denial of free expression, the ostensible denial of the very possibilities of 'confession'). The simple issue here is that, even in a culture that ostensibly praises common life and its expression through poetry, we face a major problem if the subject of that confession is essentially null, zero. In this present chapter, I shall be exploring some of these vexatious issues; and, importantly, we will need to investigate what we might term the status of the private life.

In Lowell's case, the poet's aim 'is to catch himself in the process of becoming himself';[9] and, in doing this, 'The "myth" that Lowell creates is that of America ... whose history and present predicament are embodied in his own family and epitomized in his own psychological experience'.[10] Interestingly, the substance or semantic content of the poems seems also to be important here, for it is *because* of the way that 'Lowell brought his private humiliations, sufferings, and psychological problems into the poems [that] the word "confessional" seemed appropriate enough'.[11]

Here, then, we have the collocation of several important issues. First, the poet reveals himself, 'confesses', and in so doing, establishes and yet simultaneously breaches the dividing line between a private and a public realm. This confessional discourse presupposes that something that has been occluded is now revealed: the occlusion requires a realm of privacy, often considered simply as the interiority of a subject; and the revelation requires the existence of a sphere that is public, that is constituted by discourse or dialogue, and that transcends the private domain. In this set-up, the private is a realm that secretes itself away from the social: it is a space characterized by secrecy, in that sense; in Lowell's case, it is the realm of family history as well as the darker corners of his own depressive psyche. However, such secrecy is always under intrinsic threat: a secret is only a secret once it is revealed, for, unless and until it is revealed, it has no real existence (or is at best just private thought; but even then, to be a thought, it has to be expressible, available and comprehensible *as if* already made public).

Second, confession as described by Rosenthal in his critique of Lowell is marked by humiliation: it is a confession of something that demeans the private self of the poet in some way; and yet the writing of the poetry is the redeeming factor – that is, the confession 'clears' him, purifies him. As de Man showed in his essay on Rousseau's *Confessions*, the very act of writing undoes the confession, for the confession is always marked by 'excuse': *qui s'accuse s'excuse*, he points out. He goes on, 'in terms of absolute truth, [this] ruins the seriousness of any confessional discourse by making it self-destructive'.[12] As I have argued in earlier chapters, there is a certain inauthenticity that is necessary and integral to a discourse of confession that would be truthful.

Joyce is aware of these two paradoxes. In his story 'Grace', he explicitly places a confessional act at the heart of a public sphere. In the story, Tom Kernan falls down the staircase of a pub, drunk. He faces arrest but is saved at the last minute by two men: one is a young man on a bicycle, who promptly disappears from the story, having helped Kernan to his feet; and the other is Mr Power, a local gentleman who offers to see him home safely. In falling, Kernan has bitten off a part of his tongue, and so he cannot speak. He cannot bear witness, as it were, to his accident.

Mr Power, along with Martin Cunningham and Mr McCoy, hatches a plot to try to turn Kernan around from being something of a wastrel. While he is recuperating in bed, Kernan is visited by the group of men; and, as they share a bottle of stout, the three men hold a conversation together. Kernan, excluded, asks what's going on; and they reveal that they are going on a retreat on Thursday night, that they are going to confess and 'to clean the pot', as Cunningham puts it. Kernan agrees to come along.

The retreat begins with a sermon; but it is a sermon for businessmen. The priest acknowledges that there is a potential discrepancy between the life of a Catholic conscience and the life of being in the practical world of commerce and business-relations. In my terms here, he is aware of the discrepancy between the demands of a confession based on conscience, and a confession that is essentially a conversation with the world. He invites the men present to think of their lives in terms of accounts: and, if there is something untoward, then they should 'by the grace of God', rectify their accounts.

The confession being made here is, as it were, a bringing together of private and public spheres: the men present share a worldview, that of the businessman whose task it is to make financial profit. Yet, the task of the retreat is to find a way of reconciling this capitalist economy with their consciences, which tell them that they should be more just. Kernan, a convert to Catholicism, sits in the midst of this. Importantly, as a convert, he is part outsider to the entire enterprise; and he is essentially conned into attending the retreat. Further, his damaged tongue is extremely important. Throughout the story, he cannot speak properly; and, as the men trick him into coming to the retreat, what is happening essentially is that they are speaking on his behalf. They are *representing* him; but they are, of necessity, *misrepresenting* him, and putting wishes and ideas into his head, or rather ascribing to him wishes that they themselves have. In order to maintain the community or to keep in with the public sphere of these men, Kernan allows himself to be 'represented' as if he had spoken assent. He is thus brought back into a public life again.

The question posed by the story is not just that of representing in our own voices those whose voices cannot be heard; it is also a question concerning grace itself. Is it a gracious act to try to 'save' Kernan for the public sphere, as it were? In fact, though it may appear so, it is not: the tricking of him is done for ulterior motives, and is thus inserted into an essentially commercial economy of investment and return. This is why the sermon makes sense: the soul is treated as an accounts book. If there is grace at all in this story, it lies elsewhere: it has left the story at the early stage with the young man on the bicycle who had helped Kernan, uncalled for, and who rides off, seeking no reward.

The retreat is grounded in a basic falsehood, for it fails to accommodate grace such as that shown by the young man: an act that is essentially for the good of another, but entirely gratuitous, like a gift. It is in this way that grace disturbs a capitalist economy, as it also disturbs a narrative economy here. If Kernan is temporarily silenced, the young man – grace itself – is, as it were, conditioned entirely by silence. Where the sermon offers a chiasmus between justice and economics, grace cycles off and plays no further part in such a confession. This is a silent witness, as it were, to the wrongs carried out in the capitalist economy that shapes the lives of these Dubliners.

I as we: first confessions and beginnings

More recently within this Catholic tradition, Seamus Heaney finds a 'pattern' for confession, in which the confession is always belated, a pattern where, the first time one confesses, one falls into 'truthfunk' as he calls it, because of a certain unreadiness for the act. He describes a first confession scene, where the confessant has to walk the length of the aisle of the church to tell his sins to the priest who sits as confessor at the altar. The speaker of the poem, called 'The Pattern', describes how he walks down this aisle, in a state of unpreparedness:

> Unready as I was if much rehearsed
> In the art of first confession.

What transpired next was meltwater,
A little trickle on the patterned tiles,
Truthfunk and walkaway, but then

In the nick of time, comeback
And a clean breast made
Manfully if late. The pattern set.[13]

The pattern for confession, then – in this case religious and Catholic confession – is marked by a repetition, but one where the story is never properly told first time, needing a 'comeback', through which a clean and clear identity (the clean breast made, the manful stance) can be established. Confession, as it were, at best stammers its beginning, and certainly has difficulty in knowing how to begin, no matter how well prepared for, no matter how well rehearsed. It is less a question of *why* confess, and more a question of *how to begin* a confession. At one level, it must always begin with 'I'; but what if this 'I' is not the 'here-now', and what if it is also a covert 'we', a *representative* I or even a particular kind of *democratic* I?

It follows from the predicaments that I have described above that there is now a question regarding the very singularity of the poet. In what ways can his own specific life, 'cleansed' by confessing, become representative; in what way can the essentially private be always already somehow public or at least communal? How can Kennedy's 'I' be 'America', or what is the founding condition of the possibility of this 'democracy'? In the poetry discussed by Rosenthal as paradigmatic of the confessional trend, we find that the particular is always already universal, that Lowell (and also Plath, Roethke, Bishop and perhaps especially Berryman) become the democratic representatives of the whole that is America. Single becomes general. To put this more pointedly for the terms of this chapter, one becomes many.

We see this kind of thing clearly in a poem like 'The Far Field', published by Roethke in 1964. The concluding lines of the poem are both personal and yet oddly addressed to a national condition in the wake of the Kennedy assassination, and they use words that are themselves keenly reminiscent of Kennedy's inauguration:

I am renewed by death, thought of my death,
The dry scent of a dying garden in September,
The wind fanning the ash of a low fire.
What I love is near at hand,
Always, in earth and air.[14]

Similar attitudes are to be found all the way through Berryman's *Dream Songs*, perhaps especially in his addresses to the many other poets – Plath,

Delmore Schwartz, Randall Jarrell, William Carlos Williams and many others who actually constitute what he calls his 'inner resources' –in which he uses his own response to these poets and their writings in order to construct a version of an entire American culture, a cultural memory that constitutes a present identity for an entire community.[15]

Another way of saying all this is that, in this poetry, the I more or less systematically becomes or is displaced on to the we; that the confessing I, in the very process of confessing, becomes communal – even to the point that we could say that this confessing I is that which establishes a specific community (in this case 'America') as such. In this, we see a particular confounding of two possible grounds for the establishment of the social, a confounding that is of the essence of modernity: on one hand, the social is grounded in the *conscience* of the individual, the individual who becomes a 'citizen' precisely to the extent that they express that conscience in the agora (Aristotle); on the other hand, the social is established through the very fact of *communication*, not conscience as such, and in this communicative action (Habermas) we see the gradual move towards the intersubjective establishment of the public sphere in a rational dialogue.[16]

In one variant of democracy, this move (in which a single I becomes the multiplicity of we) is indeed how such a procedure of confession would be legitimized. The answer to the '*cur confiteor*' question posed by Augustine is answered: I confess as one, as myself, in order that a voice may be given to the many. Nixon, in an uncanny prefiguration of actual historical events, expressed it simply in his inauguration: 'For its part, government will listen. We will strive to listen in new ways – to the voices of quiet anguish, the voices that speak without words, the voices of the heart – to the injured voices, the anxious voices, the voices that have despaired of being heard.'[17] Whitman, as the rather more stentorian poet, had expressed it differently and succinctly: 'I contain multitudes',[18] as if his single voice was always filled with the voices of all others. One becomes many; and, by corollary, the many can be voiced in the one, the generality of a community can be voiced by a unified voice.

Yet this is also clearly a problem: by what right can the I arrogate to itself the humiliations, the suffering, and/or the guilty acts of a community? In one way, Derrida (and behind him Heidegger and Levinas) is wrong when he asserts in *The Gift of Death* that dying is the one thing that no one else can do in my place: confessing is also one such act, something to be done, in Heaney's words, 'Full face, four square, eyelevel'. In confession, I am called to some kind of absolute singularity – what I have been calling the assertion of the 'I-here-now' – and therefore the 'I' in such a confessional mode *cannot*, by definition, be in any way 'representative' of a whole. That, in fact, would be the structure not of confession but rather of sacrifice, of the scapegoat; and confession is and remains, at one level, a seemingly solitary act. Yet, at the same time, it must be addressed to an other, to a community of sorts.

On this sacrificial structure, anathema to confession, Agamben offers a useful gloss. He argues that religion is that which 'removes things, places, animals, or people from common use and transfers them to a separate sphere'. That is to say, religion is that which mediates in some way between what might be called the sacred and the profane; and religion effects a transfer from one to the other, usually through this medium of sacrifice, which 'always sanctions the passage of something from the profane to the sacred, from the human sphere to the divine'.[19] In the terms that I have been using earlier, sacrifice here would be that which transfers something whose proper domain is that of communication into the domain of transcendence and thus of conscience.

Roberto Esposito has exposed at least one of the flaws in such a position, in his exposition of the word 'community'. Through an exploration of etymology and a fuller consideration of the history of the term, he shows that the real meaning of community – or *communitas* as he prefers to call it, maintaining the etymological origin of the word – is 'I owe'. 'The subjects of a community,' he writes, 'are united through a "debt" – in the sense of "I owe *you* something", but not "you owe *me* something".'[20] Such a debt is aligned with the grace of my previous chapter and with grace as explored in Joyce's great story of that name. Esposito goes on to argue that the foundational existence of such a debt, constitutive as it is of the subject as such, shows that the subject in such a community is never his own proper master; the debt in question 'separates' the subject from that which is 'proper' to himself. In a community, this thing of darkness that I call mine own has no place, as it were. As Esposito has it, 'the common is not characterized by the proper, but by impropriety – or more radically by the other'.[21]

Earlier in this study, I argued that there is a sense in which confession originates and has to originate in the I-here-now. However, it is now becoming clear that this I-here-now is itself dependent upon something that pre-exists it. There is, as a precondition of the very possibility of saying 'I-here-now' (*je suis seul ici, maintenant*), a realization that the real origin of confession, its real beginning, lies in something greater than I, greater than conscience: it lies in the community, the 'we' or at least the I as it is displaced in narrative on to some other grammatical person (you, he, she, it, they).

Such a position shows that a community cannot be an aggregate of 'ones', that it is not the sum of its parts, if we think of the parts as being self-contained and autonomous subjects. There would then be a difficulty with the idea of how confessional poetry works; and, more pertinently for my present purposes, a difficulty in seeing the relation between confession and the democratic impulse. It is this that I shall be exploring in the rest of this present chapter.

That exploration will require a meditation on the nature of 'one' and its relation to 'zero'. At least two things follow. First of all, we need a consideration that will turn however briefly and inexpertly to mathematics – to a consideration of the philosophy of number – that asks whether numbers 'begin' at one or at zero. Secondly, we will be looking at a relation of the one to the many, a consideration, fundamentally, of the opening of fragment 418 of the *Pensées*: '*Infini rien*' ('Infinite nothing').[22] At one level, this is clearly a question concerning the political, concerning democracy (and specifically a kind of bourgeois representative democracy where one voice stands in for many voices). However, in its manifestation as a question of the relation between particularity and universality, it is also a question of aesthetics or of what I have called elsewhere an *aesthetic democracy*.[23] Such a democracy has an intense relation to the confessional impulse.

Down to zero

In his analysis of the Henry James story, 'The Altar of the Dead', J. Hillis Miller finds a strange property of zero. The altar in question is the one at which George Stransom lights candles in memory of his dead friends, including his fiancée, Mary Antrim. The relation between these two occupies a kind of 'now-time', a dilatory moment, for 'She had died of a malignant fever after the wedding-day had been fixed, and he had lost before tasting it an affection that promised to fill his life to the brim.'[24] Stransom is caught forever in this odd moment, a moment 'between times' as it were, a kind of eternally recurring now-time that hovers between a past and a not-ever-realizable future. Miller describes Stransom's dead friends as being, like Mary, 'still alive, or dead-alive, hovering somewhere as ghosts or specters'.[25] They are neither dead nor alive, in a particular sense, but hovering, as a zero hovers, between states, between negativity and positivity. Stransom always has to light 'one more' candle, as if he will never reach the end of a series; but, as Miller points out, the moment when there would be no more candles to light – the zero moment – would need to be the moment of Stransom's own death. In this case, then, zero is equated with death itself, and James, like the reader, according to Miller, 'wants, understandably, to put off' the direct confrontation with zero. Miller then relates James's reluctance to finish this particular story (as noted in his *Notebooks*) to James's attitude to his own death, 'the Distinguished Thing' that he eventually did confront – and survive – on the occasion of his first stroke. How, asks Miller, does Fred Kaplan, James's biographer, know what James 'thought to himself' on that occasion? He goes on:

> Kaplan knows presumably because James told someone that is what he thought. James bore witness to it, but can we believe James' testimony? To know for sure another person's interiority would be like knowing death through the death of another. This is an impossibility, alas. Perhaps all biography, along with all stories, like 'The Altar of the Dead', that end with the death of the protagonist, are attempts to do the impossible, that is, to experience the death of another from within and to survive that death.[26]

According to Edith Wharton, in *A Backward Glance*, the person James told was Lady Prothero. Wharton's description is important:

> He is said to have told his old friend Lady Prothero, when she saw him after the first stroke, that in the very act of falling (he was dressing at the time) he heard in the room a voice which was distinctly, it seemed, not his own, saying: 'So here it is at last, the distinguished thing!' The phrase is too beautifully characteristic not to be recorded. He saw the distinguished thing coming, faced it, and received it with words worthy of all his dealings with life.[27]

In this, we should note that, according to this version, the voice that utters the phrase is *not* that of James himself: it is exactly as if his voice has been displaced into that of another; but another who speaks a phrase that is 'beautifully characteristic', and thus *like* the voice of James himself. If this is a confessing moment, then it is so precisely as I have been describing it: a confession but not in the voice of the subject confessing.

In Miller's reading of this, and in its relation to the candles in 'The Altar of the Dead', the zero is located explicitly as a kind of liminal point, a liminal point related to biography and autobiography. To be reduced to zero is, as it were, to confront one's own death. This, in many ways, is also the story of Blanchot's obsession with reduction, with the search for 'man at point zero', for simplicity or for obsequies and last words. More importantly, however, the relation of zero to one is a relation that makes possible the surviving of one's own death: if one can reach zero, but can also 'begin' again, as 'one' or as the start of number, then one can reach the point of death and yet also reveal the confession of a life that occurs properly at such a moment.

In short, confession is the rhetorical move that allows the self or subject *to survive its own death*; it is the movement from zero to one, and back into speech from the silence of death. It is the new beginning of which Kennedy speaks; it is the individual talent of an Eliot; it is the voicing of self that lies within Lowell or Heaney or Berryman. The survival of the subject beyond its own death is, as it were, a manifestation of grace.

Further than this, confession also becomes here a primary example of a specific type of witnessing. Agamben, in his *Remnants of Auschwitz*, makes a distinction between the *terstis* and the *superstes*. Both words are related to testimony, he points out. The *terstis* gives us a third or adjudicating voice between two other competing versions of events. More important for our purpose here is the *superstes*, described by Agamben as one who has survived something and who can thus bear witness to it. The grace of which I write in this present chapter is, as it were, the gratuitous 'living on' beyond a trauma, the survival of a subject beyond its own zero-point and its return to the positive realm of number. Having reached point zero, this subject 'counts' again, so to speak,[28] and they count as a matter of grace, the opposite of historical *Ananke* or necessity.

Grace is something that disturbs an economy, and above all it disturbs a capitalist economy. Capitalism requires a sense of equivalence and balance in its exchanges; and when there is imbalance, the supplement it produces is called 'profit'; but this profit is profit if and only if it also contributes to the growth of the economy in question: that is, it needs to be reinserted into the next level of exchange. This is capital's view of 'progress'. By contrast, grace works very differently. In a capitalist economy, there is no possibility of giving, no room for the 'gift': its offering, within capitalism, always calls for a balancing opposite, so to speak. That is to say, if I give you 'one' thing I make a 'one' from a zero, then capital says that you must 'owe' me 'one' back, you must reimburse me with something that is equivalent to my 'one'. It cannot accommodate pure giving, a pure one that does not call for debt or balanced repayment, a one that does not call for a matched future or, in short, a one that genuinely moves away from the balance and neutrality of zero. Grace, like gifting, is a giving that makes a radical break into the possibility of a future that cannot be accommodated within an existing system.

The relation of confession to one and zero is what we need now to explore; and, in the following argument, I shall do this through a close attention to Miller's work from the 1960s, the period in which confessional writing in American cold-war democracy becomes culturally significant.

One is, in arithmetic and the law of number, a way of beginning. So, 'Let me begin at the beginning.' This, of course, is and is not 'my' beginning: I am quoting from very near the beginning of Miller's 2001 book, *Speech Acts in Literature*,[29] a book that is in some ways precisely about the question of how we might begin to speak, to express the self, in writing. That beginning comes after the book's introduction, on page six. How does it take so long to begin? Haven't we already begun by page six of Hillis Miller's book; or by the sixth chapter of this book? 'And how shall *I* begin?' – this too a quotation, as T.S. Eliot 'quotes' the imagined J. Alfred Prufrock, again offering a question of beginning in the midst of things.

Let us note, in passing, that these beginnings are all versions of a stammered beginning; and, further, they are always beginnings that start in the voice of another. We are, as it were, in the presence of that vocalized 'distinguished thing', spoken for us even as we ourselves will speak.[30]

Beginning is always the problem; and I want to suggest that, especially in Hillis Miller's early work, most particularly the books made in the 1960s, *The Disappearance of God* (1963) and *Poets of Reality* (1965), such beginning – the question of how we inaugurate a speech act (such as confession) in which the I is radically implicated – was a presiding issue, and one from which we can still learn a good deal about our present topic. My focus on Hillis Miller, while appropriate because he has recently written about 'zero', is meant to have a greater significance. I will focus on his work from the 1960s, that is, work from within the very moment that I have described in my opening section above as symptomatic of a shift (especially in American culture) towards confessional surveillance. Although he does not write explicitly about confession as such, nonetheless I want to take him as paradigmatic of a particular trajectory within criticism.

The question of beginnings and of the sources of literature (or of the beginnings of voicings, the linguistic inauguration of literary acts) is more fundamental in Miller than it was in Said's great exploration of beginnings.[31] In *Beginnings*, Said was concerned with the questions of authorship in writing, with cultural authority, and with what he called 'inauguration'; and the beginning in question, while always being a beginning 'in the world', as Said would always have it, was considered in a fairly formal manner, one that found its core in the emergence of the form of the novel.[32]

In many ways, Said's meditation on this theme can itself be referred back to Frank Kermode's 'Mary Flexner Lectures', given in Bryn Mawr in 1965, ten years prior to the first publication of *Beginnings*, and subsequently published in 1966 as *The Sense of an Ending*. There, Kermode pointed out that 'It is worth remembering that the rise of what we call literary fiction happened at a time when the revealed, authenticated account of the beginning was losing its authority', and that, now (in 1965), 'beginnings have lost their mythical rigidity'.[33]

These, clearly, would be ponderous words for a reader such as Said; and, in many ways, this brief passage can be seen as a kernel of thought from which *Beginnings* emerges. For Said, however, the Kermodian formulation, focused at least tacitly on the primacy of sacred texts and sacred beginnings, is combined with a fully secularized thought that Said derives from the determinedly historicizing influence of Foucault. Where Kermode would next turn explicitly to an analysis of the Gospels, in *The Genesis of Secrecy*, Said would find that his own work would turn to questions of moral freedom and political liberty, so admirably explored in his subsequent and more overtly political work.

It is interesting to note that in the preface to the 1985 edition of *Beginnings*, Said explicitly distinguishes his own position from the kinds of 'uncanny' criticism described by Hillis Miller at that time, on the grounds that Said's own project was resolutely historical in ways that the typical kinds of criticism described and admired by Miller were not. Said was determinedly secular in these matters, his historicism being one that saw his writings as being intimately related to material actualities that were not in themselves necessarily literary: that is to say, though aware of how texts refer to each other, he always stood by the ground that his own writing had non-linguistic (even if signifying) referents in the world and that these referents were more or less directly accessible via language. On the face of it, this seems straightforward: a claim for the demands of history against aestheticist formalism.

However, I shall argue here that the question presiding over Miller's work, specifically in relation to the question of beginnings and to the act that we might now call the inauguration of the confessional impulse might be expressed as something yet more fundamental than anything seen in either Said or Kermode. The question will be shown to be at once, and paradoxically, both more historical than Said and more theologically driven than Kermode.

For the moment, and as a kind of opening gambit to the substance of the thrust of my argument here, we can formulate this question in its basic and beginning sense – the sense that some of Miller's work explicitly addresses as we will see – as the question 'How can anything come about or come into being at all?' We might gloss this: 'How do we reach "one" from "zero"?' or, better, 'How, if at all, is something that we might call an *event* possible?' By 'event' here, we mean, broadly, a something that happens whose outcome could not have been predicted from what was the given case prior to its taking place. Thus, in other words, our gloss might properly read, 'How is *history* possible?' Assuming that it must be possible, there arises the further question: what is the relation between history – or an event's 'taking place' – and our understanding of it – our grasp of it here, now (which as we know from Miller, requires patience, a laborious and industrious 'taking time' that is required for any serious reading).[34]

The assumption here is that a confession requires as a first operational move a moment of self-contemplation, an attempt to 'read' the self and its past actions, an attempt at self-understanding. Miller is at the forefront of those who would see this as anything but straightforward. It is not, as the Catholic Church used to have it, a simple matter of 'examination of conscience'; as we have already seen, some of the key questions depend upon the confounding of conscience with communication as the ground for any event at all, especially any event that tries to relate a private to a public sphere.

The focus is less on where speech, writing and actions originate, and more on how we get from the state of affairs in which there is nothing – zero – on the page to that different state of affairs in which there is something there.[35] In the terms that are pertinent to Miller, especially to his recent meditations on the zero, where is the beginning: do we start from zero or do we start at one? As Lear himself was forced to ponder: how might something come from nothing? As I might myself phrase it, in the context here, 'How do we get to "one" from "zero"?' Given that a confessing subject must, by definition, be 'peculiar' or singular, then how might 'one' confess itself, assuming that it has survived its own reduction to zero, to the bare and unadorned self?

If one returns to Hillis Miller's own beginnings, to those earlier works of criticism, we can see these questions being asked. Interestingly, they are being asked precisely at the same time as the coming to prominence, even to normality, of the confessional mode in American poetry. Let us trace the movement between *The Disappearance of God* in 1963 and *Poets of Reality* in 1965. In the earlier of these texts, Miller describes a literature that struggles with an increasingly transcendental Christian tradition. There, God is a foundational ground that guarantees value; but God is a ground beyond human grasp, and so, a ground that is distanced and removed from human 'experience'. God is a ground 'outside' the human system, but nonetheless vital to it, precisely as the ground that makes such experience possible (as a deviation from, a derivation from, an outgrowth of that ground to which it is structurally indebted for its very being and doing) in the first place. On the other hand, *Poets of Reality* traces the paths of writers who find that, if there is to be a God, 'it must be a presence within things and not beyond them'.[36] As, in their different contexts, Virginia Woolf and Richard Nixon both famously put it, we must learn to 'look within' if we are to find what constitutes reality.

We can understand this Millerian shift as a movement between two attitudes to the literary: the first – the one that we see in *The Disappearance of God* – prioritizes the definitive relation between sign and thing. That is to say, it seeks truth, value and meaning in the possibility of a grounded and grounding referentiality. The second – the attitude that prevails in *Poets of Reality* – prioritizes a constantly varying and unstable relation between signs (which we have learned to call *différance*). The first finds a ground for writing somewhere outside of writing, and it rests its case for legitimacy on the writer's determination of authenticity: it is, as it were, writing as a matter of conscience, in which the conscience tries to bear witness to (or to confess) the reality that transcends it. The second is content with a realization that there may be no such transcendence available; but, in the place of a grounding conscience, it places the sincerity of communication, and the consequent values of a community that will seek to legitimize the conversation, the communications (especially confessional revelations) among subjects.

In these texts from the 1960s, written alongside the democratic poetry of common life, we might begin to see an analogy or at least a parallel in which Miller's thinking on the power and meaning of 'zero' is already silently at work. That is to say, metaphorically at least, the problem of the relation of zero to one was already there in his writings. A transcendent God would be akin to the 'zero' as described by Miller: it is somehow 'within' the system as a sign, yet is also outside of the system, as that which grounds the very possibility of signification, even if any reference to it must be a catachresis. This is, as it were, Miller's version of Pascal's *Deus absconditus*, a God whose presence is verified, paradoxically, by absence; and whose absence, paradoxically, confirms the eternal presence. The relevant passage in Pascal is in the *Pensées*:

> *S'il n'y avait jamais rien paru de Dieu, cette privation éternelle serait équivoque, et pourrait aussi bien se rapporter à l'absence de toute divinité, qu'à l'indignité où seraient les hommes de la connaître; mais de ce qu'il paraît quelquefois, et non pas toujours, cela ôte l'équivoque. S'il paraît une fois, il est toujours; et ainsi on n'en peut conclure, sinon qu'il y a un Dieu, et que les hommes en sont indignes.*

> If nothing of God had ever appeared, such eternal deprivation would be equivocal, and could equally well tally with the absence of all divinity as it could with

the unworthiness in which we would find men who know it; but, given that he appears sometimes, and not always, the equivocation is removed. If he appears once, he always is; and thus one can only conclude that there is a God, and that men are unworthy of him.[37]

This hidden God, as Lucien Goldmann refers to it in his 1955 study of *Le dieu caché*, is like Miller's zero.[38] A God 'outside' or beyond the totality of experience is, as it were, like 'zero', structurally analogous to the operation of zero within number systems; while a God 'within', or a God that has been perceived somehow even once, is a zero so interiorized or experienced that it becomes 'my' ground or grounding, what legitimizes me and my actions, speech, writings within the system itself: 'one'.

A classic example of this – and one that is at least a silent target of Pascal – is Descartes. Crudely put, Descartes might be characterized in this way: having doubted everything external to the self, and then doubting the very self that thereby reduced the exteriority of the world to zero, Descartes is faced with a basic problem of how to reconstitute a world or how to begin it again. Fundamentally, what he does is to elide the difference between God and 'I' such that, while the *being* of the world might still depend on God, at least the *meaning* of the world becomes apparent to and through Descartes, I. In this, there is a silent identification of the self with God, and the one ('I') with the zero (the hidden number, the *dieu caché*, that grounds every possibility of numbers being in the world at all); and the consequence is that the world becomes less characterized in terms of its ontological substances or its being, and more in terms of its epistemological significances or meaning. Like Lowell, Descartes is 'catching himself in the process of becoming himself', finding or making the reality of a selfhood through an examination of the possible meanings of the subject, 'I'. The zero (or transcendent identity, 'God') *inhabits* and, as it were, speaks through the voice of a now representative (if special) 'one', the heroic Descartes. Augustine's worries from the opening of his *Confessions* are answered; and, with this answer, the entry into a specific modernity (with the prioritization of point of view, character, the autonomous self-as-such) is guaranteed.

Thus we have the creation of what we have long since come to term 'point of view' that so dominates modern literature and criticism (and which, it might be argued, gives us the very idea of 'character' that grounds the modern form of the novel, or 'identity' that governs so much contemporary literary and cultural criticism); and, further, we deal with the identification of God and subject by effectively allowing that the world might be reduced to the condition of zero while yet remaining not only pertinent to, but also absolutely the ground of, 'one', of me, of the individual.[39]

In this argument, in which we relate Miller's consideration of zero to his earlier work, we see that the zero argument is a metaphorical revisiting of some concerns that have been presiding and central to Miller's work as a whole. 'One', then, we might describe as 'zero' interiorized, a zero that grants autonomy and that thereby enables the very possibility of history, of the unpredictable event, of the un-preprogrammed, of that which requires theorization precisely because it cannot be theorized.[40] In this way, however, not only via the consideration of Miller's 1960s work but also via this explicatory detour in Descartes, we can see that there is a theological imperative behind the mathematics; and I will return to this. It is important in Pascal, too, who figures at the root of Miller's thinking on zero, at least in the specific inflection given to Pascal by Miller's one-time colleague, Paul de Man.

We can see right from the start that a question of 'displacement', the displacement or not-quite-disappearance of God, the 'one' that is also already a 'zero', has been there always (and, of course, to disappear is precisely the trope of appearance, too). In the much later *Ariadne's Thread*, Miller identifies the displacement more precisely as a structure of allegory:

> The name of this displacement is allegory. Storytelling, usually thought of as the putting into language of someone's experience of life, is in its writing or reading a hiatus in that experience. Narrative is the allegorising along a temporal line of this perpetual displacement from immediacy. Allegory in this sense, however, expresses the impossibility of expressing unequivocally, and so dominating, what is meant by experience or by writing[41]

In some ways, this is also a description of the confessional impulse. It depends upon the facts of experience (I really did this); and the telling of it involves not just narrative but also a kind of 'messianic' hiatus in experience (I stop – I arrest the flow of time, or at least slow it down – in order to tell the confession). And yet, as we have seen, precisely because of this divergence of experience and its relating, we cannot ever satisfactorily or adequately confess: at best, like Lowell, we provide an allegory of a sin that is not ours to commit in the first place, as it were.

Here, in these lacunae or hiatuses, are precisely the specific and incidental zeroes that interest Hillis Miller: moments of rupture that, on the one hand, are figurations of allegory and thus ripe for rhetorical analysis; moments that are also, on the other hand, moments of the possibility of autonomy, of self-starting, of beginning one's own beginning, of grounding oneself not in something outside the self but rather in the very fact of searching for a ground for the self itself, thus involving the self necessarily in a structure of narrative repetition (which is, of course, analysed most closely though not exclusively in Miller's *Fiction and Repetition*).[42]

I started this part of my investigation with Miller's opening sentence on J.L. Austin. There, in *Speech Acts in Literature*, Miller points out that Austin's most influential text, *How To Do Things with Words*, is the narrative and enactment of a necessary failure. Austin had set out to establish a taxonomy of 'performatives', but as he tries to do so, the work signally fails. Austin, despite himself, 'conclusively demonstrated the impossibility of establishing a clear and complete doctrine of speech acts'.[43] One reason for this is that Austin can't properly get started, because he keeps commenting on himself: 'Austin has a habit of commenting on what he is doing, to some degree from the outside, as though he were two persons, the one doing it and the other watching the first doing it. These comments are often wryly ironic, modest, or comic.'[44]

Commenting on what one is doing is, almost by definition, the act – the performative act – of confession itself. Its contemporary technological equivalent is given by the phenomenon of 'tweeting' or that of texting or of posting status messages on Facebook pages. It requires, on the one hand, that the realm of action in the public sphere continues (I communicate with someone), while yet slowing time down or arresting it in the messianic style I described in my opening chapters. In some ways, this is also the structure of that mode of critique that sees itself as being based upon the necessity of disagreement, opposition. When Said described his position as being one that prioritizes criticism over solidarity, he meant to indicate the necessity of ongoing critique, 'even in the very midst of a battle in which one is unmistakably on one side against another' given that 'there must be critical consciousness if there are to be issues, problems, values, even lives to be fought for'.[45] Such a position puts the critic in exactly the position of one who confesses: maintaining a solidarity with or fidelity to the truth of certain events, while at the same time being able to distance oneself sufficiently to comment upon them; and to do this in ways that might expose the subject themselves.

Behind Miller's commentary on Austin, yet more importantly for present purposes, it is almost impossible not to hear the ghostly echo of the voice of another, that of Paul de Man. In 'The Rhetoric of Temporality', de Man examines Charles Baudelaire's great essay on comedy, 'De l'essence du rire'.[46] He focuses at one key point on Baudelaire's consideration of the problematic comic nature of a fall, a stumble in the street. For de Man, there is a *dédoublement* here such that there are, as it were, two men in the case: there is the man who falls, empirically grazing his knees; and there is the man who is conscious of himself falling, who watches himself falling, who might even be able to comment on himself falling ('I fall'), but who, even armed with the knowledge of the fall, can do nothing to prevent or arrest it ('I am fallen'). In this, we have a one that already becomes two, and thus opens our political issues here. This latter 'linguistic self', condemned by self-consciousness to inhabit the temporality of an ever-spiralling irony, is forever divorced from the 'empirical self' who escapes, as it were, from knowledge.

In the terms I used earlier in my brief description of what is at stake in Descartes, there is a fundamental and absolutely definitive distance now between the ontological and the epistemological. In his essay de Man effectively drives a wedge between knowledge about the world on one hand and the world as such on the other. As we might now phrase it, more succinctly, he establishes the fact of a difference between consciousness and history, between, we might say, zero and one.[47]

This is also the problem that we might call the problem of the 'speech act', of the word that is also simultaneously deed, of *logos* as *ergon*.[48] Yet the source of Austin's problem, as Miller must always have known, is precisely mathematical. In 1950, Austin very certainly 'did things with words', with his own and with those of another: he translated Gottlob Frege's *Die Grundlagen der Arithmetik*.[49] Through this, I will aim to show that Miller's work, in its continual beginning, is driven fundamentally by a demand for singularity and, less immediately intuitively, a demand for an ethical democracy.

Of persuasion and the confessional ground of judgement

In Joyce's *A Portrait of the Artist as a Young Man*, Stephen discusses aesthetics with Lynch; and the vehicle of the discussion is an upturned basket on a butcher-boy's head:

> Stephen pointed to a basket which a butcher's boy had slung inverted on his head.
> Look at that basket, he said.
> I see it, said Lynch.
> In order to see that basket, said Stephen, your mind first of all separates the basket from the rest of the visible universe which is not the basket. The first phase of apprehension is a bounding line drawn about the object to be apprehended ... You apprehend it as *one* thing ... That is *integritas* ... Then ... you pass from point to point, led by its formal lines ... Having felt that it is *one* thing you feel now that it is a *thing*. You apprehend it as complex, multiple, divisible, separable, made up of its parts, the result of its parts and their sum, harmonious. That is *consonantia* ... [Then] you make the only synthesis which is logically and aesthetically permissible. You see that it is that thing which it is and no other thing. The radiance of which [Aquinas] speaks is the scholastic *quidditas*, the *whatness* of a thing.[50]

It is worth comparing this passage with the version as written in the first draft of this novel, *Stephen Hero*. There are a number of significant differences to be noted. In the earlier draft (the stammered beginning, as it were), there is no actual object operating as the focus of perception and as the occasion for the 'lecture' as given by Stephen; rather, the conversation is held in abstract terms concerning the status of the 'object' as such. Further, Stephen is using the armature of Aquinas in the early version in a purely instrumental fashion, in order to allow him to advance his own aesthetic theory of the 'epiphany'. An object 'achieves its epiphany', we are told, when its 'whatness' or absolute specificity 'leaps to us from the vestment of its appearance'.[51] Finally, the conversation in the early draft is between Stephen and Cranly, not Stephen and Lynch. Cranly is hostile to the proposition and even to the very fact of the discussion taking place at all. In the later version, Lynch is much more sympathetic, much more companionable and indulgent. This last fact will be seen to be of great significance in what follows in my own argument here.

In the 'lecture' he gives, in both versions, Stephen is at pains to isolate the object/basket in space, and also to isolate the moment of perception of it in time. The argument is that the aesthetic moment is extraordinarily *singular*, unamenable to simple repetition. What, however, is the purpose of the argument or discussion in the narrative itself? The ostensible point of the exercise is, in fact, the same as is at stake in the essay by de Man that is at the heart of 'zero', a Pascalian *art of persuasion*. Joyce is proffering a version of critical debate, critical argument; and the point of it is to reach agreement between the two different characters, Stephen and Lynch, on aesthetic judgement. In one way, then, this is a version of deliberative democracy at work, or at least of a Habermasian theory of communicative action. This, though, is why it is important to compare the two versions of the scene. In the first version, with Cranly, Stephen immediately senses Cranly's hostility and their radical separateness from each other. He not only fails to persuade, he fails even to engage. The latter version, with Lynch, is much more positive, with Lynch encouraging Stephen on through the argument: 'Bull's eye again! said Lynch wittily. Tell me now what is *claritas* and you win the cigar.'[52]

Yet, this art of persuasion is conditioned by its intrinsically problematic status, given the alleged non-iterability of the aesthetic event, given its unamenablity to repetition. To persuade, in a sense, would be to allow Lynch, say, to echo verbatim, as if the words and thoughts were his own, Stephen's aesthetic theory. However, if the argument itself constitutes the aesthetic event (as it certainly does in the text and narrative of *A Portrait*), then, axiomatically, it cannot be reiterated in this way. What is being sought here is something that cannot itself be stated, cannot itself be articulated, but can only be felt (and thus present) as something not yet realized (as absence). What is sought is a ground that can be shared, between Stephen and Lynch, a ground that they can take for granted as a shared terrain or foundational land, and on which they can build something that we could call friendship, community or, in the end, society. Such a ground is absent in the *Stephen Hero* draft, but present in *A Portrait*. However, its very presence cannot be stated explicitly: it can only be known without being seen or shown.

In other words, at stake is the problem of how we would legitimize or provide the foundations, *Die Grundlagen*, of our judgements: how, that is, we would focus on the 'one' (the singularity of the basket or other aesthetic object) while revealing the 'zero' (the guaranteed truth of our judgements). Further, how might we do this in such a way as to preserve the empirical *fact* of the substantive existence of zero while yet not requiring its empirical visibility or presence? How might we see or at least *infer the presence* of a zero that underpins the clearly visible and substantial entity that is the one? How might we be sensitive to the fact of the zero within the one even when it remains unarticulated, when it remains silent, when it has a zero-degree of existence? The important paradox here is that, while having a *zero-degree* of existence, this entity nonetheless *has an existence* even if its existence is as a non-existent or zero-degree existent.

We might refine this further if we recall from the Joyce example that, through the act of critical persuasion or argument, Lynch (assuming that he finds a common ground – a zero – to share with Stephen) becomes *as* Stephen himself. That is, the two would then share their own source or originating impetus: the two are *as* one, while yet remaining themselves absolutely differentiated and singular. There is a mathematical issue lying behind this, to which I will return below.

The question of what might be at stake in an act of persuasion is also what is at stake in much of Pascal. Here is an excerpt from the *Pensées*, another text (like Austin's) where we have but a beginning, a pre-text (a kind of zero-ground) for Pascal's great projected but never written apologia for Christianity. My passage comes from *liasse* number II, headed *Vanité*. Pascal writes:

> *Nous ne nous tenons jamais au temps présent. Nous rappelons le passé, nous anticipons l'avenir... C'est que le présent d'ordinaire nous blesse. Nous le cachons à notre vue parce qu'il nous afflige, et s'il nous est agréable nous regrettons de le voir échapper... Que chacun examine ses pensées. Il les trouvera toutes occupées au passé ou à l'avenir. Nous ne pensons presque point au présent... Le passé et le présent sont nos moyens; le seul avenir est notre fin. Ainsi nous ne vivons jamais, mais nous espérons de vivre*

> We can never remain within the present time. We recall the past, we anticipate the future ... It's that the present uually hurts. We hide it from view because it afflicts us, and if it is agreeable to us we hate to see it go ... Let each person examine his thoughts. He will find them all caught up with the past or the future. We hardly ever think of the present ... The past and the present are our means; only the future is our end. Thus we never live, but rather we hope to live[53]

In this, the present moment is one that we run or fall away from. By not thinking in, of, or to the present, we also cannot live in the present; and yet the present is also the ground of our past and future, the ground, therefore, of all the moments in which we *can* live or know. The present, here, becomes a 'zero' that hovers, as in Miller's consideration of zero, between the negative and the positive numbers, an asymptotic point on a potentially infinite line.

'Zero' would thus always be precisely the midpoint of any such line, the point *in medias res*, the mirroring-point of a representation that would also be the point or locus of the possibility of transformation or of change itself. Our 'beginnings' thus are always Horatian: *in medias res*. Beginnings have always already begun and have always already been begun; and beginnings thus forever disappear. The name we usually give to this is *nostalgia*, that painful voyage homewards in which Joyce, for one, was always engaged. In the search for the origins of an act for which the subject seeks redemption, in whatever form, we find a confessional impetus that is shaped by such nostalgia, a desire for the supposedly 'clean breast of it' that we allegedly once had. This is why, as in Heaney, confession is not only always to be repeated, but also always belated: 'In the nick of time, heelturn, comeback / And a clean breast made / Manfully if late. The pattern set.'

Zero is the disappearing God that makes it possible, in its very asymptotic disappearance, to transform a negative into a positive. In mediating, literally, between the negatives and the positives, it operates like Milton's Satan, able to say, 'Evil, be thou my good', to turn a No into a Yes. What is this if it is not an act, as in Satan, of *persuasion*? Zero, in short, is that which structurally permits us and even enables us to *persuade*; or, in short, to bring about change or empirical history itself. Further, that change is substantively the change in the relations between those engaged in the acts of persuasion, those – like Stephen and Lynch – who can form a community of sorts or, at the very least, who can form a friendship. Zero, as the impossible point whose very impossibility makes possible – even necessary – the fact of change itself, becomes thus also the ground of our historical – and no also our social – being.

In 'The Rhetoric of Temporality', de Man had found that irony (in whose temporal order the philosophical falling subject is condemned forever to live) named 'a problem that exists within the self' for it demonstrates 'the impossibility of our being historical'.[54] By returning to zero, we find that that history is not only possible but also necessary again, redeemed now in a form that suggests two fundamental conditions of the historical.

Firstly, history is always already begun. At one level, obviously, this is banal; but at another level it is significant, for it precludes any revolutionary thinking that would proclaim a 'Year Zero', such as we might find it in myths of political movements (from the liberatory origins of the French Revolution to the abominations of a Third Reich) or religious movements (such as those that date history from the times of a guru or leader). The zero of the alleged year zero was always already there, and past, as the very ground and possibility of our being in the first place. It follows from this first condition not only that revolutions are structurally impossible, but also that 'new starts' or 'clean breasts' – fresh beginnings, including theological fresh beginnings – are also structurally impossible. The ghosts of the past, the guilts of the past, must weigh forever on what it is that gives our present condition its specific character: *there is no excuse*, as it were, despite whatever de Man might try to show in his 'Excuses' essay on Rousseau.[55]

This – the fact that *there is no excuse* – is the scandal that simultaneously demands confession while also negating its power. There are major political consequences for this, not only in courts of law but also in major political settings such as those that shaped Arendt's descriptions in *Eichmann in*

Jerusalem.[56] There are also major theological consequences for any who would proclaim confession as a way of redeeming the self. In both cases, a certain idea of grace becomes a disruptive element.

Secondly, the history that has always already begun is one that can never be 'mine', for it is always necessarily conditioned by friendship or at least by the relatedness – the *Zusammenhang* – that we call the social. It follows from this second condition that, in a very strict sense, 'autobiography' is also impossible, and never more impossible than in those stories of a life that centre upon a transgression, an apostasy, a 'turning-point' or personal revolution. The autonomy that would ground an autobiography as the tacit condition of its possibility is itself now dubious.

Instead of considering the importance of autonomy in our modernity and in our modern cultures, we ought rather to be focusing more intently and seriously on those moments of singularity, those unrepeatable moments or, better, 'occasions' when our autonomy is called into question precisely by the *demand* for persuasion. Such a demand is of the order of ethics, for it inevitably situates us in the social position where, like Stephen and like Lynch, we have *something to say*, where we have to make that beginning that constitutes a mark on a page, a mark upon another consciousness. We must make there be something rather than nothing; but, in so doing, we also constitute the 'we' that shapes the occasion itself, an occasion that we can now identify with our being historical and our social being at once.

Confessing friendship and democracy

We need, clearly, to look more closely at this 'one'. Following Frege (as Austin did in translating him), we can see that there is a problem with the basic formulation 1+1=2. That formulation is fundamental not only to arithmetic, but also to any democracy that prioritizes 'the many' or the majority within a community. Frege argues that, in the case of 1+1=2, the two 1s would have to be different (in what follows, let us think of these as Stephen and Lynch, say). If they were not different, then, asks Frege, how could they be distinguished from each other as separate 1s in the first place? That gives us a problem with 2, which can no longer be seen simply as the summation of 1+1. For Frege, 'number is not simply an agglomeration of things', and:

> If we try to produce the number [say, 2] by putting together different distinct objects [say you and me], the result is an agglomeration in which the objects counted remain still in possession of precisely those properties which serve to distinguish them from one another, and that is not the number [i.e. the 'meaning' of 2 is not and cannot be 'you and me', or 'Stephen-and-Lynch']. But if we try to do it the other way, by putting together identicals [I and I, say], the result runs perpetually together into one and we never reach a plurality.[57]

In this formulation, we see the difference between the two accounts of Stephen's aesthetics in the two versions of *A Portrait*. The first version, *Stephen Hero*, delivers its aesthetic theory in purely abstract terms; the second, in the published *Portrait*, gives, by contrast, a very specific substance to the abstraction by imaging for us the upturned basket on the head of the butcher's boy. The mathematical account of reality – in which 1+1=2, for example – depends, for its working, on something that evades the possibility of historical specificity by remaining purely formal and abstract. In this, therefore, we have the *form* of an arithmetical sum *without any content*.

Thus, it follows that it is correct – or '1+1=2' is true – if and only if there is no specificity, no historical substance, to the 1s that are thus being 'counted' or accounted for in the 2. By simple analogy, most political constructions that we consider as 'democratic' are, at best, only formally democratic. Their democracy has no content. As Rancière has it, 'Societies, today as yesterday, are organized by the play of oligarchies. There is, strictly speaking, no such thing as democratic government. Government is always exercised by the minority over the majority.'[58]

Frege complicates our thinking of number here by offering us a version of mathematics that is historical in that it has substantive content; and, when number is given a substance in this way, we find a certain impossibility or negation of formal arithmetic and its certainties, its formulaic truth. This is obviously important in its potential effect upon political considerations. This, of course, is not a justification of the totalitarian thinking of O'Brien and the Party in Orwell's *1984*: in that text, where 2+2=5, or where 2+2 can be made to equal anything the Party wants it to equal, we have precisely the validation of arithmetic as a purely formal and vacuous game. As Winston knows – and as O'Brien also knows – as soon as you give substance to 2, things become more complicated. Indeed, it is *only* if 2 remains pure vacuous form that 2+2=5.

While Rancière analyses this as a profound hatred of democracy, it might be equally useful to consider the matter in less extreme form. We do not need any explicit (or even implicit) government by oligarchy to see the stakes of our question for a culture that vaunts itself as democratic by virtue of its release of many voices, in the Nixon mode. Today, the less offensive way that we consider these matters is by vaunting a mode of cultural relativism. However, such relativism, while ostensibly giving voice to the previously unheard, is itself intrinsically totalitarian insofar as it remains within the bounds of a merely *formal* democracy. Relativism is that state of affairs in which we claim that truth depends for its validation upon situatedness or upon ethnic or other 'norms' as agreed by any group. Thus, Pilate-like, we all have truths, but 'mine' may differ from 'yours', though we can make claims for the alleged validity of both. Obviously, this is a trivialization of truth.

Alain Touraine is useful as a guide here. He points out that democracy is, as we have always known, threatened by various forms of oligarchy. However, in addition to this, democracy is also threatened precisely by the consequences of a philosophy that sees the point of democracy as being the simple release of many confessional voices in a society of 'deliberation', the kind of deliberative democracy that Martha C. Nussbaum places at the centre of a democratic education.[59] The name he gives to this threat is not relativism, but 'culturalism'.

In this 'culturalism', he argues, we push the respect for minorities to the point where we effectively suppress the very idea of there being a majority at all, the consequence of which is that we reduce the efficacy of any idea of there being a domain of a general law at all (what we might once have called a universalizing principle). The danger is that, in this extreme respect for differences, for cultural differences, we establish and encourage the formation of localized 'communities' which impose, within their own milieu, an antidemocratic culture; As he glosses this:

La société politique ne serait plus alors qu'un marché aux transactions vaguement réglées entre des communautés enfermées dans l'obsession de leur identité et de leur homogénéité.

Political society would then be nothing more than a market of vaguely regulated transactions between communities that are locked within an obsession with their identity and homogeneity.[60]

That is to say, it can be that the very principle of identity leads to an antidemocratic condition. Against this, Touraine argues, rightly in my view, for a mode of democratization that is concerned with emancipation, rather than with 'mere' deliberation. To ground this more fully, we need a fuller consideration of the status of the subject in democracy, and the status of the individual, the one.

Democracies, in general, depend upon forms of counting and accountabilities. If we are to explore the political effects of Frege's thought, we might begin from a consideration of the idea of a one that is identical with another one: that is to say, we need to revisit the idea of duplication and reproducibility in what is Benjamin's most cited essay on 'The work of art in the age of mechanical reproduction'. Part of the drive behind that essay lies in Benjamin's awareness that the work of art made for reproduction is a work that endangers the 'aura', which he defines as 'the unique phenomenon of a distance'.[61] That which is 'unique' in this way – in my terms here, that which occasions the singularity of an event, especially of an aesthetic event whose substance is such that it requires *a change in the identity of the subject of perception* – is unique precisely because of its location in place and time. Such a location or situation is, by definition, unrepeatable.

However, modernity wishes to overcome this distance, to become more intimate with the objects that organize the levels, hierarchies and priorities within the values of its society; and Benjamin explicitly relates this desire to overcome distance with the rise of 'the masses'. Blanchot is useful here in his devastating examination (taken from the work of Hubert Damisch) of the bogus democracy offered by 'paperback culture'. The invention of the paperback proposes a state of affairs where, ostensibly, everyone now has free access to culture in its widest sense: culture, as it were, has become transparent, and we are entering the age of a so-called 'transparent society' in which everything is available, and available or accessible *immediately*, without mediation. Culture becomes precisely the substance of the 'I-here-now', as it were.[62]

This, liberal thought argues, is the very basis of a deliberative democracy, and is thus a good and progressive thing. However, this occludes what is really operational within such a culture, and especially within its economic realities. Here is Blanchot:

> The paperback publisher ensures his profit not by selling many printings of any particular book but by procuring a large market for the entire series. Here we detect cheating: the series must reach the most varied public; it must therefore be made up of many things, heterogeneous, superficially broad, of a deceptive eclecticism and without any unity aside from its presentation – the colorful cover whose scintillation attracts the gaze and gives the buyer a luxurious pleasure: a luxury and quality within the reach of everyone.[63]

In reality, this ostensible pluralism is deceptive. To work properly, this market needs extremely fast turnover: the books appear in the shops but for a limited period of time. You must rush to buy them, before the common interest has moved on to the next items. In short, according to Blanchot, distances of space and time are reduced to zero.

A very generalized 'culture' now 'acts as a substitute for each person'; and thus, difficult works are reduced to 'values', values that are always already known in advance, values that are confirmed by the works or by our alleged common understanding of them. Further, and even worse:

> the work's *irreducible* distance, the approach of which is the approach of a remoteness and which we grasp only as lack – a lack in ourselves, a lack in the work, and a void in language – the strangeness of the work, the speech that can be spoken only a little beyond itself, is reduced to a happy familiarity, commensurate with possible knowledge and unutterable language. Culture is substance and full substance; its space is a continuous, homogeneous space without gap and without curvature.[64]

This 'culture', then, is entirely anti-democratic. It works as a scandal allowing individuals to believe that they exist within a democratic condition, while simultaneously working in totalitarian fashion to reduce their heterogeneity and to fashion them as undifferentiated one from the other. If they are 'individuals' at all, they are so only in a purely formal and abstract way. In the reduction of time to instantaneity, and the reduction of distance to zero, they give a false or bogus version of democracy. This reduction of space and time to the instantaneously available is what we usually refer to as a culture of *transparency*.

The culture of transparency means the end of our right to a private life: in this state of affairs, we are forced to confess all, eternally and totally. In some regimes, this is called surveillance or, in more extreme and less quotidian form, the wringing of betrayals by political torture. In some situations, it is thought of as standing bare before a deity. But in other societies, (and this is especially so within modernity) it is called consumerism, a consumerism that pretends to offer a condition in which culture is available as a mass-effect. It is akin to what we have already seen in Perec's *Les choses*.

Benjamin writes that 'Every day the urge grows stronger to get hold of an object at very close range by way of its likeness, its reproduction.'[65] If we, in mass society, cannot hold the *Mona Lisa* before our eyes in the intimacy of a private epiphany, then we can at least have access to the reproductions of the image. Something inevitably happens, however, as we saw in the case of Jérôme and Sylvie in Perec's novel. According to Benjamin:

> Unmistakably, reproduction as offered by picture magazines and newsreels differs from the image seen by the unarmed eye. Uniqueness and permanence are as closely linked in the latter as are transitoriness and reproducibility in the former. To pry an object from its shell, to destroy its aura, is the mark of a perception whose 'sense of the universal equality of things' has increased to such a degree that it extracts it even from a unique object by means of reproduction.[66]

Here, Benjamin identifies the logic of reproduction (the logic of formal arithmetic, as it were) with a mode of perception that has given up on the possibility of evaluative differentiation, or of aesthetic discrimination and judgement. All things become universally equal; and all are equally worthy of critical attention.

Interestingly, there is a rather unquestioning acceptance of this mode of thinking among those critics who have abandoned the literary in favour of something called the cultural, especially in the form of 'cultural studies' or, more recently, 'cultural criticism'. In cultural studies, reading becomes essentially a content-free activity, a formal methodology whose modes (derived from a 'theory' that has fundamentally been reduced to semiotics) can be applied equally 'to Canaletto and to Corn-Flake packets – why not?', as in the recent journalistic formulations of Catherine Belsey, for example.[67] Those engaged in this kind of activity proclaim that it is critical and even radical in its political roots as well as in its implications and consequences. However, given that it is content-free in this way (unable or unwilling to distinguish the singularity of Canaletto from that of Corn Flakes), it is actually entirely complicit with the conservative politics of those governments that conceive of education in purely instrumentalist terms, where the formal acquisition of rather neutral 'skills' replaces the content and substance of 'the pursuit of knowledge'.[68]

More important still is what these critics ignore in Benjamin, which is that the alleged equality of aesthetic (and other) objects is a by-product of the fact that in mass society, such objects – reproduced objects – have been denuded of their content which, for Benjamin, means essentially that they have been stripped of their historical being, substance and location. We attend, then, to the form of an object ('what an enigmatic image is that of the *Mona Lisa*', which we can compare *as an image* with all the other paintings in this or that volume of reproductions, say) while being denied its content (the historical struggles, plays of force and of powers that made the painting possible and even necessary at a certain place and in a specific moment – which is unrepeatable, difficult of access, distant and certainly not available for us-here-now).

In contradistinction to all this, my case is that the critical point about art is its difficulty of access. A critical approach that subscribes to the possibility of an art 'confessing' itself is a critical approach that will eventuate in only one thing: the 'confessions' of the subject of criticism who falls into autobiography instead of criticism. Worse, this mode of critical practice proceeds as if the I-here-now that constitutes such a subject is constitutive of identity and not of difference. In this valorization of a critique that is essentially a modulation of identity-politics, we end up with a claim for a democracy that attends to individual acts of reading, but that does so in a purely formal and vacuous manner. Further, this 'democracy' believes that a social formation is made up arithmetically of the sum of its individual parts, whereas a society that is a genuine social formation is always geometrically formed as a structure that cannot be reduced to constituent elements in this simplified way.

In Benjamin, this reduction of the content of an object to its pure form might be used to explain the difference between the two versions of aesthetics in Joyce. Filled with content (the basket), friendship, communication and the socially historical become possible (Stephen and Lynch finding their common ground). Denuded of content, by contrast, and left as pure abstraction, friendship and the social – in sum, the grounds of our being or becoming historical – are denied (Stephen and Cranly).

When the objects of perception become formally equalized in this way, then so too do the subjects of perception; and this is what we see in the cultures of transparency. There can now be no perception better than any other, for the subjects of perception have themselves been abstracted from history. This gives us all a purely formal equality before the text, as it were, in a gesture that can only be described as a 'bogus democracy'. We are all now equally 'one' so to speak. Yet now, how would we evaluate and discriminate? How do we make judgements at all in such a case? More fundamentally still, how might we validate such judgements or give them a legitimacy that transcends 'my' own subjectivity?

However, if we are to establish community at all, in the sense of those historical and social friendships to which I have adverted above, then it follows that we must seek to persuade: we cannot accept the absolute relativity of all judgements, for to do so would be a denial of our historical and social being. Yet we lack the grounds – the zero – on which to formulate our separate 'ones'.

At this point, we reach one root of the mathematical politics here. The usual resolution of the problem is not one where we genuinely try persuasion by argument; rather, the majority wins out. We simply count those who have similar judgements and call the resulting majority view 'truth' or at least the authoritative or legitimized version. This, obviously, is not too far removed from the totalitarianism criticized in *1984*. One other name for this state of affairs, of course, is ideology. However, within humanistic studies, we have tended to confound it with 'democracy'. The problem, as we can now see courtesy of this detour via Benjamin, is that we have the *form* of democracy without any *content*.

A fuller reading of his essay reveals, further, that Benjamin identifies the condition in which we evacuate objects (and people, subjects) of their recalcitrant substantive content, replacing that content with the more easily manipulable vacuities of form, as a condition in which we are complicit with those forms of fascist thinking which, while acknowledging as Benjamin puts it that 'the masses have a right to change property relations', nevertheless see their fascist salvation 'in giving these masses not their right, but instead a chance to express themselves'.[69] Benjamin famously goes on to say that 'All efforts to render politics aesthetic culminate in one thing: war'; and, by analogy, all efforts to evacuate objects of their content and to evacuate the singularity of an aesthetic occasion of its content also culminate in this same thing.

Yet, in this final section of my argument, I want to revive the idea of an aesthetic that can drive politics: an aesthetic democracy. Our 'democracies', such as we know them, depend upon an arithmetical falsification, for they depend upon eliding the singularities of the various subjects whose voices can be 'counted'. In this, the formality of the count trumps the content of the vote, as it were. Instead of an arithmetical democracy, which has the defect that it elides historical content from the democratic act, we might start to consider the possibility of a redefinition of what constitutes a democratic relation among human subjects. In the light of foregoing chapters, such a relation might be thought of not just as an *intimacy* but a friendship or even a relation of love.

Love and friendship do not depend upon the confessing or telling of our loves, nor on the revelations of the contents of individualized consciences. Rather, both friendship and love are relations in which 1+1 does not ever arrive at 2 in any simple way. This is so because these relations give full regard to the absolute disjunction between the two 1s in the case. In friendship, neither one tries to subsume the other; instead, friendship is conditioned precisely by the constant awareness of alterity as such, while yet demanding greater and greater intimacy. In friendship, it is not the case that one 'confesses' oneself to another; rather, it is the case that the relation itself is conditioned by forms of *persuasion*, sometimes construed as seduction. In this case, therefore, the very fact of relatedness or friendship makes it possible for each several human subject within that relation to realize herself or himself precisely as a subject in the first place.

The resulting subject is marked by two things: a) the action of developing *as* a subject (the conversion of selfhood that we argued earlier is constitutive of the confessional act); and b) the ongoing demand for persuasion or change as a structural condition of the subject's emergence. From the first condition here, we have a subject marked not as a being (or identity) but as a becoming (or difference); and from the second condition, we have a subject that is necessarily structurally communal and in pursuit of freedom, in open pursuit of non-determination, in open pursuit of seeking to emancipate their others.

In this form of democracy, we acknowledge difference as well as unity. Indeed, for a thinker such as Touraine, democracy properly understood is that system that allows a society to be both one and diverse simultaneously. Democracy '*est définie par la combinaison de l'universel et du particulier*' (Democracy 'is defined by the combination of the universal and the particular'); and this, for Touraine, does not eventuate in any kind of homogenizing drive at all (that is to say, a resolution of the conflict individual-universal in favour of the universal) but rather results in what he calls a release of '*individus-sujets*' or subject-individuals.[70]

Two things need explaining. First, the question of the aesthetics that lies behind this democracy, this regulation of the claims of individual and universal; and secondly, the nature of this '*sujet*', the nature of the subject of this new democratic condition, a democracy of action.

Aesthetics begins, at least in its modern formulations, precisely as a question of how we might regulate the competing claims of the individual and the universal, the particular and the universal, as a location for the perception of beauty and, behind that, of truth. Francis Hutcheson argued that the perception of beauty lies within the relation of what he called 'variety within uniformity' and vice versa. In this, he finds a quasi-mathematical foundation for aesthetics:

> The figures which excite in us the ideas of beauty seem to be those in which there is *uniformity amidst variety* ... what we call beautiful in objects, to speak in the mathematical style, seems to be in compound ratio of uniformity and variety: so that where the uniformity of bodies is equal, the beauty is as the variety; and where the variety is equal, the beauty is as the uniformity[71]

Aesthetics then begins as a mathematical problem concerning the regulation of particular and general, variety and uniformity. What Hutcheson is trying to do here is to find a mode of legitimization of our statements regarding beauty: do we ground the truth or value of those statements on the individual (conscience) or upon the community (communication, discussion)? If based on the community (or the primacy of the uniform) then we eschew experience and give up on the idea that beauty is something that can be experienced or perceived by the individual subject as a condition of their living; if based on the individual (variety) then we eschew law and thereby suggest that beauty is so entirely in the eye of the beholder that we cannot seriously discuss it, or its occasions and objects, for we have retreated into a solipsistic view in which there can be no possibility of deliberated agreements.

To maintain the proper democratic relations between law and experience, then, we need to find what is essentially an *aesthetic* basis for our democracy. The proper such basis, I claim, is that which releases as much variety as possible while still maintaining the necessity of law: that is to say, we need to maximize human experience but to do so in a fashion that acknowledges that experience has a grounding in law.

Law, in this, is not and cannot be grounded in a simple arithmetic majority. We do not vote on truth, as it were. Frege has already shown us that this is illegitimate for any such positing of a majority is based upon the ignoring of actual experience, of actual subjects, based on the evacuation of experience from the lived existence of those subjects.

What, then, is the nature of the subject of democracy? Arendt and Touraine would agree with the philosophy of a much earlier thinker, John Macmurray. Macmurray's entire philosophy was based upon the idea of the 'person in action'. True to a Scottish tradition of philosophy, he saw thought not as something abstract but rather as something practical. Further, the most serious way of validating action was in terms of its contribution to freedom, which he argued was something that not only 'has a higher value than happiness' but also 'is the defining character of man'.[72] Interestingly, he describes the paradox of freedom in ways that are reiterated in some of the thinkers discussed earlier in this book. First of all, he points out that freedom is indeed 'conditioned' and is thus relative rather than absolute: it is an ever-ongoing negotiation between potentially unlimited technological advance and potentially always unsatisfied desire (given that our desires, insofar as we are human, always transcend our present condition or state). He describes this paradox as that which lies in the difficulty we find in being ourselves', reminiscent here of Rosenthal's description of Lowell above. Further, he traces this to St Paul whom he cites to the effect that '"it doth not yet appear what we shall be"' and he goes on in his own words, 'We are and yet are not ourselves; and in this is our freedom'[73]. Our human nature is something not given as such, but rather something that we must fight for, or, as Touraine would have it in his description of the human subject:

> *J'appelle sujet la construction de l'individu (ou du groupe) comme acteur, par l'association de sa liberté affirmée et de son expérience vécue assumée et réinterprétée. Le sujet est l'effort de transformation d'une situation vécue en action libre; il introduit de la liberté dans ce qui apparaît d'abord comme des déterminants sociaux et un héritage culturel.*

> What I call a *subject* is the construction of the individual (or of the group) as an agent, by the association or its affirmed liberty and its lived experience that is both acknowledged and reinterpreted. The subject is the effort of transformating a lived situation into a free action; it introduces freedom into that which first of all appears to be social determinations or cultural heritage.

Or, more succinctly still, the subject '*est ce travail, jamais achevé, jamais réussi, pour unir ce qui tend à se séparer*' (the subject 'is this work, never completed, never achieved, to unite that which tends to atomization').[74]

This subject of freedom, then, is both single and diverse, both individuated and communitarian at once. It is a one and a many; and it is a recognition that it is the many that allows for the possibility of the emergence of a one. Macmurray is helpfully clear on this:

> Freedom is our nature. But our nature lies always beyond us, and has to be intended and achieved. The obstacle lies in our fear, and the craving for security which expresses it. So at every crisis we are faced with a free choice between freedom and security. If we choose security, and make that our aim, we lose freedom, and find in the end that security eludes us. If we choose freedom, then we are debarred from aiming at security; for that would mean imposing our bondage upon others.[75]

In this, we see an attempt to persuade us to a generosity; and such a generosity not only acknowledges alterity as a founding condition for the subject, but also a founding condition for the possibility of freedom. Freedom is not that which is achieved by speaking in my own voice; rather, freedom requires the voice of the other, and a listening as well as a speaking. It is, as it were, a confession of community as such.

There is an example of the kind of thing I am arguing for here in the fully developed reading protocols of Hillis Miller, whose work is often marked precisely by an attention to singularities: to the singularity of the work of art, the singularity of the subject engaged with it, the singularity of the many diverse occasions of reading. The resulting 'democratic reading' is one that will not 'theorize' in the sense that it will not elide differences in the name of abstraction; but instead will maintain and even multiply differences, with all the attendant difficulties. The democracy that results is a kind of 'aesthetic democracy', depending upon a rigorous attention to the kinds of alterity invited by a meditation on the anomalous position of 'zero', upon its relation to any and every single 'one'. The persuasions effected between participants or readers here depend upon a respect for '*le tout autre*' (or 'completely other'), for a maintaining of their singularity, while yet also striving to effect what is an impossible possibility: communication between a 'one' and another 'one' who, in being disjunctive with respect to each other, cannot possibly add up to a '2'. The name that we usually give to such a relation, of course, is love (which, as Miller indicates, is another word for 'zero').[76]

Consider Miller's readings of Johann David Wyss's *The Swiss Family Robinson*, described with great affection in his *On Literature*. There, we find someone with a basket not on their head (as in Joyce) but on their back. Miller describes one of his earliest memories 'of being carried in a "pack-basket" on my father's back on a camping trip with the rest of my family and another family to the Adirondack Mountains in northern New York State'.[77] It would be only through legerdemain that I would claim that we have here taken Joyce beyond Joyce, as it were, in finding a content for that butcher-boy's basket; but it is as if the content of the basket, tumbling out as it is upturned, is nothing other than Hillis Miller himself, son not of a butcher but of a minister. Yet, in this 'addition' to the Joyce story, wherein I seek to give yet more content to the original object than was originally the case, I am following a beginning provided for me by Miller in his own beginning act of reading *The Swiss Family Robinson*.

Looking back at the text now, Miller finds that one of its defining characteristics is:

> the way reader after reader has been so taken by the virtual reality *The Swiss Family Robinson* reveals that he or she feels authorized to extend the original with new episodes. It seems as if, once you are inside this alternative world, you can explore and record even those parts of it Wyss did not happen to write down, so powerful is the reader's persuasion of its independent existence[78]

Addition and persuasion here are central to the singularity of the occasion of reading. Indeed, they are what constitute its singularity as an event. This, though, is an addition with substantive historical *content*, however ostensibly anecdotal or conventionally 'confessional' it may be; and, more importantly, it is a persuasion made in the interests of friendship (the families camping together), hospitality and the historical sociability to which we properly give the name 'democracy'.

Finally, then, let me return to *De l'art de persuader*. There, Pascal knows that:

> *quoi que ce soit qu'on veuille persuader, il faut avoir égard à la personne à qui on en veut, dont il faut connaître l'esprit et le Coeur, quels principes il accorde, quelles choses il aime*

> whatever it is that one wants to persuade someone about, it is necessary to have regard to the person who is to be persuaded, and you must be familiar with his mind and Heart, with what principles he holds to, what things he likes[79]

Persuasion is always historical, always social, always partly demanded by the other; and, in fulfilling such a demand, it becomes possible for the subject to articulate their own 'becoming', their own historical mutability. A culture of transparency, in which all is supposedly revealed, is a culture of anti-democracy. It proposes, falsely, that the primary condition of human being is the interiority of a self-contained subject that is purely individuated, and whose 'freedom' is assured solely by the choice between revelation and concealment. The result becomes a society whose abased 'democracy' is founded upon a condition of an alleged equality, grounded in the rhetorical trope of a near-chiasmus: 'I'll show you mine if you show me yours'; and such a culture can only be based, in fact, upon inequality and shame. It is always unequal because of the preconditions on which a human relatedness is based (the 'deal' between the two confessing selfhoods); it is shameful because it always presupposes that the interiority, if revealed, can only be humiliating.

Agamben, following Levinas, has refined our understanding of this kind of shame. He points out that Levinas had argued, in 1935, that shame 'does not derive ... from the consciousness of an imperfection or a lack in our being from which we take distance'. Rather, shame is in many ways precisely the opposite of this, deriving instead from what I called in earlier chapters a crisis of intimacy, but an intimacy of the self with the self, an intimacy that proclaims a full self-possession grounded in what must always be a false idea of self-coincidence. As Agamben has it, 'shame is grounded in our being's incapacity to move away and break from itself.[80]

Against this, we might usefully consider confession as an act that is primarily one of persuasion; but a persuasion whose impetus is to persuade us to a freedom, and a freedom that is necessarily conditioned by our always becoming, always differing, always releasing more and more diversity, always pursuing freedom – and above all, pursuing the freedom of the other. Confession is always, or should always be, about the release of the prisoners and perhaps, first and foremost, about the release of the self from the imprisonment of the culture of transparency. Behind the alleged transparent nudity of the self lies nothing, in fact; for the self is always preconditioned by its relations to other selves. As Beckett so rightly knew, there is, as it were, 'nothing to communicate', while there is also simultaneously an absolute demand to communicate. Confession, thus, is always the profession of a relation to alterity; and, properly understood, it is thus akin to love and to the democratic drive that shapes the very possibility of love, understood now as the elaboration of freedom.

PART THREE

7

Witnessing and Literary Confession

Or, Confessing and Modernity:
The Troubling Witness

In previous chapters, I have suggested that confession is an act of communication before it is a matter of conscience. This presupposes that a confession must be attended to or must be *witnessed*; and, further, given the importance of alterity to the construction of a self, the witness becomes a primary constituent of any confessional discourse. In this present chapter, I shall explore the role of witnessing and the function of testimony; and I shall concurrently advance further the argument relating to the question of whether it is ever possible to confess in one's own voice or whether the confessing 'I' must always be displaced on to an other person (both grammatically and substantively or ethically).

We can begin by looking at two literary examples of a confessional act, in writings by J.M. Coetzee and Seamus Deane; and we will then explore the questions thrown up by these examples in a more theoretical fashion. This latter will require some thought on the nature of translation and its effects on evidence. We will look briefly at a passage from confession of survival, Derrida's *Demeure*, and at a less familiar feuilleton by Robert Scheu, *Die Konversation in der Ehe*, where we can explore further the idea of confession being essentially akin to love.

Fictional testaments

In 2009, J.M. Coetzee published *Summertime*, a characteristically clever novel which, like a number of Coetzee's texts (especially, of course, *Boyhood* and *Youth*, the two earlier companion texts to *Summertime*), plays with the status of autobiography and character in fiction. The story is one involving a biographer who is putting together a volume detailing a key period in the life of one John Coetzee, a South African novelist whose life story matches fairly precisely the life story of J.M. Coetzee himself. At one level, this is characteristic of many late modern texts: the attention to a kind of hyper-reflexivity and self-consciousness, learnt from the moderns, that has the effect of leading us into paradoxical thought. At another level, it is more serious than this: it addresses the question of what it might mean to tell the story of one's own life and, very specifically within that, to confess.

Near the end of the novel we find ourselves reading Coetzee's 'Notebooks: undated fragments'. In this section, by John Coetzee himself, we find what we must infer to be a clear act of confession. Although clear, the confession in question is neither direct nor straightforward, for in these 'Notebooks' Coetzee refers to himself in the third person. The confession is, as it were, displaced from the I to the he. The substance is as follows: after the Second World War, John Coetzee's father, who had been serving in Italy after the capitulation of Mussolini in 1944, had developed a 'newfound passion for opera'; and had bought a long-playing record of Renata Tebaldi singing various arias, especially arias from Italian opera. Coetzee himself preferred Bach, he tells us; and so there was a kind of musical war, between Tebaldi and Bach, between Italy and Germany and, of course, behind this between father and son. Then we find Coetzee's confession, in a voice displaced on to third-person narration:

> One day, while no one was around, he took the Tebaldi record out of its sleeve and with a razor blade drew a deep score across its surface.
> On Sunday evening his father put on the record. With each revolution the needle jumped. 'Who has done this?' he demanded. But no one, it seemed, had done it. It had just happened.[1]

Thus, we are told, Bach triumphed over Tebaldi; and son over father. However, it is not as straightforward as that. For decades, Coetzee has felt remorse; and the confession recounted in *Summertime* represents a kind of unfinished business. The business is unfinished for the simple reason that, after the damage to the record, the father simply stopped listening to Tebaldi, even after the son, feeling guilt and shame, buys a new and unblemished record of her singing. In doing this, the father denies the son the possibility of redemption or of re-establishing a kind of economic balance between act and forgiveness; in ignoring the act, the father effectively precludes the possibility of Coetzee's confession having any efficacy or purchase on their relations. There is a kind of incompletion in this confessional act. It is, as it were, something begun, but left hanging because of the father's disregard or refusal to witness the confession.

According to what I have already described as an economy that shapes a certain idea of confession, the act of confessing 'works' if and only if it is recognized, if and only if it is witnessed, as it were. When, as in this case, the ostensible required witness (the father) refuses to witness, then it follows logically that the speaker himself acts as a silent witness to his own voice. This partly explains that displacement from the I to the third-person narrative at work: J.M. Coetzee acts as witness to John Coetzee's confessional act in an effort to redeem him. In the refusal to witness adequately, the father in this case refuses to acknowledge his own pain and misery. The son's initial act, intended to cause pain and suffering and to assert power and primacy within the relationship, is emptied of significance. However, the act has been committed and, unless and until its effect is recognized through an act of witnessing, it remains in a kind of historical vacuum or void, a now-time that lacks substance. This causes a literally untold misery in the son.

There is a parallel but different case in Seamus Deane's *Reading in the Dark* (published in 1996, just prior to the 1998 'Good Friday agreement' that heralded one proper attempt at starting a democratic organization for the north of Ireland). Again, in this novel, a father and son have a difficult relation. At the very heart of the novel, the son tries to assert his power and authority in a particularly nasty act that is parallel to that of Coetzee in its fundamental destructiveness. The son (the Deane figure) has brought shame on the family by appearing to collaborate with the police in June 1951. Threatened in the street by a gang who are going to beat him up, the son finds an escape by throwing a stone at a passing police car and thus drawing the attention of the police to what is going on. In the fraught and divided north of Ireland at the time of the novel's setting, this is a profoundly troubling thing to do. He has been forced into it essentially as an act of self-preservation; and the vindictiveness of the police ensures that his appeal to them for safety becomes fully apparent. However, the father's view is straightforward: the son should have taken a beating from his Protestant tormentors and the matter would now be over. By involving the police, he has brought shame and fear into the Catholic household.

The son tells his father that it is stupid to suggest that he should just have taken a beating; and, in a moment of fury at his insolence, the father strikes him: 'He hit me so fast, I saw nothing. My shoulder felt hot and broken. I got up, hating him … My father looked at me, his face suddenly sad as well as angry. He was sorry he had hit me; but he wanted to hit me again.'[2] To ease his frustration the father goes out to prune and tend to the roses that he lovingly grows in the house's backyard. A short time later, in anger at his father's treatment of him, the son deliberately and savagely cuts down the rose bushes. In both this case and that of Coetzee, the assertion of filial identity depends upon a destruction of paternal identity. The Freudian and Oedipal aspect of this is less important, for present purposes, than the observation that, in both texts, the question of a necessary confession is tied to a breaking with the immediate forebear: the confession is called into play by a temporality that requires a breaking of the *Jetztzeit*, as it were.

In *Reading in the Dark*, the boy is exacting already what he thinks of as a kind of revenge on his father, who has struck him already for an act of insolence. The response of the father to the boy, after the roses are battered down with a spade and covered in concreting powder, is complex. First, the father tells the boy that he will be made to remember the act every day from now on. Next, with the help of some friends, he concretes over the entire yard where he used to grow the flowers. Now, every time the boy plays there, or even walks there, he is reminded of his action: it becomes a kind of permanence of the moment, the cemented path a kind of monument or memorial. Later that same day, though, the boy lies in his room, half-asleep, and is disturbed by the realization that someone else is there in the room.

> It was getting dark when I woke. Someone had touched me. I opened my eyes a slit, stared at the wallpaper and closed them again as my father bent over me. He kissed my hair. I slowly stiffened, from the toes up. In a moment, I would cough or cry; but the bed rose as his weight lifted, and I rose lightly with it, like a wave lifting. He thought I was still asleep. He whispered to himself something I didn't catch. The bedroom door closed and the stairs creaked their old familiar music as he went down.
>
> That more or less ended it.[3]

The scene here depicts a love here that is not a forgiveness, but a kind of grace; and it depends upon the permanence of this *Jetztzeit*, the now-time of the savage act in the garden. Although we are told that 'that more or less ended it', we are also immediately reminded that the yard 'remained concreted' and that whenever the boy played on it or even walked on it after this time, it was 'like walking on hot ground below which voices and roses were burning, burning'.[4] There is no excuse here; but, instead of a logic of accusation-exculpation, a logic of a capitalist economy, we have here another example of grace that disturbs such an economy. Here, though, the effect is salutary, in reminding us that the confession is, in a certain sense, not recognized: it is as unfinished, in its way, as that of Coetzee; and this is why it demands the typically stammered retelling or rehearsing in this fictional form.

The son is shocked by the generous grace of the act. By contrast, Coetzee is tormented by the non-recognition of his transgression; and that non-acknowledgement means that he is unable to confess directly, and that he has to have recourse to this fictionalized autobiography to do it. In the Coetzee case, the economy of confession is disrupted by a failure to recognize or witness the confession; in Deane, the economy is fractured by grace.

In his earlier *Youth*, Coetzee addresses also the fragility of any kind of confessional writing. Early on in the text, we hear of John's encounter with Jacqueline, the nurse who makes a sexual advance on him and then moves into his flat. He rapidly tires of her and one day comes home to find her about to leave, packing her bag in a fury. The trouble is that she has read the diary that he has been keeping, a diary that seems to comprise basically the pages that we ourselves have just read. John asserts his right to write and to confront what he calls the truth in that writing. However, there is a problem with the kind of confessing of the truth that he writes in a diary, a diary that is ostensibly meant for his own reading only:

> who is to say that the feelings he writes in his diary are his true feelings? Who is to say that at each moment while the pen moves he is truly himself? At one moment

he might truly be himself, at another he might simply be making things up. How can he know for sure? Why should he even *want* to know for sure?[5]

In the next paragraph, we find him pondering why Jacqueline would believe him, given that 'he does not believe himself. He does not know what he believes.' This is one of the great paradoxes of the diarist, the confessional writer par excellence: we cannot know the truth of what we write. This is so because, as I have now amply demonstrated, confession is not a matter of conscience, it is instead a matter of communication; and the meaning of communication is never given by a solitary conscience, but is instead a product of the negotiated linguistic exchange. As Coetzee writes in the same passage from which I have just quoted him, 'when all is said and done, the fact remains that his first try at living with a woman has ended in failure, in ignominy'. This, the fact, is what constitutes the 'truth', not the materials stated in the diary: the failure of the relation is, as it were, the event that constitutes truth here; and that is a social matter.

These fictional tales, both of them marked by autobiographical impulse, set up the question of confession in relation to judgement, justice and witnessing. It is this that I want to address in this chapter. In what follows, I shall attempt to link confessing to modernity; and, perhaps not entirely obviously, my way into this will be via the question of translation. Although this is not immediately obvious, it should become clear that it is relevant as soon as we remind ourselves that confession is primarily an act of communication and not a prioritization of a conscience that communes with itself in some entirely interiorized realm of being. Translation, in fact, becomes a paradigm case of confession. It involves the speaking in a displaced voice; it involves a communication between different tongues, and all the struggles that ensue given such a lack of immediacy (or of unmediated transparency); and it involves a certain logic of love and of grace as a determinant of the equalities required for democracy in our relations to have any material substance.

Translation and witnessing

If modernity means anything, it implies making a break with the immediate past, a break that will allow for an alignment between the present and a more archaic origin, a more distant past. It is fundamentally an act of transformation and is thus akin to confession construed as an act that is constituted by a fundamental conversion. It is a kind of shot across the *Jetztzeit*, as it were; and in these cases just discussed, the question at stake is the relation between the now-time of the son and the immediate past of the father.

But in this, a new question of economy arises, akin to the structure of 'owing' that we saw at work in Esposito's version of the *communitas*. In this case, the economics derives from the temporal relation: to what is the now-time of the present indebted and where does it find its grace or its possibility of advancing to futurity? There is a politics to this as well; and it depends upon the matter of testimony and surveillance. It is this that will form the cornerstone of my investigation of witnessing here.

The witness is the one who can say, 'I was there.' Yet, as witness, this subject cannot themself be directly engaged in the action to which they bear witness. That is to say: the witness must have been there, but at the same time must also have been somehow distanced from the act being confessed. We see this enacted clearly in Coetzee's example. It is a confession told in the third person: 'he did this'; and that converts the confession into a witness testimony.

Agamben is helpful here. He considers the notion of the witness as martyr. As is commonly known, the Greek word *martis* means both martyr and witness: to be a martyr is to bear witness to a faith, in these terms. Agamben points out not only that martyrdom and witnessing are linked, but also indicates that there is an act of memorization going on here, an act that works across time, for the Greek term *martis* derives from a verb meaning 'to remember'. In his consideration of Auschwitz, he discusses a certain kind of 'impossibility' of testimony.

His argument rests on the figure of the 'Muselmann' (literally 'Muslim') in the camps. He writes that the most likely explanation of this nomenclature 'can be found in the literal meaning of the Arabic word Muslim: the one who submits unconditionally to the will of God'.[6] In the camps, the *Muselmänner* were those who could be defined by 'a loss of all will and consciousness'.[7] They occupied a kind of interstitial state between living and death, or between the human and the inhuman, as Agamben prefers to term it. This is an important figure for the question of testimony and witnessing.

The argument goes that the witness of what actually went on in Auschwitz, the one who can testify in all truth to the fatal acts there, is, by definition, dead. Those who survive are, again of necessity, at a small remove from the central atrocity,[8] and, thus removed or distanced, they cannot testify: they 'were not there', as it were. However, Agamben (obviously horrified at the banality of this argument) goes on to point out that we are essentially here in the presence of two types of testimony. Testimony, he writes, invokes two modes of subjectivity, two different subjects. Firstly, there is the survivor, 'who can speak but who has nothing interesting to say'; but secondly, there is this figure of the 'Muselmann', the man who 'has touched bottom' or, in the terms from my earlier arguments above, the 'man at point zero', and who therefore 'has much to say but cannot speak'.[9] The question of witnessing relates, therefore, to both survival *and* to the necessity of finding the voice of another in which the events witnessed can be narrated. That is to say: the question of witnessing depends upon an act of *translation* in which a voice of another speaks and allows that which has happened to be re-presented.

To advance this case further, I will repeat (in a kind of stammering of beginnings, as it were) something that I already said in the last chapter: I will begin with a beginning that is not my own, and a beginning that is in translation and that speaks of translation. Here is a brief passage from Derrida's *Demeure*, a text that is both an act of a certain confession and of a testimony that witnesses the self surviving its own death:

> This instant, at this very instant, I am speaking French, we are speaking French. This is a testimony. And this instant, as I am saying this, I pass and I have already passed from *I* to *you*. I am speaking French, we are speaking French. I can only say I am speaking French if it is assumed, as soon as I speak, this instant, in this very instant, that someone here, now, at least someone is able to understand this language that I call and is called French, and is able to form from the outset a *we* with the one who is speaking here this instant, with me, consequently.[10]

'I am speaking French, we are speaking French.' This is a testimony. In translation, it is a false testimony; and yet it is a false testimony to an event that, at the time when it was spoken, was true. '*Je parle français, nous parlons français*' is what Derrida said (if we believe him, of course). There is here, in the act and fact of translation, a problem concerning time. As in any confessional writing, there is that odd temporal narrative disjunction between two moments: the moment when the act is committed, and the moment when the confession of that act is pronounced. Although both are governed by an 'I', the 'I' in the case must be marked by an internal fracture or difference, and that difference is a kind of conversion. In this, the confessional I becomes the site, if you will, of *translation as such*. The translation occupies the position of the I that confesses; and the text translated occupies that of the original sin, the original act or transgression. Further, the text translated is said not for the first time, even if it attests to something happening for the first time. Translation is the site of an encounter, and in this kind of case, it is an encounter between an event that happens for the first time and (if you will) the second time of its happening for the first time. It thus calls into question the singularity of any event, and bears witness to something that *is* and *is not* true at the same time.

Not all encounters, especially those happening for the first time and in an international or translational (inter-lingual or trans-lingual) context, are encounters between equals. Landfall studies make it clear that those whose feet fall upon the land that has been trodden for years by others is often the more powerful foot, against which the native has to kneel, or before which the indigene is made to lay not a foot but a knee. This is so, further and perhaps especially so, precisely in encounters across time, between an I-then and an I-here-now. The I, translated across time, becomes problematic, as in the context of *Demeure*, say, the context of a survival and a witnessing of the self as it confesses and that thus survives its own death.

Things and persons, that is, can be brought together in ways that might even resemble an erotic encounter (as in the history of comic fiction, of course) but as with many such encounters in an international context, the parties are not always equally free parties to the encounter. English can be brought together with India, and with Indian literature, for example; or Spain can be brought together with a certain 'Latin America'. I am inviting here questions regarding the status of translation; but I wish to hear the term in at least two ways: firstly, as meaning the use of a language that is not my own or my first, but that I use *as if for the first time*; secondly, as a word that involves *transformation*. At this point, we need also to bear in mind that I have already shown how any confessional text has to be a *conversion* narrative; and here I want to widen the idea of conversion to that of transformation.

I have argued in previous pages that there is, especially in any text related to confessional discourse, a problem regarding experience. What is the nature of *literary* experience? Experience as such, we usually intuitively claim, is a deep marker of the self, even to the point of being constitutive of the self. Character, we think, is nothing more or less than the sum of experiences that accrue to a particular individuated body. Experience, thus, is what makes 'me' different from 'you'; and yet, oddly, for an experience to be an experience in material terms, it must also be shared. Experience always involves a relation between a world construed as interiority and that construed as exterior to that interiority: self and other, in an older vocabulary. This is especially so in the kind of encounter of which I will write here, the literary textual encounter that constitutes the event of reading.

Perhaps paradoxically, it is the most intimate of experiences that we assume must be shared, such as love. On one hand, then, experience is what brings the self into an intimacy with itself, assuring the self of an identity and thus severing it from contact with the exterior world. It is intensely and constitutively private. Yet, at the same time, it is in experience that the self that engages with the world 'confers' with the self that knows about or that witnesses such an engagement. Experience is, in fact, that term that we use to describe such a conferring, a conference or a relation. This is another, but very different way, in which we see the kind of *dédoublement* of the self that de Man saw in his analysis of Baudelaire.

Yet literary experience is also, first and foremost, a linguistic experience or an engagement with language. I began earlier with a question concerning translation; and I want here to develop that thinking a little. The example that I advanced – 'I am speaking French, we are speaking French' – was one involving what Derrida called a testimony; and it was a testimony, as I indicated, that was at once both true and false. It is an intriguing example in that when it was said for the first time, it was said differently – *je parle français, nous parlons français* – and it was true; when it is heard by us, received by us, 'read' by us, it is in these different translated words – through words that are semantically equivalent – and yet it is false. The reading or translation falsifies the testimony. Is that what is involved in all reading? It is an act of translation that falsifies a testimony?

It is useful here to turn to Theodor Adorno. In 1959, Adorno wrote a small piece, 'Worter aus der Fremde ('Words from abroad'), for a radio broadcast (for Hessischer Rundfunk). In it, he defended himself against his detractors and especially against those who had criticized him for his alleged fascination with 'words from abroad'. His case is that what irritates people who complain about 'foreign linguistic imports' is not the fact that foreign words are being used; rather, what they find troublesome is that they are being asked to comprehend *ideas* that are outside of their usual linguistic range of reference. That is to say, they are afraid, according to the logic of the Adorno talk, of the new *experience* of thinking that is invited by the words. Adorno thinks back to his own youthful fascination with words from abroad, and he explains it thus:

> the fact that we happened upon foreign words in particular was hardly due to political considerations. Rather, since language is erotically charged in its words, at least for the kind of person who is capable of expression, love drives us to foreign words ... The early craving for foreign words is like the craving for foreign and if possible exotic girls; what lures us is a kind of exogamy of language, which would like to escape from the sphere of what is always the same, the spell of what one is and knows anyway. At that time foreign words made us blush, like saying the name of a secret love. National groups who want one-dish meals even in language find this response hateful.[11]

In this passage – a passage in which he 'confesses' his craving for girls – Adorno makes explicit the relation between translation and a certain kind of erotic intimacy. The experience of the foreign word, like the experience of an erotic encounter, transforms the self, allowing it to escape from 'the sphere of what is always the same' into a mode of difference, transformation.[12]

I can introduce a final text here that will allow us to explore this issue of translation and testimony more fully. Sometime around 1920, Robert Scheu published a short text, *Die Konversation in der Ehe* (*Conversation in Marriage*). In his splendid introduction to his translation of this piece, Gilbert Carr astutely matches the business of translation directly on to 'the themes of erotic attraction and spiritual communion' that are actually contained in the narrative within the text. A text about conversation in marriage becomes also a text about translation or about the marriage of conversation in different voices, different tongues. For our present purposes, it also becomes a text about confession. If confession is communication before conscience, as I have been arguing, this text gives us an example of a specific kind of communication, in conversation. Conversation becomes a kind of bond between at least two people in a 'polar relationship of two beings, which conversation does not so much develop anew as make manifest'; and, as Scheu puts it:

> When two people of the opposite sex observe such a polarity in themselves, that magical power which conversation has cast over them, they are at that point already in an intimate, erotic relationship, even if they do not at all care to admit it to themselves, even, indeed, if they consciously resist it.[13]

We might notice in this language a foreshadowing of D.H. Lawrence, who will also write at length about the polarity that constitutes love and erotic desire; but more importantly for present purposes, we should note that it is conversation, construed as a dialogue between two individuals whose dialogue *constitutes* the ostensible revelation of their souls, as it were. That is to say: confession here is a matter of communication, certainly; but it is also a communication that constitutes the very experience or possibility of love.

These cases all effectively recast a certain Kant. Kant makes a distinction between two modes of judgement, which are actually two modes of thinking. The first, which he calls determining judgement, is the kind of judgement that we make when our judgements are governed by rules or criteria. These might be rules such as those that shape Montaigne's idea of law in 'De l'expérience', as we saw in my opening chapter. Agamben offers a useful contemporary gloss on this when he points out that,

> As jurists well know, law is not directed toward the establishment of justice. Nor is it directed toward the verification of truth. Law is solely directed toward judgement ... The ultimate aim of law is the production of a *res judicata*, in which the sentence becomes the substitute for the true and the just, being held as true despite its falsity and injustice.[14]

Another way we have of expressing this is in terms of the predilection for conformity with ideology in our judgements: a refusal, as Adorno would see it, to entertain the possibility of a new and perhaps exotic thought.

The second mode, which Kant calls reflective judgement, is that which happens when we are called upon to make a judgement, *but without rules or criteria* – as in judging whether a painting is beautiful, say, or as in judging whether or not to continue with an erotic relationship. The first kind of judgement, made in conformity with a rule and designed to consolidate it, gives us back the world that we already knew; the second, by contrast, forces us to expand our consciousness, to shape the world anew, to think of the world differently and from the point of view of another (or of the self-become-another). The former, in short, takes us back into our own conscience; the latter makes a virtue of the fact of our communications with each other and the necessity, therefore, of attending to the other: listening in the conversation that constitutes marriage, as it were.

In literary terms, this Kantian opposition is the difference between a criticism that is organized around a politics of identity and one that is organized around a politics of difference. Reading according to a politics of identity is a reading that will confirm our already existing prejudices about the world, a reading that will validate our everyday experience (but only an experience without content); reading according to a politics of difference is uncomfortable, in that it offers – or forces us to have – a new experience. This latter is the 'exogamy of language;' of which Adorno writes.

Thus, literary experience – writing and reading – becomes experience if and only if it is an act of translation. If we widen this, we can say that literary experience necessitates transformation; and if we narrow it back to our present concern, confession is always necessarily translation.

Blanchot helps us advance this further. For Blanchot, literature was firmly tied to what he called 'the right to death'; and a way of understanding this is to see that writing involves us in a paradox:

> a person who wishes to write is stopped by a contradiction: in order to write, he must have the talent to write. But gifts, in themselves, are nothing. As long as he has not yet sat down at his table and written a work, the writer is not a writer and does not know if he has the capacity to become one. He has no talent until he has written. But he needs talent in order to write.[15]

Blanchot's writer here is precisely in the position of one who would confess: the problem is how to begin, as we have seen. Trying to make sense of the paradox, Blanchot offers an analogy with the primitive man who builds a stove or oven. The person who does this transforms certain raw materials (wood, iron, say) into a new thing, and a new thing that can do much more than the untransformed raw materials could ever have done. He has added to the world; and had added a certain potentiality. As Blanchot has it, the building of the stove 'affirms the presence in the world of something which was not there before, and in so doing, denies something which was there before'.

More importantly still, however, the making of the stove transforms the conditions and being of its maker as well, for the resulting heat 'will also make me someone different': where I was cold, I am now warm. Writing, argues Blanchot, is the scene of this kind of transformation writ large and aid bare, and the book that the writer makes 'is precisely myself become other'.[16] This is exactly akin to the position that we have seen in a poet such as Lowell, for whom confessional writing was a process in which he catches himself in the process of becoming himself, as Rosenthal described it.

Thus, the making of the stove is like the procedure of beginning that we see described by Arendt, a process that aligns transformation and freedom. It is an act of inauguration in which the subject makes themselves, but makes themselves by transforming themselves (displacing their person, as it were), and in which simultaneously they assert a freedom. Yet it is also an act of inauguration that does one further significant thing: in transforming the self, it retroactively and paradoxically also creates an original self that was in need of transformation. This is exactly like that mode of expression or conversation that I describe as integral to confessing. Confessing is itself a beginning act; but it has to be a communication and not something that originates from within a discrete conscience. Rather, it creates that conscience through the act of confessional communication in the first place. In doing so, we also get an act of translation: the translation, however, is not just that which goes on between two speakers trying to understand each other; rather, it is a translation of the entire arrangement in which the two find themselves in the first place. It is a *Konversation in der Ehe* that makes of the marriage a new thing.

Reading, a process in which the self becomes other, is always this mode of translation: always a displacement of the self that constructs the possibility of a freedom and a relation with alterity. Properly done, reading is always an encounter with foreign words. It is an act that bears witness to a self that can no longer be there; and in this regard, it is also a witnessing of the voices of the dead.

Witnessing the dead

At this stage, we have a number of interlocking strands in our argument. First, reading can be described as 'precisely myself become other'; and in this regard, it is a procedure in which the voice of the self is displaced on to other voices, other persons. Next, we have confession as a mode of writing in which the self somehow paradoxically appears to survive its own death. Third, this relates explicitly to witnessing, a witnessing that involves memorization or memorial of that which has gone before. Finally, the witness is those who testify, but who testifies as from a kind of median position (like an interpreter or translator) between what Agamben called the survivor and the 'Muselmann', between one who can speak without substance and one who cannot speak the substance that constitutes the bare self or self at a point zero.

We should now seek to bring these strands together yet more tightly; and we can begin from translation and reading the voices of the dead. Literary modernism has made much of this. While it is the case that a common sense tells us that, in the usual course of things, we cannot 'encounter' our own death as a kind of material experience, we do frequently encounter the dead; and we sometimes call that encounter 'literature'. Consider, for example, the opening of Eliot's *The Waste Land*. When Eliot opens that text by writing that 'April is the cruellest month', he is 'translating' (and, of course substantially transforming, even reversing) Chaucer's *Canterbury Tales* for us; and his text 'converses' in a kind of marriage with Chaucer's opening ('Whan that Aprille with his shoures soote / The droghte of Marche ...'). Eliot bears witness to the ghost of Chaucer, whose testimony regarding the nature of April is transformed. This is exactly like Derrida's 'I am speaking French', a text and testimony transformed through translation – or simply through reading.

This, however, is not at all unusual as a literary operation. In fact, it is essentially normative and thus constitutive of our reading act itself. Our encounter with all and any literature, I shall now claim, is precisely such a witnessing of death, a bearing of witness to the testimony of the dead, the dead who are the limit-point of experience. However, for this to be the case, we need as readers to be open to the possibility of the encounter itself: we need to constitute identity through a transformative conversation that may reveal or confess (and thus retroactively construct) our self.

To write is to be in intimacy with death in a certain sense; and to read is to bear witness not only to the fact of our own impending death, but also to bear witness to the testimony of those who have gone before. We can advance this further, bearing in mind the issue of translation that I have raised here. Consider Jorge Luis Borges, who will in some ways make this a theme of some of the stories in his *Labyrinths*. In 'Pierre Menard, Author of the *Quixote*', we are presented with what is essentially a parable of reading itself. Pierre Menard sets himself the task of writing *Don Quixote*, the great text by the long-dead Cervantes. The task is unfinished, but perfect as far as it goes: 'Needless to say, he never contemplated a mechanical transcription of the original; he did not propose to copy it. His admirable intention was to produce a few pages which would coincide – word for word and line for line – with those of Miguel de Cervantes.'[17]

Yet this, of course, is in one way a perfect description of Menard actually *reading* the *Quixote*. The reading act here operates exactly like an act of translation; but the point that Borges makes here is that writing itself is always already an act of translation in any case.

Let us turn, though, to a more explicitly confessional text in Borges, 'The Shape of the Sword'. This is a confessional text, but it is anything but straightforward. As in Heaney, it is a stammering confession that needs to be re-read once one arrives at the end; and it is written in a fashion that is full of potential error and marked by a fundamental displacement of person. It is the story of 'the Englishman from La Colorada' who, it turns out, is not English but Irish. The Irishman tells the tale of how he got his facial scar, a kind of crescent-moon shape across his face; and he tells it in polyglot manner, in a Spanish that is rudimentary, cluttered with Brazilian and Portuguese, and in one brief but important moment, French.

The tale is a one of betrayal. This English-Irishman tells Borges of his history as a republican in the fight for Irish independence. His group is joined by one John Vincent Moon, who is presented as a Marxist and a theorist: that is to say, Moon is a Marxist who fears the material history that involves fighting and action, preferring books and, at a crucial turn in the tale, the telephone. The Irishman recounts the story of how, one evening, he saw an example of Moon's fear and cowardice. Walking late one night, Moon and the Irishman-narrator are confronted by a soldier. Standing petrified, Moon takes what turns out to be a superficial wound in the shoulder. Our Irishman says that 'This frightened man *mortified* me, as if I were the coward, not Vincent Moon'[18] (stress added). That is to say, this frightened man effectively brought the Irishman into a proximate intimacy with death itself, and in such a way as to transform one man into another, the Irishman into Moon. At this point, the Irishman offers a philosophical gloss on such a situation:

> Whatever one man does, it is as if all men did it. For that reason it is not unfair that one disobedience in a garden should contaminate all humanity; for that reason it is not unjust that the crucifixion of a single Jew should be sufficient to save it. Perhaps Schopenhauer was right: I am all other me, any man is all men, Shakespeare is in some manner the miserable John Vincent Moon.[19]

We come close here, in this quasi-philosophical interruption of the narrative, to the core of the matter. It will turn out, in fact, that the Irishman is John Vincent Moon himself: he has 'displaced' or *translated* his confession from a first- to a third-person narrative; and, oddly, this makes theoretical sense, if we accept the logic that says that the narrator of a confession is distanced from – translated from, and transformed from – the person who committed the acts that are being confessed. The tale has been told from the point of view – and indeed in the very voice of –the man who has been betrayed and shot by the British. That is to say, the tale is told by a man who is proximate to death; and the telling of the tale is an enactment of betrayal as well, precisely *because of* its confessional nature. One can confess only the fault of another; literature (and especially literary confession) is the self-become-other.

The testimonial confession here is at once true and false: true when it is spoken for the first time, false when it is translated. This is not the first time that the tale has been told. We know, if we return to the opening of the story, that it has been told already, to one Cardoso; and that that was how the English-Irishman came to be here, owning the fields to which Borges has come, this very night.

As in the case of Menard, reading/writing the *Quixote*, the reader of this tale is also thus translated in their act of bearing witness (or simply listening). A kind of chain of translations is set up: Cardoso becomes Borges; Borges becomes the reader; the reader becomes everyone. As in the brief moment of philosophizing, all other men are me. I am foreign. I exist only in translation, even for the first time, between Spanish and Brazilian, Portuguese and French, British and Irish. Literature translates its reader and its writer; or, more fully expressed now, confession *allows one thereby to survive our own death; and it is thus a testimony to our having been there.* To write is to be in intimacy with death in a certain sense; and to read is to bear witness not only to the fact of our own impending death, but also to bear witness to the testimony of those who have gone before.

When Adorno spoke of his love for foreign words as an exogamy of language, it is this that he meant. The foreign word – as most explicitly in the voices of others, the voices especially of the dead – is a kind of event, disrupting the categories of our stale thinking, of the mentality that we have been given by a language with which we are all too familiar. The foreign word forces us to listen, as if for the first time; and this is what we call witnessing. If literature can be thought of in this way, as the site where we stage the death of the self, it is also the site of testimony. For it is here that we bear witness to our own death, to ourselves become ghostly: we are like Stransom in 'The Altar of the Dead', the James story I discussed earlier. We survive in the text as the record of our transformation: the text is our confession, and we need a listener, a confessor.

Listening, uttering: the question of evidence

If confessing is always displaced, then what might we say of witnessing the confession, in the sense of hearing it or just listening to it, 'attending' to it? The scene I have in mind to explore this is *King Lear*, Act 4, Scene 1, where Poor Tom witnesses the suicidal Gloucester in a near-death scene. Poor Tom says:

> O gods! Who is't can say 'I am at the worst'?
> I am worse that e'er I was ...
>   ... And worse I may be yet: the worst is not
> So long as we can say 'this is the worst'.

Here, saying 'this is the worst' is, of necessity, according to Poor Tom, a false testimony. If we can continue to speak – if literature survives – then we are not yet at death, not yet at the end, not yet at the worst or the point zero that has been reached by the figure of the 'Muselmann'. Yet the scene is more complex than this suggests. Poor Tom is, of course, not Poor Tom: he is Edgar transformed or translated; and Gloucester's death does not yet take place.

The entire scene resembles a Catholic confession, as recounted by Heaney in 'The Pattern' discussed earlier. The annual requirement for Catholic confession was set and established at the Fourth Lateran Council of 1215; and the scene here more or less accurately figures what that Council had put in place. Tom here is in the position of the confessor (like the priest who is and is not himself), Gloucester that of the confessant, revealing his innermost self to one whom he cannot see, and then doing a kind of penance (that imagined suicide) which for a moment at least purges and cures him, absolves him. Edgar here is not himself; rather, he appears – or, better still, *disappears* – into the figure of Poor Tom. It is as if witnessing, such as takes place in this literary confession, requires such a distance in which the confessor – and here we can substitute the term 'reader' – must distance themselves from themselves if they are to gain access to an experience that is truly recounted or narrated. This scene thematizes that distancing from the self, that transformation of the self, that is of the essence of the literary experience; and that experience is now, paradigmatically, the confessional experience.

As I have previously argued, there is a peculiar sense in which a confessional text cannot be unproblematically true. For example, given that Augustine's *Confessions* is a text that narrates a conversion, then the Augustine who signs it is not the Augustine who lived the story that he tells as the story of his life. The very act of writing transforms him; and he ponders explicitly what it might mean to say the words of a confession, or to write them, as opposed merely to communing directly with God in his thoughts.

It is in Book X, Chapter 3, of his *Confessions* – written obviously long before the Lateran Council – that Augustine asks himself what might be the point of confession and, more directly, the point of his writing this text. Why, he asks, does it matter if I speak my confessions aloud to other people? How would those people, his readers, know that he is speaking or writing the truth, he asks, and he quotes from Paul's first letter to the Corinthians: how do they know whether I am telling the truth, since no one *knows a man's thoughts, except the man's own spirit that is within him'*. In this Book of the *Confessions*, a book in which he famously confronts the conundrum of time, he asks:

> what does it profit me ... to make known to men in your sight, through this book, not what I once was, but what I am now? ... many people who know me, and others who do not know me but have heard of me or read my books, wish to hear what I am now, at this moment, as I set down my confessions. They cannot lay their ears to my heart, and yet it is in my heart that I am whatever I am.[20]

Here, we see confession as determined by communication; but it is a communication that can never be direct, given that it is a communication across time. Such communication, of course, is literature: a writing as from the dead to the living.

However, we are also seeing something else going on in these passages. Firstly, we see a kind of demand for utterance: the requirement to confess aloud. Secondly, however, we also see a real uncertainty about the status of confession, especially confession that is (as I have argued) necessarily done in voices other than that of the self. In the introduction to his *Troubling Confessions*, Peter Brooks adverts to the legal case concerning Bill Clinton and Monica Lewinsky in 1998. The editorial of the *New York Times* of 12 December that year was, in the words of Brooks, 'a plea for Clinton "to say the words" – that he had lied under oath'. The editorial was pointing out that 'there could be no true contrition, and thus no pardon and no reconciliation, until Clinton said "the words," until he explicitly gave public utterance to the statement: "I lied."'[21]

As Brooks makes fully clear, however, the story could not ever end just there. Quite apart from the Cretan liar paradox that sits at the base of this particular confessional statement, there are other reasons for uncertainty:

> Unless the content of the confession can be verified by other means, thus substantiating its trustworthiness, it may be false – false to fact, if true to some sense of guilt. The law records many instances of false confessions – and no doubt many have gone unrecorded. What is the truth of confession?[22]

As I have argued in these pages, however, truth (considered as some kind of correspondence to fact) is actually less important here than something else: evidence itself. Let us then pose the question concerning the nature of evidence, or of testimony, in relation to confession as a communicative act.

At one level, we expect evidence to substantiate and to corroborate 'a truth universally acknowledged', so to speak. If it works to establish such a truth – that is, if it substantiates something that is essentially 'self-evident' or self-evidencing' – then can it become something that is so taken for granted that it requires no further gloss or commentary; and if so, how close is it to ideology? In a court of law, evidence is that which is admitted in order to prove a case or a proposition. For instance, in the propositional statement: 'I accuse you of killing this individual', I might educe in evidence your fingerprints on a gun, a bullet-wound in an individual corpse and a forensic demonstration that shows incontrovertibly that this gun fired this bullet. These would be evidences in that they are themselves objective facts or singular states of affairs from which we can make implications or draw inferences.

W. V. Quine finds the nature of evidence such as this troubling, and, essentially, he replaces it with what he calls 'observation sentences'. Such sentences might be, in his examples, 'It's raining' or 'That's a rabbit'. Sentences like these he refers to as 'occasion sentences': they are true on some occasions and false at others. After all, sometimes it is raining and sometimes not, as he puts it. Then he gets to the core of our question here: 'Briefly stated, then, an observation sentence is an occasion sentence on which speakers of the language can agree outright on witnessing the occasion.' He will then add to this, first by claiming that observation sentences 'are the link between language ... and the real world that language is all about'; before finally getting to the main issue for us: 'An observation sentence for a community is an occasion sentence on which members of the community can agree outright on witnessing the occasion.'[23]

This last refinement makes it clear that evidence is linked to two things: the first is a community and the second is instantaneity or a moment in time. With respect to the first of these, we have already argued that confession being a matter primarily of communication must also therefore be a matter pertaining to the construction of a community. It is a community that confesses, and that thereby produces individuals as such in a retrospective construction of the unreformed and untransformed self, the self that needed the confession for redemption in the first place. Further, the community in question is therefore understood to be made up of speech negotiations (or literature) and not of individuated consciences. The Borges tale just analysed shows this; and the earlier Coetzee and Deane examples indicate that this happens not only in a political context but rather, more forcefully, that it is actually constitutive of that political context. Confession constructs the community, but these are in a dialectic that constitutes the self that we recognize as the very foundational cornerstone of cultural modernity itself. With regard to the second point, the issue of truthful evidence becomes problematic, we have seen, as long as it happens in time: truth, in these terms, is of the moment. Perhaps we need therefore to ditch the idea of truth and to settle instead for evidence, in what will necessarily be something of a lesser formulation.

In my hypothetical example, I might say that undeniably 'this is your fingerprint'; and undeniably, 'this is a bullet-wound containing traces of a bullet fired from the gun that bears your prints'. From these two observation sentences, we can then imply a narrative that allows us to say, 'You pulled this trigger and fired this bullet from this gun into this body, causing death. That is, I accuse you of murder'; but the 'I' in this case needs to be 'all men' as Borges has it, a community or society that requires this guilt for whatever set of reasons. This is problematic if the accused denies the sentences. In that case, either they indicate that they are not a member of the community, or they imply that there is another community that can be organized around different observation sentences.

The question here really pertains to the relation between two phrases: 'I accuse' and 'I confess'. I have indicated that there is a kind of economy at work in confession; and I used the examples of Deane and Coetzee to indicate this or, more precisely, to indicate its failure. Essentially, my argument is that 'there is no excuse'. If this is so, then the appropriate response to a confession turns out to be something akin to grace. In many cases, we behave as if confession closes the case, closes the deal, as it were. That is to say: a wrong is done and reparation comes when the response to the 'I accuse' is an uttered 'I confess', in some sort of balanced economy. However, in that case, the confession falls precisely into the kind of paradox drawn by de Man in his reading of Rousseau – *qui s'accuse s'excuse* – and the confession undoes itself by fulfilling the economic demand placed on it through the *j'accuse*. As Brooks puts it:

> Confession of wrongdoing is considered fundamental to morality because it constitutes a verbal act of self-recognition as wrongdoer and hence provides the basis of rehabilitation. It is the precondition of the end to ostracism, re-entry into one's desired place in the human community ... Refusal of confession can be taken as a defiance of one's judges ... whereas confession allows those judges to pass their sentences in security, knowing that the guilty party not only deserves and accepts but perhaps in some sense wants punishment, as the penance that follows confession.[24]

This is a form of legal confession that presupposes and accepts the presiding idea of cultural modernity: that the self is autonomous, that it chose to do the action it did and that it exists entirely independently of the society upon which it exerted the act. The argument of the present book is designed to counter virtually all of this. Further, the argument of this book helps explain the more general tendency now towards a kind of acceptance, in grace, of guilt.

I pointed out above that we have a problem if an accused denies the observation sentences of his accuser. We have the possibility that either the accused belongs to a different community organized around different observation sentences or that they are simply not a member of the community that makes the observation sentences. In short, we have the situation of a kind of *apartheid* here. The 'solution' to that problem is not to be found in the covert acts of economic and moral revenge that goes under the name of 'reparation'; rather, the solution is the discovery of new conversations, new observation sentences, that will allow both for truth (an acknowledgement of things that were done) and also for reconciliation, without the economy of modern 'justice', a justice that turns out to be not modern at all but rather more indebted to Old Testament versions of vengeance (the perfect match of eye for eye, tooth for tooth). This is the meaning of the truth and reconciliation committee. There is no excuse; but there is, instead, the attempt at the construction of a new community, a new time.

Evidence nonetheless has some intimacy with truth, and to what Davidson calls a correspondence theory of truth.[25] In this, evidence is meant to display the nature of the facts of a case in such a way as to yield one and only one possible version of material fact; and the fact has to be considered as both true and truly understood by all parties to the case. Yet, as we know from literary criticism, fact always gives way to interpretation, and to interpretation based upon the 'one' or the point of view. In short, evidence has a relation to the disappearing God that has made itself apparent again: the zero becomes one, as it were. Evidence is tied firmly to *display*, or to the 'self-evidencing' that we have already explored under the sign of 'transparency'.

At this point, we should turn to Rousseau, though not to his *Confessions*. In the 1750s, Rousseau established himself as a public figure through his first two great discourses, the *Discours sur les sciences et les arts* and the *Discours sur l'origine et les fondements de l'inégalité parmi les hommes*.[26] In these discourses, Rousseau begins to articulate a version of democratic human relations, and he finds an abiding problem in human relations of what we might call 'theatricality'. Briefly, the argument is that for the social as we know it to exist at all (i.e. for there to be a viable public sphere), 'politeness' is required; but for Rousseau, it is in such politeness that we see the emergence of insincerity (or an opacity that is the opposite of transparency) in human relations and, yet more importantly, a dissociation of the human subject from itself.

This – an early version of inauthenticity – is the state of affairs that we have come to know from T.S. Eliot and Friedrich Schiller as a 'dissociation of sensibility'. In such a dissociation, it is not simply the case that the subject is able to watch himself 'at a distance', as if the subject exists like some puppet-master pulling the strings of a Lacanian mannequin whose function it is to represent the subject there where they are not. More telling than this is the fact that, for Rousseau, such a dissociation of the subject with respect to itself introduces into the very constitution of human subjectivity itself a *temporal* difference or distance, such that the being of the subject is now marked by temporality – and thus by becoming – rather than by the essentially timeless continuous and homogeneous present tense of existence in Rousseau's conception of the state of nature.

The subject-in-time is one which cannot actually sensibly experience anything: its very interior temporality effects a rupture in the now such that the subject can never be found *in* a present moment. Politeness, it follows from all this, might be necessary for the social or public sphere; but it denies the possibility of our ever experiencing that public sphere in the first place. The social – the agora – is now an empty space, surrounded by vacuous subjects, subjects whose constitution is that they are continuously becoming, in search of an always elusive being.

It is in these great discourses that we can see the emergence of a logic that drives Rousseau to write his polemical *Lettre sur les spectacles* against Jean Le Rond d'Alembert (and, behind d'Alembert, Voltaire). Theatricality, and – as Rousseau begins to think this problem more fundamentally – representation itself become an abiding problem in human and social affairs. Rousseau, too, aligned himself with the logic of a certain kind of 'observation sentence' version of evidence and truth. His attitude to the growth and development of language as a mode of representation – a language that could re-figure or re-present the world as it is – was odd. It is developed in the second great discourse, the *Discours sur l'origine de l'inégalité parmi les hommes*.

In this discourse, Rousseau claims that language emanates originally from some great '*cri de la nature*', and he then derives from this a mimetic view of language in which a speaker represents a world outside the self by making a noise from within himself that somehow accommodates and represents that exteriority. We are back again at the old Augustinian and Cartesian questions of space, but this time construed as issues that will explain how it is that language can tell the truth or not. Rousseau then essentially makes every single utterance an observation-sentence that is tied firmly and absolutely to the singularity of its own specific occasion. As he put it in his description of how language evolved:

> *Chaque objet reçût d'abord un nom particulier, sans égard aux genres, et aux espèces, que ces premiers instituteurs n'étaient pas en état de distinguer; et tous les individus se présentèrent isolés à leur esprit, comme ils le sont dans le tableau de la nature. Si un chêne s'appelait A, un autre chêne s'appelait B: de sorte que plus les connaissances étaient bornées, et plus le dictionnaire devint étendu.*

> Each object received first of all a particular name, without regard to genres or species, which these first teachers were not in a state to be able to distinguish; and all individuals presented themselves isolated in spirit, as they are in the tableau of nature. If one oak was called A, an other oak was called B: such that the more limited knowledge was, the more extended the dictionary became.[27]

In this, we have an attitude to truth that is *entirely* occasional and self-evidently true for each occasion. However, we lose the possibility of there being any law at all, for there is no possibility of a general applicability of any statement. This is the condition of absolute transparency: but it is a condition in which society itself becomes absolutely impossible.

This, in fact is a condition in which everyone must axiomatically confess or reveal themselves transparently; but in which no one is able ever to listen. This is all utterance; and, as in our contemporary cultures where the demand for confessional transparency has become entirely normative, we end up only with insincerity and hypocrisy for, as I have shown, the culture of this mode of 'revelation of conscience' is condemned to inauthenticity. Rousseau saw this exactly: for society to exist and to persist, we need those forms of insincerity that we call politeness; or, in my preferred terms here, a kind of *Konversation in der Ehe*, an erotics of translation that effects future possibility, that keeps a society going.

Hypocrisy, in fact, becomes a condition of any confession that subscribes to the view that the act of confession is the expression of a conscience. We might turn here to Pierre Teilhard de Chardin:

> *Comme toute autre connaissance humaine, la Psychologie religieuse se construit sur des expériences. Elle a besoin de faits. Et puisque, en l'occurrence, les faits n'apparaissent qu'au plus profound des consciences, elle attend, pour se développer, des 'confessions' individuelles.*

> As with any other human science, religious Psychology rests on experiences. It needs facts. And since, as it happens, facts are apparent only to the most profound consciences, it has to wait for individual 'confessions' in order to develop.[28]

The greatest or most authoritative evidence has often been taken to be this kind of confession. The text of a confession must axiomatically be sincere; but as it enters the public sphere (that is, as it is communication) it must also of necessity be not just absolutely singular but also (thereby) absolutely hypocritical, an enactment of the truth rather than a statement of a precedent truth. Confession, thus, is not and cannot be a statement of the truth; rather, it is that which produces the truth.

In my closing chapter below, I will thus write such a confession.

8

My Language!

The first time I read Shakespeare was in August 1967. The first play was *A Midsummer Night's Dream*. I was twelve, having just entered the second year of my secondary schooling at St Mungo's Academy, Glasgow. The school was run by Jesuits of the Marist Order and its main aim, grounded in a sense of charitable mission, was to give a Catholic education to the under-privileged boys of Townhead, a working-class area of tenements whose people were marked by a high degree of economic poverty. In addition, though, the school also admitted a small number of boys from elsewhere in Glasgow – often, in fact, from even more disadvantaged areas – through a scheme that allowed the Jesuits to cream off what it saw as academic talent at age eleven; and these boys were to be given a more advanced academic education. I was one of these, joining the school from the East End of Glasgow initially in August 1966. For those of us who were selected in this way, school was already 'marked' in the sense that it was equated with ideas of escape, primarily the escape from poverty through a good education. Shakespeare, as I discovered in 1967, was supposed to form part of that education.

In what follows here, I want to explore how it is that I moved from what was my initial profound dislike of Shakespeare – more than, and different from, stereotypical schoolboy griping. How did I move from such dislike of *A Midsummer Night's Dream* that autumn to an entirely different point of view, now, as one who 'professes' literature and who thinks something of Shakespeare probably quite literally every day? The route, insofar as I can reconstruct it from memory, is rather indirect – or it will at first appear so. We will pass from Parkhead in the working-class East End of Glasgow, via Lisbon and Paris, to my present position. On the road, we will find out what Shakespeare might mean to one who teaches and thinks about English and other literatures: me. The Shakespeare who emerges is different from the Shakespeare of 1967, obviously; and so am I different and still differing, sensing this differing as something that stems from Shakespeare and that is equated in my mind with a kind of freedom.

A dream of availability

Why did Mr McDermott, our English teacher, decide to start with *A Midsummer Night's Dream*? What is it that makes this play so often the first play that schoolchildren read or study when they encounter Shakespeare? After all, although a comedy, it is actually a rather difficult play. It involves, among other things, fairies who seem keen on child abduction, a nether-world that parallels the real world, an Indian boy who is stolen by fairies and then fought over, the usual Shakespearean troubled parenthood and childhood, with anxiety-driven relations between fathers and daughters, a queen playing about with ideas of bestiality, a self-reflexive play-within-play motif, gender and class troubles and so on.

Perhaps needless to say, this is not how it is usually presented to a twelve-year-old; or, at least, it is not entirely how it was presented to me. Rather, this play was essentially to be viewed as a harmless comedy, a romp of sorts, through which a moral message about love, duty and a social order of things was to be conveyed. In this reading, the central character is always Bottom; and he is followed closely by Puck. From the point of view of Bottom, it is a comedy of character: the man is an ass, and Shakespeare is showing him up as such, but in an affectionate manner. Puck is slightly more devilish or mischievous: a prankster-director whose practical joking makes for comic difficulties in which he finds himself having to resolve complications of his own making.

Who might find these kinds of thing *available* at the age of twelve or so? I think it is fair to say that there were some governing assumptions going on in the distribution of this play to the allegedly academically gifted in a partially selective-intake school. (I say 'partially selective' because the actual school-mix was very extensive, reaching across from the economically disadvantaged of the centre of the city through all social classes to boys who commuted in from rather more posh suburbs near the West End.) Those assumptions might have held true for some readers but not for others; and, where they held true, the play would have been more easily and readily accessible than it would be for those – among whom I number myself and my classmates – for whom the assumptions were simply false.

Imagine a certain kind of childhood, where the house you live in stands alone, apart from other houses, and enjoys a good deal of space. Imagine, further, that your parents actually own the house and the land on which it stands. Outside, there is a garden, where you have domesticated parts of a wilder nature. Inside, you have your own room. Maybe there are books in your room, for there certainly are books elsewhere in the house. At night, your parents do not seem to be exhausted; but have time and energy to read to you. They read from books of fairy-tales, perhaps, or romances that involve princes whose wealth, while greater than that of your parents, is not different in kind. Here, heritage will be important; for love-relations will probably be tied to land or power and will certainly be tied to questions of authority. Here, moreover, people may seem to change partners, their amorous commitments being somehow more open, more liberal. In this household, in some cases, children go away from home for long periods, to be cared for by others while living together in a kind of nether-world, the childhood-world, of a dormitory. The child brought up in such an environment has a way in to *A Midsummer Night's Dream* simply in terms of a certain set of expectations of what one does with its story and language.

Now imagine something different, even opposite to that described above: a house in a tenement block shared with seven or more other families; the house rented from the council, not owned; no private space and certainly no garden; noise of neighbours above, below, beside you; not many books, if any; parents working overtime, sometimes in hard physical labour, maybe weaving or as joiners, carpenters and the like, and not having endless reserves of energy to read to their children; and so on. The child of this house, Bottom's house, has to find or make an entirely different route into the play, for there are probably no normative expectations at all regarding what one does with its story, its language, its problems. The play is simply less *available* to this child; or, at best, it is available in entirely different ways. This child reader of the play is 'located' by the norms and expectations that are taken as standard by the more advantaged child described above, in ways that that more advantaged child is not.

In short, then: *A Midsummer Night's Dream* is offered *not* to all twelve-year-olds; rather, it is understood that a certain kind of twelve-year-old is the norm; and the play is set in the curriculum for them. The interesting issue here is what happens when you take the second kind of child and treat him as if he were of the first. This is one part of the background to my engagement with Shakespeare. My dislike of Shakespeare was not at all dislike of the play, even if I thought it was: in fact, I couldn't *read* the play at that time. Perhaps I still can't. I do not wish to make the issue of class central to the presentation of my predicament here; yet I will stick with it for one moment longer to suggest something that I did learn about how we read Bottom.

Bottom is, of course, a hugely interesting character. The play mocks him in some ways for his sense of self-importance; but we are certainly never encouraged to despise him. On the contrary, Bottom is probably the most well-liked of the characters for any audience. Why is that so? The man is an ass, certainly, and at one point literally so. Although he has a little learning, he does not wear it as well as the lords and ladies, Helena and Hermia, or Lysander and Demetrius, whose very names indicate that they are at home in the foundational myths of entire civilizations. Bottom is aspirant as well; and, although he shows himself up, it would be wrong – the play seems to suggest – for us to mock such a person. They may be asses, but it is not their own fault that they are thus. My contention is that the point of view that thinks thus sits more comfortably in my first childhood scenario than it does in my second. And, who am I – child of that second scenario – who am I, I think, as I read this play? Am I not also an aspirant, not-yet well-enough educated person; isn't my mother a tailor, like Starveling; and isn't my new best friend's father a joiner, like Snug; my neighbour at home a carpenter, like Quince? If I mock this Bottom, however gently, what am I doing in relation to my founding environment? What values am I starting to imbibe here?

When the education authorities set this play as a set text for eleven- and twelve-year-olds in the 1960s, they had in mind a very specific audience: the benignly conservative middle-classes. And, when my school set it for us, they were inculcating us into the norms of that audience. For me, it was an exercise in dealing with certain kinds of unfamiliar value-systems. The school streamed and set its classes: 1:A1 was the 'advanced' first-year class; and we heard speak of the legendary 1:Z10 where the boys did not have the chance to read Shakespeare. Instead, those in this 'bottom' set engaged in things like woodwork or joinery and so on while we, by now in 2:A1, read plays about, well, joiners and woodworkers, Bottoms, Snugs, Quinces and the like. The setting of the play in the curriculum was part of a structure that established a social organization in terms of a stratified, sedimented and layered society.

I don't want to make too much of this, except to say that the educational thinking that lay behind the setting of Shakespeare for us is a mode of thinking that persists and lingers to the present time, despite the many critiques made of it all through the 1970s and 1980s. Education, if anything, has become *more* a matter of socialization than ever before; and its politicization is, of course, now more and more explicit. Part of the shift in my attitude to Shakespeare over the years came about by my realizing – and this is partly due to this first engagement with his work – that the plays might help offer a critique as well as an endorsement of established social orders. That is what I need now to show.

Mr McDermott, then, came into the classroom armed with the books for the year's work. Top of the pile was *A Midsummer Night's Dream*. We knew that this was the serious business, more serious than the J. Meade Falkner *Moonfleet* that followed. Had I known about Bourdieu, I would have understood issues of cultural capital. If we were indeed to make it in the world (whatever that meant, probably that notional escape from poverty), then we'd need to get on top of this, to get Shakespeare under our belts. The book looked unattractive: the edition was 'the Junior School Shakespeare' edition. To my amazement, when I received my own copy, there was already a familiar name – not just that of Shakespeare – inside it. It was traditional for many pupils to write their names on the inside cover of their books, so that, often, you'd receive a book with about a dozen names all inside, all scored through except the last one. I myself preferred not to do that: I already had a fetishistic respect for the material object of the book which prevented me somehow from writing in it. Yet this copy had obviously been sitting in the school cupboard, untouched, for about a decade.

The name inside was that of my own brother, who had gone through the school ten years before I did. There he was: his name, his class. He had also signed the book about halfway through, with a flashy autograph that he was obviously trying to perfect. He had left a little graffiti on the pages and, tellingly, on the inside back cover, the details of his financial position. It was not good. He owed a friend 6/11d (six shillings and eleven pence: about 35p in today's money, but a huge sum in 1957, when he had the book); he owed my sister 7d (about 3p) and my other brother 2/- (two shillings: 10p). His total position was a debt of some 9/6 (47p or so). These would have been extremely significant sums for a boy of his age in 1957. As I sat there, I thought that these figures might help to explain why he had decided not only to abandon Shakespeare and any further midsummer night's dreaming, but also to leave school just a year further on, following my father into the shipyards where he could make some money to help clear his debts.

And now, I still have the book in my possession. At the end of that year, Mr McDermott was more lax than he ought to have been about collecting the texts back in. I could have taken it into school and made sure it was returned; but I didn't. Instead, I kept it. Given that I hated Shakespeare – indeed the whole Shakespeare experience – so vigorously, it is interesting that I nonetheless stole this bit of cultural capital: a small piece of cultural capital detailing the lack of economic capital that helped determine the life of my brother, but that also determined my own life very differently.

Mr McDermott struggled to get us to engage with the opening scene where Theseus tells Hippolyta that 'our nuptial hour / Draws on apace ... but, O, methinks, how slow / The old moon wanes! She lingers my desires, / Like to a step-dame or a dowager / Long withering out a young man's retinue.'

'Why is it "like to", sir? Why not just "like"?'

'It's needed for the scansion.'

'...'

'Scansion,' he repeated.

'What's that, sir?'

'The rhythm of the lines. The beat.'

'Rhythm?'

'Yes: five beats to the line. Pentameter. Hasn't Mr McConville started you off on this in the Latin class yet?' We were beginning to 'read' Virgil's *Aeneid*, Book 2. 'You know,' he went on, 'dactyls, spondees, trochees, all that malarkey.'

We groaned. But two things were being driven home: firstly, the ostensibly unwelcome news that English could be as foreign as Latin; and secondly, more positively, that there was a semiotic aspect to language – rhyme, rhythm, sound – that helped carry the semantics. Needless to say, we hadn't a clue what was going on – yet. Mr McDermott had to demonstrate, placing the stresses in an exaggerated fashion: 'Four DAYS will QUICKly STEEP themSELVES in NIGHT,' he sang, his hand cutting the air with each beat or stress.

We started to sing along, making fun of the text and emptying it of whatever semantic content it had under our steady beat. We could make neither head nor tail of the text; but it sang to us in some way. Then, scene two comes along, and we're in prose, not singing. This, of course, is the realm of the workers. This is where the complications start for us. These workers are recognizable, given that we are all, or mostly, from such working families. Yet, the play is presenting them as odd in some way, as an anomalous deviation from certain norms that have been set up in the opening. Above all, this is a question of language: while the opening scenes were incomprehensible semantically to us, we at least found a solace in the regularity of their semiotic aspects. Here, we are among people whom we should recognize, but it is their language that is alienating us all the more, now that we have been given a means of grasping the opening scene with its rhythmic verse.

It is not the case that we had some strong class allegiance that made us feel insulted or anything of the kind. Rather, the difficulty is that we understood so little of what was going on. We also knew that we were in the presence of high art, a high art that was to become part of our identity through our acquisition of it as cultural capital. Thus, the linguistic difficulties that we have here become redeemable, in that we see that we are not yet adequate to the text. In short, what is going on, as I now understand (but at the time only vaguely felt), is that we are about to become mildly alienated from our backgrounds: we were to start to become the norm, singing along, five beats to the line, as we prepared ourselves to assume the commanding roles of the normative verse-speakers. The singing was more important than it had first seemed, after all: it gave us a solidarity, even the identity to be found in a mindless solidarity, such as we knew and recognized from Saturday afternoons at football matches.

Yet I resisted. The play was about fairies but my objections to it had nothing to do with the subject-matter, which I simply didn't understand. My objection, voiced loudly in class discussion, was about the language, which I described as 'flowery'. Why did Shakespeare have to go all round the houses in saying whatever it was that the characters had to say? I had so little understanding of the operations of poetry, so little awareness of the history of the language, that I simply would not believe Mr McDermott when he suggested that the language I was reading here was somehow readily understood by an earlier audience. He conceded readily that ordinary folk didn't speak like the characters in the play – not even those working weavers and joiners. The language was contrived, certainly – 'poetic', he called it, even in the prose passages. However, he maintained that the language did not occlude the sense for Shakespeare's audience, for his contemporaries; and that it should therefore, in principle, be understood by us.

To the extent that we did manage to glean some understanding of the subject-matter (admittedly not much), again we found reason to object.

The driving force in our education – why we had given up our friendships in our locality to attend this school – was aligned to a sense of growing sophistication. We were about progress, especially progress as achieved through the intellect and reason. We were certainly not at this school to read fairy-tales or to be seduced by the irrational world of this play. The play was rank with superstition: by contrast, we were entering the realms of science and analysis, a realm that rejected the world of fairy as something childish and unsophisticated.

So we began the process of analysis, admittedly in a naive fashion. We turned to the characters we found interesting, especially Bottom. We knew we were supposed to laugh at him, in his earnest desire to be the most important and the most noticed of the actors, in his keen eagerness to be in a lead role and so to be someone, to be noticed and to feel he *exists*. Yet we already had a double attitude to him, partly given by the language problem. As we tried to paraphrase, we began less to laugh *at Bottom* and more to laugh *with Shakespeare*, we felt, as he encouraged us to laugh *with Bottom*. We looked closely at the characters as they prepare to rehearse in Act 3, Scene 1. There, their concern is about illusion, and about the possibility that they will upset their audience, especially the ladies. In what is actually a sophisticated discussion of the theatrical *bienséances* – dramatic propriety – we are invited to laugh *with* these characters at ourselves, at the possibility that we can be deluded by mere theatre. Importantly for my present case, the other major element of comedy in this and other scenes is the malapropism. As the characters say the opposite of what they mean, we see their own struggles with language; and we recognized those struggles, for they are the struggles of people who are aspiring to escape from their everyday circumstances and to identify themselves with another class of people. Like us schoolboys, they know a little; and they strive to know more. The key to their elevation and freedom will be the mastery of a language, of the adoption of a role that is, for the moment, beyond their capabilities. We were watching ourselves. Given this, and given that we were laughing, we were also learning a fundamental rule of critical analysis: the avoidance of pomposity, the avoidance of an unjustified self-assurance, the avoidance – in short – of the kind of judgements practised by the lords and ladies of the play.

Thus, we began to learn that Shakespeare, while certainly a major element in an arrangement by which social order was to be maintained, also gave us a way into criticize that order, even as we were entering it. In a word: he gave us the possibility of difference. Needless to say, at the time, we did not use this kind of language to describe what was going on; but it was important to us that we found such a way to do two things: firstly, to deal with our discomfort when we saw the rude mechanicals; secondly, to find a means of engaging with questions of language, comprehension and misapprehension.

A detour

At the time, however, we had other things on our minds, things that seemed infinitely more important than all this.

The single greatest event of 1967, as we all know, took place on 25 May that year, in Lisbon, Portugal: Glasgow Celtic, effectively a local team from Parkhead in the east of the city, won the football European Cup, the first British team ever to do so, beating the famed Italian side, Inter Milan, 2–1. The event was important because it was not simply a game of football. It will sound pretentious to claim but this match was part of a series of historical and ideological events of some magnitude that would lead to attempted political revolutions across Europe just one year later, in the famed *événements* of May 1968. More locally, it was also a formative event in terms of my relations to culture, to language, to my schooling and to Shakespeare.

We should not forget that Shakespeare himself knew about football, a game that, in his time as in ours provoked strong responses from the public. Dromio of Ephesus, kicked around in *The Comedy of Errors* by Adriana, protests, asking 'Am I so round with you, as you with me, / That like a football you do spurn me thus? / You spurn me hence, and he [Antipholus] will spurn me hither: / If I last in this service, you must case me in leather.' Yet more directly, Kent, in *King Lear*, commits a professional foul or, more precisely, a 'sandwich tackle', with Lear himself, on Oswald. When Lear strikes the brazen Oswald, Oswald objects, saying 'I'll not be strucken', to which Kent replies, tripping him up, 'Nor tripp'd neither, you base football player.' Perhaps more relevant to the upcoming revolutionary spirit of May 1968 was Camus, the goalkeeper, who famously asserted that all that he had ever learned that was of value in the field of ethics and human relationships, he learned from football. His Algerian descendant, Derrida, whose own thinking was to prove so revolutionary in the field of literary criticism, also had dreams, like my friends and I had in Glasgow, of becoming a professional footballer. Like him, 'we would play until the dead of night, I dreamt of becoming a professional player'.[1]

What happened in Lisbon that day in 1967 was part of a spirit of the times; and it was to affect the core of my own literary and critical development. Revolution was already in the air and the match was a part of it; but, for us in St Mungo's Academy, it was a very special part and very pertinent to us. As many will know, Glasgow at the time was riven by religious division and bigotry: traditionally, Roman Catholics supported Celtic (a team established by priests in the working-class community in 1888); and Protestants supported Rangers. The boys in my school were, for the most part, passionate supporters of Celtic, football being the main component of our mental and physical activity every day. But what was at stake was not just the destination of the European Cup; rather, what was at stake was an entire attitude to life. Inter Milan were famous for their extraordinary success, grounded in a system of play that was based on solid defence: the system of *catenaccio* ('door-bolt') devised by their manager Helenio Herrera. Their back line of four players (novel at the time, but more or less standard now), with an additional sweeper, was impenetrable; and they depended on ensuring that the opposition could not score. The opposition, unable to score, would grow frustrated and impatient, allow concentration in their own defensive lines to lapse; at which point the Inter Milan sweeper would push the ball forward, releasing and launching the solitary attacking move of their game in which they would score. 1–0 was the usual result. It was dull, the dourest and cynical pragmatism; but it was effective, machine-like in its near-industrial grinding-out of victories.

By contrast, Celtic were making a reputation for adventurous play. Their manager, Jock Stein, was a man who saw the romance of ambition. His team were all more or less exclusively born within a couple of miles of Celtic Park (Paradise, as it was known to supporters); and so this was essentially a local team, drawn from the tenements, almost like the scratch-teams that played all over Glasgow on Saturday mornings. They played as if they had nothing to lose but were willing to risk it all. We identified closely with them.

In the match, Inter Milan took an early lead and Celtic went in at half-time that dreaded single goal down. What followed in the second half was a relentless assault, attack after attack on that famed defence. It wasn't quite all caution thrown to the wind: the forty-one year-old Ronnie Simpson (known as 'Faither' because of his age), the Celtic goalkeeper, did stay in his own half; but he was virtually the only player there for much of the game (keeping an eye on the dentures that belonged to the Celtic players, apparently all left in his cap behind the goalposts). When Celtic won, it did not just signal the first ever British team to win this most challenging of competitions; rather, what was signalled was a new future for the game, the validation of an adventurous sense of life's possibilities, a belief in the local people of Glasgow that they were capable of anything, if they could just allow their wild Romantic selves to flourish. 'Total football' and 'the beautiful game', as Pelé referred to it, was just around the corner: and we, in the East End of Glasgow, had turned that corner first. As it happened, Tommy Gemmell, the left-back who scored the equalizing goal, wore suits that were made-to-measure for him by my mother. Starveling's son, as it were, was that close to the match and its adventure.

Had we been more knowledgeable, we would have perhaps cast this as a contest between ruthlessly efficient Enlightenment models of the industrial grinding out of results, set against an untutored romanticism, full of spirit, imagination – and, crucially, *poetry*. It was also much more than this: it gave us a sense of the aesthetic – the sheer beauty of the Celtic style of play, the very fact that there *was* such play, playfulness, like Friedrich Schlegel's *Spielen*. This aesthetic adventure was to triumph over the dull but ostensibly successful modes of industrialization: those brought money, but ours brought happiness and joy. Industrialization, of course, was the daily routine for the families I knew from our school: my own father (two years dead by this time) and brother in the Clyde's shipyards; the fathers of my friends working as boiler-makers in the railways; sometimes (if they were lucky), others working as craftsmen (carpenters, plumbers, painters and decorators). Aesthetic play and the play of aesthetics was more than just football: it was politics, and we sensed this, even though we did not have the vocabulary at the time to articulate it.

As a schoolboy in St Mungo's, this game marked 1967 as special. More than this: it marked *us* as special. For the first time, we became visible on a world stage where we were validated, and we were validated through our identification with the spirit of romance, adventure and a style that could even trump Italy (itself a by-word for style from the 1950s). And we were visible also in Shakespeare: remember, in the following August when we read the *Dream*, we realized that Shakespeare has the audience watching itself. But, at the forefront of our minds was the fact that the summer of 1967 was truly a summer of love: love of football. We returned to the new school year in August of that year, charged with a new sense of ourselves: as Catholics, as working-class boys who were on their way to make good in the world, as adventurers.

It was thus that we approached *A Midsummer Night's Dream*.

The notes

Struggling with the play, I turned to the Notes at the back for help. Sure enough, my earliest fear – that this is as foreign as Latin – was confirmed. The first note in my edition explains 'nuptial hour', calling it 'wedding hour' and stating that it comes from 'Lat: *Nubeo, nupsi, nuptum*, to marry'. So far, so helpful; but foreign. I started to hear again how foreign 'my language' was to me. As a child, in working-class Glasgow, I was aware (actually quite explicitly) of at least three modes of speech, three Englishs. There was the language we spoke at home; then there as the slightly more formal language – polite usage, really, with a slightly modified accent – that I used when speaking to my teacher or to the doctor or priest; and finally, there was the BBC, as it were: a world of televised English. Whenever I watched TV (probably too much), I was aware of the authority of that voice, that speech. I also knew that I would one day be able to speak it, or would need to speak it if I were to accede myself to such authority (the authority, sought by Bottom, that means you count, you exist, you are listened to). The change would come about as a result of my education, an education that was partly built upon that incipient multilingualism. I inhabited different languages and changed as a person depending on which one I spoke. However, in Shakespeare, there was as yet no question for me of accent or propriety: this was a different kind of foreignness; and it irritated me that I felt excluded.

The feeling of exclusion lingered for some time. However, relatively early on in my engagements with Shakespeare, we read *The Tempest*, another play that I found very difficult, but one within which I found the importance of translation. When Ferdinand meets Miranda, in Act 1, Scene 2, he hears her speak and exclaims, 'My language? Heavens! / I am the best of them that speak this speech, / Were I but where 'tis spoken.' He is surprised that this foreign, wild, untutored girl speaks his language. What was important to me, though, was that he claims the language as *his*, that it is a matter of ownership; and that he distinguishes the quality of speakers dependent upon that ownership ('I am the best of them'). My shock at this passage derived from the fact that I have never felt that language is a matter of ownership; rather, for me, it has always been a matter of imagination, something for the lunatic, lover and poet who can inhabit a philosophy undreamt of, in imagination. My attempt to learn French had already shown me that there were things that could be said in French that were, strictly, untranslatable: to speak French was to 'think' it, to inhabit the mind of a French persona, even to re-mould the shape of one's lips, mouth and facial expression. Maybe to 'hear' Shakespeare was the same, I realized: a matter of acting, borrowing a persona, standing in the skin of someone I was not.

The note for line 11 put me in my place, telling me how to pronounce 'Philostrate' ('in three syllables', we are told, in case we need tuition on how to speak). But hold, what next? At line 14, we get a note on 'companion', which means 'fellow, used contemptuously'. The note firstly affirms Latinate roots but then promises something more interesting: 'Originally, one who ate with another. (Lat. *cum*, with, *panis*, bread.) *Fellow* and *companion* have exchanged meanings since Shakespeare's time.' What interested me here was that the meaning of a word changes with time, even to the stage where two words can exchange meanings: white becomes black, as it were. This opened up for me the question of translating from this Shakespeare-Latin: it is now a question of how a culture 'lives' a language, lives its words, and how those words can change meanings across time. Suddenly, the play opened to the real world in all sorts of ways, and told me that my language was a living and changing organic thing, tied to communities but open to difference.

At line 69, we are told that 'Whether' is 'to be pronounced "where" as it is still in many parts of the country'. Now, there is a 'correction' of pronunciation, but a correction that allows for dialect variants, that even legitimizes the possibility that those with dialects have an authentic relation to the play and its language. Finally, in this brief introductory section of Notes, we get a note referring to lines 74–5 that tells us 'Elizabeth was unmarried, and nothing pleased her more than to hear praises of a single life'. Shakespeare had a specific audience, then: the Queen, the famed Virgin Queen. Now, we can take our distance from this; but at least we have a place to stand, a language to speak and a sense that things in this text are not as solidly monumental an authority as we had thought.

Concluding, beginning

In sum, from these notes, we realized that Shakespeare was a foreign language, that the language required us to change (even to change physically) in order to inhabit it and that its standing as a culturally authoritative monument was not unchangeable: we could have a relation to that authority, we could make the words change meaning.

We were profoundly aware of the cultural authority of 'Shakespeare'; and yet we resisted it to some extent. It would be many years before I realized what was going on in this preliminary series of engagements with these plays. Hannah Arendt helps explain. When she considers the fraught question of what constitutes 'authority', she points out that 'Since authority always demands obedience, it is commonly mistaken for some form of power or violence.'[2] She is adamant, however, that authority in fact both precludes the use of external or coercive force (for then authority as such would have failed) and that it is incompatible with persuasion 'which presupposes equality and works through a process of argumentation'.[3] Neither Mr McDermott's physical threats, nor his arguments, would persuade us that *A Midsummer Night's Dream* was good or enjoyable; for that, we would rely on Shakespeare himself. Here is the rub: as Arendt puts it, 'Authority implies an obedience in which men retain their freedom'[4] – or, I might add, in which we *find* our freedom. We can acknowledge an authority here, via this play, that allowed us to gain a freedom, the freedom conditioned by difference, by differing or, as Rainer Maria Rilke would have had it, by changing our life. By constantly changing language – that is, by continually reading – it has become possible for me to change my life and its possibilities. Shakespeare has been central to the edification of a self that constitutes itself as differing, as freeing itself from the tyranny of identity; and in that freedom is the sharing of languages.

Notes

Introduction: The Philosophy of Transparency

1 Peter Brooks, *Troubling Confessions* (Chicago, IL: University of Chicago Press, 2000), p. 6.

2 Giorgio Agamben, *Remnants of Auschwitz* (trans. Daniel Heller-Roazen; New York, NY: Zone Books, 2002), p. 24. There is an interesting trend here, one that might deserve further consideration. First, legal culpability shrinks to the admission of moral or characterological shortcomings; but this in turn is erased from consideration. As in our recent crises of capitalism, caused by bankers, we have, at best, a 'displaced' acknowledgement of the shortcomings: as Fred Goodwin said, when asked to apologize for the failures of the Royal Bank of Scotland, 'There is an apology' – the phraseology is important, and is certainly not 'I apologize'. Then, beyond this, 'the time for apology is over', as Bob Diamond put it in his meeting with the UK House of Commons Select Committee, just weeks before collecting a personal bonus reputed to be of the order of £8 million, and while many UK citizens faced the prospect of job cuts and reduced public services as a result of the bankers' behaviour.

3 See Wolfgang Sofsky, *Privacy: A Manifesto* (trans. Steven Rendall; Princeton, NJ: Princeton University Press, 2008).

4 On the idea of a transparent society, see Gianni Vattimo, *The Transparent Society* (trans. David Webb; Cambridge: Polity Press, 1992), where Vattimo traces the idea back to a certain Hegelian notion of the fulfilment of *Geist*, the moment when Spirit comes to Absolute Self-knowing, as it were, and thus where the subject coincides entirely with its presentation.

5 See Naomi Klein, *The Shock Doctrine* (Harmondsworth: Penguin, 2007). The collocation of disaster capital and redemption here is, of course, not to be ascribed to Klein: I mean simply to indicate coincidental overlap.

6 I have explored this in detail in Thomas Docherty, *Criticism and Modernity* (Oxford: Oxford University Press, 1999), especially chapter 2, 'Love as the European Humour' (pp. 39–68), and chapter 5, 'The Politics of Singularity' (pp. 116–60).

Chapter 1 Now

1 Paul Auster, *Sunset Park* (London: Faber, 2010), p. 308.

2 Alain Robbe-Grillet, *Dans le labyrinth* (Paris: Minuit, 1958).

3 See Edward Said, *Beginnings: Intention and Method* (New York, NY: Basic Books, 1975).

4 I explore this much more fully in a sustained consideration of J. Hillis Miller's work, and especially his recent considerations of 'zero', in Chapter 6 of this book.

5 We should note in passing that, even in this demand for a secular criticism, a theological language nonetheless asserts itself, almost as if it were a primary vocabulary for Benjamin. It is well known, of course, that this is fairly common in Benjamin; but here, I will be exploring why this seems inevitable. In more recent philosophy, such as that of Giorgio Agamben, this messianic moment becomes

'the time that remains'. Giorgio Agamben, *The Time that Remains* (trans. Patricia Dailey; Stanford, CA: Stanford University Press, 2005).

6   See 'Theses on the Philosophy of History', in Walter Benjamin, *Illuminations* (ed. Hannah Arendt, trans. Harry Zohn, London: Fontana, 1973), p. 264.

7   Jean-François Lyotard, *La confession d'Augustin* (Paris: Galilée, 1998), p. 70; my translation.

8   It should not escape notice that Lyotard, too, in a great deal of his writing, is heavily influenced by Judeo-Christian traditions. His work on the relation of discourse to figure – work that shapes a good deal of his fundamental aesthetics – is informed by the religious question of idolatry and the ban on images of God; and that aesthetic becomes in turn a question of the problems of representation that shape his ethics and politics as well, including the delineations of postmodernism for which he is probably most famous. For more on this, see Thomas Docherty, *After Theory* (revised 2nd edn, Edinburgh: Edinburgh University Press, 1996), pp. 172–6.

9   G.W.F. Hegel, *Phenomenology of Spirit* (trans. A.V. Miller, Oxford: Oxford University Press, 1977), p. 60 (section A, 1).

10   Such a referential version of how language operates in relation to truth is, of course, not straightforward and is highly contested. For a good introduction to the philosophical issues, see W.V. Quine, *Pursuit of Truth* (Cambridge, MA: Harvard University Press, 1990); and consider especially his formulation of what he calls 'observation sentences', which he describes as '*occasion* sentences: true on some occasions, false on others' (Quine, *Pursuit of Truth*, p. 3 and *passim*).

11   Jonathan Swift, *Gulliver's Travels and Other Writings* (ed. Louis A. Landa, Oxford: Oxford University Press, 1976), p. 310. We should note, in passing, that this also effectively trashes the preceding four sections of 'A Tale of a Tub' itself. It becomes a proto-Fishian 'self-consuming artifact', a text that erases itself as it goes along, like Robbe-Grillet's *Les Gommes*.

12   See Michel Serres, *Eclaircissements: Entretiens avec Bruno Latour* (Paris: Garnier-Flammarion, 1994), p. 76.

13   See Hannah Arendt, *Crises of the Republic* (New York, NY: Harcourt Brace & Company, 1972), p. 4; and see also Hannah Arendt, *Between Past and Future: Eight Exercises in Political Thought* (Harmondsworth: Penguin, 1993), pp. 227–8.

14   Arendt, *Crises of the Republic*, p. 5.

15   Arendt, *Crises of the Republic*, p. 5.

16   Arendt, *Crises of the Republic*, p. 5.

17   See Michel de Montaigne, *Essais* (Paris: Garnier-Flammarion, 1969), vol. 1, p. 74 ('Des Menteurs'): '*Un ancient père dit que nous sommes mieux en la compagnie d'un chien cognu qu'en celle d'un homme duquel le langage nous est inconnu*' ('An ancient father says that we are better off in the company of a dog with which we are familiar than we would be in the company of a man whose language we don't speak'). This is an indirect allusion to the writings of the '*ancien père*' that is Augustine, in Augustine, *City of God* (trans. Henry Bettenson, Harmondsworth: Penguin, 1980), p. 861 (Book XIX, ch. 7): 'a man would be more cheerful with his dog for company than with a foreigner'. For a fuller understanding of the extremely complex case of Rousseau, see Paul de Man's essay, 'Excuses', in Paul de Man, *Allegories of Reading* (New Haven, CT: Yale University Press, 1979) – an essay that perhaps says a good deal more about de Man than it does about Rousseau.

18   See François Villon, *Poésies complètes* (Paris: Livre de Poche, 1972). Villon has been rather neglected in recent times; but 'Le testament' is one of our great

examples of a very specific kind of confessional text, a text written after Villon
is found guilty of murder and theft, and in which he writes his revenge on his
accusers. In some ways, it is a primary text of the kind of 'witnessing' that I
explore in Chapter 7 of this book.

19 See Geoffrey Bennington and Jacques Derrida, *Jacques Derrida* (Paris: Seuil,
1991). John Gower, *Confessio Amantis*, is widely available in e-versions: see
http://omacl.org [accessed 1 February 2012].

20 Lyotard, *La confession d'Augustin*, p. 47.

21 Augustine, *Confessions* (trans. R.S. Pine-Coffin, Harmondsworth: Penguin, 1961),
p. 266.

22 Benjamin, *Illuminations*, p. 265.

23 In passing, we might phrase this in such a way as to say that the teller of the
beads – the one who prays – holds history between finger and thumb; and, once
we put it like this, we cannot help but recall Seamus Heaney's most celebrated
poem, 'Digging', where we find the relation between digging the historical realm
and writing: 'Between my finger and my thumb / The squat pen rests: snug as
a gun.'

24 Benjamin, *Illuminations*, p. 263.

25 Benjamin, *Illuminations*, p. 263.

26 Lyotard, *La confession d'Augustin*, p. 44. We should also consider this in relation
to Samuel Beckett's 1930 study of Proust, where he sees clearly that habit, and
its relation to habitation, is at the centre of *A la recherché du temps perdu*. See
Samuel Beckett, *Proust* (London: Chatto and Windus, 1930). Finally, alongside
these, see a key element of Russian Formalism, as expressed in the writing of
Viktor Shklovsky, 'Art as Technique', in Lee T. Lemon and Marion J. Reis
(eds and trans), *Russian Formalist Criticism* (Lincoln, NE: University of Nebraska
Press, 1965), pp. 11–12: 'If we start to examine the general laws of perception, we
see that as perception becomes habitual, it becomes automatic ... Habitualization
devours works, clothes, furniture, one's wife, and the fear of war'.

27 Hans Blumenberg, *The Legitimacy of the Modern Age* (trans. Robert M. Wallace,
Cambridge, MA: MIT Press, 1983), p. 596.

28 Jean-Luc Nancy, *Being Singular Plural* (trans. Robert Richardson and Anne
O'Byrne, Stanford, CA: Stanford University Press, 2000), p. 165.

29 Jean-Luc Nancy, *The Experience of Freedom* (trans. Bridget McDonald, Stanford,
CA: Stanford University Press, 1993), p. 115.

30 'What is a contemporary?', in Giorgio Agamben, *What is an Apparatus?*
(trans. David Kishik and Stefan Pedatella, Stanford, CA: Stanford University
Press, 2009), p. 40.

31 Benjamin, *Illuminations*, p. 263.

32 Agamben, *What is an Apparatus?*, pp. 47–50.

33 See Stanley Fish, *Surprised by Sin* (Cambridge, MA: Harvard University Press,
1967). This study became the basis, in fact, for virtually all of Fish's subsequent
work. His version of reader-response criticism is essentially one in which the
substance of reading is a condition in which the reader is subject to constant
surprises; and, in turn, this becomes a paradoxical *expectation* of surprise,
the word for which is essentially 'the new pragmatism'.

34 Lyotard, *La confession d'Augustin*, pp. 72–3.

35 Lyotard, *La confession d'Augustin*, p. 73.

36 See Augustine, *City of God*, pp. 519–20; and see my comments on this in
Docherty, *Criticism and Modernity*, pp. 200–204.

37 The key texts are Alain Badiou, *Saint Paul: La fondation de l'universalisme* (Paris: PUF, 1997); Agamben, *The Time that Remains*; and Slavoj Žižek, *The Puppet and the Dwarf* (Cambridge, MA: MIT Press, 2003).

38 See Gianni Vattimo, *La fine della modernità* (Milan: Garzanti, 1985).

39 Badiou, *Saint Paul*, pp. 12–13; my translation.

40 Alain Badiou, *Petit manuel d'inesthétique* (Paris: Seuil, 1998), p. 29; my translation. See also John Henry Cardinal Newman, *The Idea of a University* (ed. Martin J. Svaglic, San Francisco, CA: Rinehart Press, 1960), p. xliv. Here, in the Preface to his lectures, Newman dismisses the idea that a university education should be about the engendering of what he calls 'viewiness', or having and expressing views that are based on opinion rather than on knowledge. For a fuller engagement with these ideas in the contemporary moment, see Thomas Docherty, *For the University* (London: Bloomsbury Academic, 2011).

41 Badiou, *Saint Paul*, p.11 (translation of all quotations from this volume are mine). For a less philosophical, but equally hard-hitting version of this, see the trenchant critique of identity-politics in Tony Judt, *The Memory Chalet* (London: Heinemann, 2010), p. 202: 'you are what your grandparents suffered'. I discuss this briefly later.

42 Badiou, *Saint Paul*, p. 13.

43 Badiou, *Saint Paul*, p. 11.

44 Badiou, *Saint Paul*, p. 15. It would also follow from this mode of thought, of course, that democracy – if it is to be characterized solely as that political mode in which I 'tell' my voice/vote – is also anathema to truth.

45 Badiou, *Saint Paul*, p. 15.

46 Badiou, *Saint Paul*, pp. 22–3.

47 See Jacques Rancière, *Moments politiques* (Paris: La Fabrique, 2009), p. 92.

48 Rancière, *Moments politiques*, p. 92.

49 I have argued this in more detail in Thomas Docherty, *Aesthetic Democracy* (Stanford, CA: Stanford University Press, 2007).

50 All passages cited here are from Judt, *The Memory Chalet*, p. 202.

Chapter 2 Official Identity and Clandestine Experience

1 Vincent Descombes, *Modern French Philosophy* (trans. L. Scott-Fox and J.M. Harding, Cambridge: Cambridge University Press, 1980), p. 37.

2 Descombes, *Modern French Philosophy*, p. 37.

3 See 'A Sketch of the Past', in Virginia Woolf, *Moments of Being* (ed. Jeanne Schulkind, London: Triad Panther, 1978), p. 81. It is important to note, in passing, that for Virginia Woolf, the 'moment' in question is not simply a temporal moment. Rather, the term is taken essentially from the discourses of physics, where it relates to momentum, weight, attitude, mood, inclination; or, in short, the moment is a play of forces that constitute a weight of the present, its pressing upon us as a sensation of being, set against the many moments of 'non-being' as Woolf calls them, describing those less marked or less intense moments as 'nondescript cotton wool'.

4 We see a similar thinking in Paul de Man, when he tries to understand the movements of allegory and of irony in his famous 'The Rhetoric of Temporality' essay, in Paul de Man, *Blindness and Insight* (London: Methuen, 1983). See also my commentary on that essay in Docherty, *After Theory*, pp. 119–26.

5 Descombes, *Modern French Philosophy*, p. 38.

6 See the passage 'An ecstatic lecture', in the 'Diapsalmata' section of Søren Kierkegaard, *Either/Or* (trans. Alastair Hannay, Harmondsworth: Penguin, 1992), pp. 54–5; and see also Jean-François Lyotard, *Le différend* (Paris: Minuit, 1983), pp. 65–6, 153–60.

7 Frank Kermode, in his memoir, Frank Kermode, *Not Entitled* (New York, NY: Farrar, Straus & Giroux, 1999), writes of the abbreviation NE, meaning 'not entitled', used by sailors when they forfeit their salary due to some misdemeanour. Being 'not entitled' was described as getting a 'fucking nor'easter'; and this relates entitlement to financial standing and to evaluation. There is a study to be done on the very idea of such titles and entitlements.

8 In this, it extends the work in my essay, Thomas Docherty, 'For a new empiricism', *Parallax* 5: 2 (1999), pp. 51–64, and in 'Aesthetics and the demise of experience' in Docherty, *Aesthetic Democracy*. For other essays on this 'New Aestheticism', see John Joughin and Simon Malpas (eds), *The New Aestheticism* (Manchester: Manchester University Press, 2003).

9 For a good guide to the operations of rhetoric in question here, see Peter Mack, *Elizabethan Rhetoric* (Cambridge: Cambridge University Press, 2002); and, for more detailed exploration on this specifically in Montaigne, see Peter Mack, *Rhetoric and Reading in Montaigne and Shakespeare* (London: Bloomsbury Academic, 2009).

10 We are perhaps more acquainted with this in recent times courtesy of the philosophy of Lyotard, whose 'postmodern mood' is one that is characterized by the necessity to 'judge without criteria'. For a straightforward statement of this, see Jean-François Lyotard, *Just Gaming* (trans. Wlad Godzich, Manchester: Manchester University Press, 1985), p. 14: 'we judge without criteria. We are in the position of Aristotle's prudent individual, who makes judgments about the just and the unjust without the least criterion'. Montaigne, like Lyotard, would have been familiar with this from Aristotle.

11 Michel de Montaigne, *Essays* (trans. J.M. Cohen, Penguin, Harmondsworth, 1958), p. 351. For the original, see Montaigne, *Essais*, vol. 3, p. 281.

12 For an exposition and occasional exploration of what is at stake in this, see H. Aram Veeser (ed.), *The Confessions of the Critics* (London: Routledge, 1996). For the autobiographical pact, see Philippe Lejeune, *Le pacte autobiographique* (Paris: Seuil, 1975).

13 I explore this slightly more fully in Thomas Docherty, *The English Question; or, Academic Freedoms* (Brighton: Sussex Academic Press, 2008), where I consider what has happened to the discipline of English studies in a politics governed by audit culture, bureaucracy and the administrative priorities of a society that has seen the rise and triumph of the managerialist class. Its consequences for education more generally are explored in Docherty, *For the University*.

14 Leslie A. Fiedler, 'Archetype and signature: A study of the relationship between biography and poetry', *Sewanee Review*, 60 (1952), pp. 253–73.

15 The periodization here, especially of the so-called 'death of the author', is important. There is a link to be made between this abstract art, the kenotic dissolution of the author, and a cold-war mentality that shaped the 1960s; and I explore this in some more detail in Chapter 6, where the reduction of the author to a 'bare self' is examined.

16 The not so silent allusion here, of course, is to Jacques Derrida's 'Signature, Event, Context', an essay that in many ways updates and extends very profoundly the insights of Fiedler (though the two are in fact unrelated).

See Jacques Derrida, *Margins: of Philosophy* (trans. Alan Bass, Brighton: Harvester Press, 1982).

17 Jean-François Lyotard, *Signé Malraux* (Paris: Grasset, 1996).

18 Jürgen Habermas, *Legitimation Crisis* (trans. Thomas McCarthy, London: Heinemann, 1976), p. 98.

19 Jacques Derrida, *Writing and Difference* (trans. Alan Bass, London: Routledge, 1978), pp. 4–5.

20 Gilles Deleuze, *Bergsonism* (trans. Hugh Tomlinson and Barbara Habberjam, New York, NY: Zone Books, 1988), p. 37.

21 Gilles Deleuze, *Spinoza* (trans. Robert Hurley, San Francisco, CA: City Lights Books, 1988), p. 18.

22 Michael Hardt, *Gilles Deleuze* (London: UCL Press, 1993), p. 61.

23 Gilles Deleuze, *Pourparlers* (Paris: Minuit, 1990), p. 218; my translation. The reference is to Bernard Groethuysen (who studied under Wilhelm Dilthey), a philosopher better-known in France than in the anglophone world.

24 Gilles Deleuze and Félix Guattari, *Qu'est-ce que la philosophie?* (Paris: Minuit, 1991), p. 8.

25 Montaigne, *Essais*, vol. 1, p. 35; my translation.

26 Jean-Jacques Rousseau, *Confessions* (trans. J.M. Cohen, Harmondsworth: Penguin, 1953), p. 17.

27 'No Messiah', in Robert Lowell, *The Dolphin* (London: Faber and Faber, 1973), p. 74.

28 'Critic', in Lowell, *The Dolphin*, p. 43.

29 Augustine, *Confessions*, p. 22.

30 Herman Melville, *Moby Dick* (London: Bantam Books, 1981), p. 11. I am indebted to Geoffrey Hartman for the speculation here about the status of nomination. In private conversation, July 1983, he suggested that 'all acts of narrative are, in the end, finally acts of nomination'. I am extending this here beyond the scope of narrative and am relating it to the status of confession. I explored what I call 'scenes of recognition' in Thomas Docherty, *John Donne, Undone* (London: Methuen, 1986).

31 Augustine, *Confessions*, p. 26.

32 Augustine, *Confessions*, p. 26.

33 Augustine, *Confessions*, p. 347.

34 Augustine, *Confessions*, p. 346.

35 Augustine, *Confessions*, pp. 346, 347.

36 Peter Fenves, 'Foreword: From Empiricism to the Experience of Freedom', in Jean-Luc Nancy, *The Experience of Freedom* (trans. Bridget McDonald, Stanford, CA: Stanford University Press, 1993), p. xiii.

37 Catherine Belsey, *Desire* (Oxford: Blackwell, 1994), p. 10. She explicitly opposes experience to 'texts'.

38 Giorgio Agamben, *Infancy and History* (trans. Liz Heron, London: Verso, 1993), p. 14.

39 Reprinted in Arendt, *Crises of the Republic*, p. 179.

40 Arendt, *Crises of the Republic*, p. 109.

41 Arendt, *Crises of the Republic*, p. 110.

42 Arendt, *Between Past and Future*, p. 91.

43 Arendt, *Between Past and Future*, p. 95.

44 Arendt, *Between Past and Future*, p. 95.

45 Samuel Beckett, *Molloy, Malone Dies, The Unnamable* (London: John Calder, 1959), p. 386.

46 I am indebted to Jim Byatt for a number of conversations through which
    this link of Beckettian skin to taboo, and to this specific taboo, came to be
    developed. Behind these formulations, I think we can hear the ghost of that
    archetypal first modern man, Hamlet, pondering his own potential for action or
    agency, pondering his identity and whether to bring it to an end or to a definite
    conclusion in his famed soliloquy: 'to be or not to be'. One reason why this is a
    question for Hamlet, and one that might yield a resolution, is that he thinks in
    terms of being itself, and not in terms of how he might *become* other than he is.
    In Shakespeare, typically, it is the *female* character who is cast in terms of
    becoming: 'I do beguile the thing I am by seeming otherwise', says Desdemona.
    Shakespeare's day, of course, called this 'mutability', ascribed it to femininity
    and devalued it. However, it is perhaps better regarded as the emergence, into
    modernity, of the pressure of an entire philosophy of difference, an ontology of
    becoming. If we attend to Agamben and Badiou, however, we now have a rival
    contender for the title of 'first modern': Saint Paul.
47 Agamben, *Remnants of Auschwitz*, p. 13.
48 Agamben, *Remnants of Auschwitz*, p. 12.
49 Arendt, *Crises of the Republic*, pp. 132–3.

Chapter 3 This Thing of Darkness I Acknowledge Mine

1 Blaise Pascal, *Pensées* (ed. Louis Lafuma, Paris: Seuil, 1962), fragment no. 64;
   Blaise Pascal, *Pensées* (ed. Léon Brunschvicg, Paris: Flammarion, 1976), fragment
   no. 295.
2 Pascal, *Pensées* (ed. Lafuma), fragment no. 113; Pascal, *Pensées* (ed. Brunschvicg),
   fragment no. 348.
3 William Shakespeare, *The Tempest*, Act V, Scene 1.
4 Georges Perec, *Les choses* (Paris: Julliard, 1965), p. 78; my translation.
5 Perec, *Les choses*, p. 65.
6 John Macmurray, *Conditions of Freedom* (Atlantic Highlands, NJ: Humanities
   Press, 1993), p. 2.
7 Macmurray, *Conditions of Freedom*, p. 3; italics added.
8 See Sylviane Agacinski, *Le passeur du temps* (Paris: Seuil, 2000), where we find
   the argument that time corrupts, certainly; but it also generates and produces.
   The ambivalences of time here – and especially the ambiguity of 'the present' – are
   akin to the ambivalence that I will find in 'zero', in Chapter 6.
9 This modern Subject requires such a fiction precisely because of one effect of
   David Hume's sceptical philosophy which, in its refusal to found thinking of
   truth upon a stable self, opens a specific antifoundationalism whose effect is
   to produce various strategies of containment advanced in the name of fiction
   rather than truth. Fictions of the self – in those biographical fictions of the
   eighteenth-century novel, say – thus answer to the anxiety that there might
   not actually be a self in the first place. The fiction constructs, and proposes as
   normative, that which it pretends merely to describe. Temporally, the novel
   predicts – or foretells – a history; and in such foretelling makes the future into
   a past, while its present remains curiously void and empty. On this, see my
   'foretelling' chapter in Docherty, *Aesthetic Democracy*; and see also 'Now',
   Chapter 1 in this book.
10 Erich Auerbach, *Mimesis* (trans. Willard R. Trask, Princeton, NJ: Princeton
   University Press, 1968).

11   Augustine, *Confessions*, p. 209. This question, of a writing in which the writer reflects on the present act of writing, became part of the staple diet of a certain kind of hyper-reflexivity often associated with postmodernism. We find it in the mid-twentieth-century French *nouveau roman*; but we also find it, before that, in the *Kunstlerroman*; and it takes a certain philosophical seriousness in Foucault and, perhaps most tellingly, in Blanchot's *L'instant de ma mort* and Derrida's response, *Demeure*. It is explored further in Chapter 7.

12   'Writing to the minute', of course, is Samuel Richardson's phrase describing the supposed transcription of the letters in *Clarissa*. For a good exploration of the issues involved in such 'contemporaneous' writing, see Lennard J. Davis, *Factual Fictions* (New York, NY: Columbia University Press, 1983); but perhaps the best single commentary on the idea is in Henry Fielding's *Shamela* and its parodying of the idea.

13   Auerbach, *Mimesis*, pp. 70–71. Forster indicates that 'and then … and then …' (as in ' The king died, and then the Queen died.') is precisely the opposite of plot, which requires consequence ('The King died, and then the Queen died of grief') (E.M. Forster, *Aspects of the Novel* (Harmondsworth: Penguin, 1927)). Frank Kermode, in Frank Kermode, *The Sense of an Ending* (Oxford: Oxford University Press, 1966), explains this in terms of a question of roused expectations, the 'tick' of a clock that is followed by or that implies a following 'tock'. The question of expectation, and its relation to the 'event' and to surprise will all figure later in this chapter.

14   Augustine writes that 'Ambrose often repeated the text: *The written law inflicts death, whereas the spiritual law brings life*', Augustine, *Confessions*, p. 116. This, from 2 Corinthians, is, of course, one of the key passages for interpretation in Paul; and it has become a crux of some current debates around the significance of Paul, especially in the work of Badiou, *Saint Paul*, and in that of Agamben, *The Time that Remains*. It is interesting to note, in passing, that Paul was also a figure of fundamental importance to Macmurray in 1949, when Macmurray sees Paul as a figure who determines identity-as-difference: Paul is and is not Paul, so to speak.

15   Augustine, *Confessions*, p. 112.

16   Augustine, *Confessions*, p. 114.

17   Augustine, *Confessions*, p. 115.

18   Augustine, *Confessions*, p. 116.

19   See Lyotard, *La confession d'Augustin*, for this idea that the text does not describe a conversion but instead enacts it at every point.

20   Augustine, *Confessions*, p. 123.

21   Auerbach, *Mimesis*, p. 74.

22   René Descartes, *Discours de la méthode* (ed. E. Gilson, Paris: Librairie Philosophique J. Vrin, 1970), pp. 44–5; these and all other translations are mine.

23   Descartes, *Discours de la méthode*, pp. 47–8.

24   Descartes, *Discours de la méthode*, pp. 64, 66.

25   Descartes, *Discours de la méthode*, p. 80.

26   Blaise Pascal, *Oeuvres complètes* (Paris: Seuil, 1963), p. 286.

27   Pascal, *Oeuvres complètes*, p. 286.

28   Pascal, *Oeuvres complètes*, p. 290.

29   Pascal, *Oeuvres complètes*, p. 291.

30   Perec, *Les choses*, p. 38.

31   Perec, *Les choses*, p. 144.

32   See Alasdair MacIntyre, *Three Rival Versions of Moral Enquiry* (London: Duckworth, 1990), pp. 170–95.

33 Descartes, *Discours de la méthode*, pp. 51–2.
34 Jean-Paul Sartre, *Being and Nothingness* (trans. Hazel E. Barnes, New York, NY: Philosophical Library, 1956), p. 566.
35 Auerbach, *Mimesis*, p. 74.
36 Jean-François Lyotard, *The Inhuman: Reflections on Time* (trans. Geoffrey Bennington and Rachel Bowlby, Cambridge: Polity Press, 1991), p. 60.
37 Lyotard, *The Inhuman*, p. 65. See also Jürgen Habermas, *The Past as Future* (ed. and trans. Max Pensky, Cambridge: Polity Press, 1994), p. 66: 'the temptation to use models from the past for the interpretation of the future seems impossible to resist'. He is speaking of the problems of Germany after reunification; but the comment has a more general applicability, in which the mood is characterized by the phrase 'Let's get it over with, just like we did once before!'
38 Perec, *Les choses*, p. 72.
39 Perec, *Les choses*, p. 73.
40 Emmanuel Levinas, *Le temps et l'autre* (Paris: Quadrige/PUF, 1991); my translation (the original: *'le temps n'est pas le fait d'un sujet isolé et seul, mais … il est la relation même du sujet avec autrui'*).
41 Virginia Woolf, 'Character in Fiction', originally delivered as a paper to the Heretics' Society in 1924, and subsequently revised and reprinted in various versions. I cite here from the version in Virginia Woolf, *Selected Essays* (ed. David Bradshaw, Oxford: Oxford University Press, 2008), p. 38.
42 Jürgen Habermas, in private conversation, University College Dublin, 14 April 1994, asserted that it was precisely this principle of autonomy as a constituent element of the movement of Enlightenment that Lyotard – at that time seen as an opponent of Habermas – 'has not understood'. Part of the argument of this chapter derives from a consideration of this claim, which Habermas also claimed as the basic philosophical – and not political – difference between Lyotard and himself. For a fuller exploration of the implications of this, see the essays collected in Seyla Benhabib (ed.), *Democracy and Difference* (Princeton, NJ: Princeton University Press, 1996).
43 T.S. Eliot, *The Sacred Wood* (London: Methuen, 1966), pp. xv–xvi.
44 Eliot, *The Sacred Wood*, p. 79.
45 Benjamin, *Illuminations*, p. 264.
46 Benjamin, *Illuminations*, p. 264.
47 For the best discussion of this, see Zygmunt Bauman, *Modernity and the Holocaust* (Oxford: Polity Press, 1989).
48 The kind of singularity in question here is that described by Clément Rosset in his many texts, but most pertinently and succinctly in Clément Rosset, *L'objet singulier* (Paris: Minuit, 1979).
49 Benjamin, *Illuminations*, p. 263.
50 Benjamin, *Illuminations*, p. 265.
51 Benjamin, *Illuminations*, p. 264.
52 See Rosset, *L'objet singulier*.
53 For a fuller description of what I call 'anatheory', see my studies, Docherty, *After Theory*, and Thomas Docherty, *Alterities* (Oxford: Oxford University Press, 1996).
54 See Jean Baudrillard, *Fatal Strategies* (trans. Philip Beitchman and W.G.J. Niesluchowski, London: Pluto Press, 1990).
55 With respect to Hopkins, the single most significant ostensible parataxis is the 'AND' that appears in 'The Windhover'; an 'AND' that actually fails to operate paratactically. The silent allusions in the rest of this paragraph are to 'Not Ideas

about the Thing, but the Thing itself', in Wallace Stevens, *Collected Poems* (London: Faber and Faber, 1984), p. 534; William Carlos Williams, *Paterson* (Harmondsworth, Penguin, 1983), p. 6; 'The Thing', in Martin Heidegger, *Poetry, Language, Thought* (trans. Albert Hofstadter, New York, NY: Harper Colophon, 1975), Chapter 5.

56 'Seeing Things' and 'The Settle Bed' in Seamus Heaney, *Seeing Things* (London: Faber and Faber, 1992), pp. 16, 28. For a fuller discussion of this 'new empiricism', as I have termed it, see my chapter on 'The Modern Thing' in Docherty, *Alterities*.

57 I have argued this in some theoretical detail in Docherty, *Alterities*, where I work through a series of examples, but especially focusing on Wim Wenders's *Paris, Texas*, as a paradigmatic example.

58 For more on the importance of the witness in relation to the confessional impulse, see Chapter 7.

59 Ian McEwan, *The Child in Time* (London: Picador, 1988), p. 105.

60 For the meaning of this 'solace of good form', see Jean François Lyotard, 'Answering the question: what is postmodernism?', in Thomas Docherty (ed.), *Postmodernism* (New York, NY: Columbia University Press, 1993).

Chapter 4 Dilatory Time

1 See Montaigne, *Essays*, pp. 42–3. The essay is from Book 1, Chapter 21. Montaigne goes on to discuss the case noted by Augustine, of a man who could control his farts; and of how that was 'trumped' by Vives, who told of a man 'who could synchronize his blasts to the metre of verses that were read to him'; but he notes that 'this does not imply the complete obedience of this organ. For usually it is most unruly and mutinous.'

2 Montaigne, *Essays*, p. 42.

3 See Fredric Jameson, *The Political Unconscious* (London: Methuen, 1981), p. 102. See my commentary on this in Docherty, *Aesthetic Democracy*, Chapter 9.

4 It is this conception that governs a work such as Milton's *Comus*, say, in which the character of the Lady 'protects' herself against rape by saying that, while her violator can touch her body, he cannot touch her mind. This becomes an assertion of a form of intellectual freedom, however fraught. The attitude in question also shapes some political fiction, such as Helen Dunmore's recent novel, *The Betrayal*, about conditions in Stalinist Russia where the demand for a private sphere becomes 'translated' into imprisonment: you cannot get more private than that; and thus this issue itself becomes worthy of exploration, which I carry out in Chapter 7. See Docherty, *Aesthetic Democracy*.

5 The conception of the body as machine has a long history; but for present purposes, it is the history of this concept from Julien de La Mettrie, *Machine Man and Other Writings* (ed. and trans. Ann Thomson, Cambridge: Cambridge University Press, 1996), through to Gilles Deleuze and Félix Guattari, *Anti-Oedipus* (trans. Robert Hurley, Mark Seem and Helen R. Lane, London: Athlone Press, 1984), that is most important and pertinent, for it is in this 'modern' version of the concept that the relation of the body to time becomes central.

6 The most formidable thinking on this is that of Paul Virilio, in a series of early texts including: Paul Virilio, *Vitesse et politique* (Paris: Galilée, 1977); Paul Virilio, *L'horizon négatif* (Paris: Galilée, 1984); Paul Virilio, *L'espace critique* (Paris: Christian Bourgois, 1984); and Paul Virilio, *L'art du moteur* (Paris: Galilée, 1993).

The philosophy in these texts derives some of its significance from Virilio's work on war and on contemporary cultures conditioned by electronic and so-called 'instantaneous' media. See, for examples of this, Paul Virilio, *Guerre et cinéma* (Paris: Editions de l'Etoile, 1984); Paul Virilio, *Défense populaire et luttes écologiques* (Paris: Galilée, 1978); Paul Virilio, *Esthétique de la disparition* (Paris: Galilée, 1989); Paul Virilio, *L'écran du désert* (Paris: Galilée, 1991); and Paul Virilio, *L'inertie polaire* (Paris: Christian Bourgois, 1990).

7   For a general approach to this question, see, for example, Jacques Attali, *Histoires du temps* (Paris: Fayard, 1982), p. 155; and Pierre Boutang, *Le temps* (Paris: Hatier, 1993). See also David Harvey, *The Enigma of Capital* (New York, NY: Profile Books, 2010), and David Harvey, *Cosmopolitanism and the Geographies of Freedom* (New York, NY: Columbia University Press, 2009).

8   See 'Modern Fiction', in Virginia Woolf, *The Common Reader* (London: Hogarth Press, 1925).

9   The coincidence of this film with the year of Nixon's resignation after the bugging scandals of Watergate is, as Coppola himself has said, just that: coincidence. He wrote the script in the 1960s, before Nixon was even elected. However, the surveillance equipment described in the film is exactly like that used in the Watergate surveillance scandals. Most importantly for present purposes is the fact that the whole issue of surveillance and the question of the relation of private life to the public and political sphere is, at this time, a matter of pressing cultural concern. Watergate may not 'explain' *The Conversation*; but they both help delineate the major and pressing concerns of the cultural moment.

10   David Hume, *A Treatise of Human Nature* (ed. Ernest C. Mossner, London: Penguin Classics, 1984), pp. 299–300.

11   Hume, *A Treatise of Human Nature*, p. 300. For the relation of this to Deleuze in particular, see Thomas Docherty, 'Accidental Conditions', in Gerard Delanty and Stephen Turner (eds), *Handbook of Contemporary Social and Political Theory* (London: Routledge, 2011).

12   For more on this (though not in ways that accord with my own argument here), see Boutang, *Le temps*.

13   Franco Moretti, *The Way of the World* (trans. Albert Sbraggia, London: Verso, 1987)

14   For a different view – philosophical rather than fictional – of how such legitimation is attained, see Blumenberg, *The Legitimacy of the Modern Age*.

15   Note here the distinction between objects and things: after Heidegger, we can think of the object as a 'thing' *reduced* to its status as an element in the subject's determining consciousness; a thing becomes an object when it is considered to be there 'for' appropriation by a conscious subject. For examples of the phenomenology of which I write here, see Georges Poulet, *Etudes sur le temps humain*, (3 vols, Edinburgh: Edinburgh University Press, 1949; Paris: Plon Méaux, 1964); Jean Pouillon, *Temps et roman* (Vienna: Gallimard, 1946); A.A. Mendilow, *Time and the Novel* (New York, NY: Humanities Press, 1952); Paul Ricoeur, *Temps et récit*, vol. 2 (Paris: Seuil, 1984). A later variant and further sophistication of this kind of work is to be found in the so-called 'reader-response' school of criticism, influenced by Roman Ingarden and often associated with Wolfgang Iser or Hans-Robert Jauss, where the subject-position in question simply shifts to be identified more fully with that of the reader.

16   Michael H. Levenson makes a similar point as a kind of precision of the way in which 'point of view' is important in modernism, in Michael H. Levenson,

A Genealogy of Modernism (Cambridge: Cambridge University Press, 1984), especially in Chapter 1.

17 Auerbach, *Mimesis*, p. 74.
18 Michel Serres, *Eclaircissements: Entretiens avec Bruno Latour* (Paris: Garnier-Flammarion, 1994), p. 72.
19 Serres, *Eclaircissements*, pp. 76–8.
20 Serres, *Eclaircissements*, p. 76.
21 Serres, *Eclaircissements*, p. 78.
22 This is akin to the position rehearsed in postmodern architectural theory by Paolo Portoghesi, who comments on 'the presence of the past' as one determining instance or characteristic of the postmodern in terms of the built environment. See Paolo Portoghesi, *Postmodern* (trans. E. Shapiro, New York, NY: Rizzoli, 1983). A variant on this is reiterated in Charles Jencks's many arguments about the importance of the neoclassical strain in postmodern art.
23 Julia Kristeva, *Le temps sensible* (Paris: NRF, 1994), p. 208.
24 Swift, *Gulliver's Travels*, p. 310.
25 Patrick Parrinder argues, in Patrick Parrinder, *The Failure of Theory* (Brighton: Harvester, 1987), that criticism depends fundamentally on disagreement. See my commentary on this position, a variant on Edward Said's claims for criticism as a mode of dissent, in Docherty, *After Theory*, pp. 249–51.
26 See Thomas Docherty, *Reading (Absent) Character* (Oxford: Oxford University Press, 1983), Chapters 4, 5 and 6.
27 See Kermode, *The Sense of an Ending*, pp. 44–5, for the outline of this plot structure; and also my commentary in Docherty, *Reading (Absent) Character*, pp. 134–55.
28 Mendilow, *Time and the Novel*.
29 André Gide, *Journal des Faux-monnayeurs* (Paris: NRF Gallimard, 1927), p. 23.
30 Michel Butor, *L'emploi du temps* (Paris: Minuit, 1957), pp. 147–8.
31 Lyotard, *The Inhuman*, pp. 65–6.
32 McEwan, *The Child in Time*, pp. 93–5.
33 McEwan, *The Child in Time*, p. 177.
34 McEwan, *The Child in Time*, p. 105.

Chapter 5 Waste and the Ecology of Anguish

1 Pascal, *Pensées* (ed. Lafuma), fragment no. 200; Pascal, *Pensées* (ed. Brunschvicg), fragment no. 347; Pascal, *Oeuvres complètes*, p. 528.
2 Villon, *Poésies complètes*, p. 61.
3 Maurice Blanchot, *Faux pas* (trans. Charlotte Mandell, Stanford, CA: Stanford University Press, 2001), p. 1.
4 Blanchot, *Faux pas*, p. 1.
5 Blanchot, *Faux pas*, p. 3. See also Samuel Beckett, *Proust and Three Dialogues* (London: John Calder, 1969).
6 Blanchot, *Faux Pas*, p. 3.
7 See Simon Critchley, *Very Little, Almost Nothing* (London: Routledge, 1997), p. 25; and Montaigne, *Essais*, vol. 1, p. 127 (Book 1, Chapter 20).
8 'Qu'il ne faut juger de nostre heur qu'après la mort', in Montaigne, *Essais*, vol. 1, pp. 123–5 (Book 1, Chapter 19).
9 Interestingly, of course, in suggesting an 'expanse' of time, there is a suggestion that Proust was thinking paradoxically not in temporal but in spatial terms.

The thinker who understood the stakes of this most fully, apart from Proust himself, was Georges Poulet. See, especially, Poulet, *Etudes sur le temps humain*, his great work in three volumes as well as his study, Georges Poulet, *Proustian Space* (trans. Elliott Coleman, Baltimore, MD: Johns Hopkins University Press, 1977).

10 For the most relevant analysis of the relation between time and productivity, see the work of André Gorz, especially André Gorz, *Farewell to the Working Class* (trans. Mike Sonenscher, London: Pluto Press, 1982); and André Gorz, *Critique of Economic Reason* (trans. G. Handyside and C. Turner, London: Verso, 1989).

11 In relation to these ideas of 'full' and 'empty' time, see Kermode, *The Sense of an Ending*; and Frank Kermode, *The Genesis of Secrecy* (Cambridge, MA: Harvard University Press, 1979).

12 Deleuze relates this most centrally to Immanuel Kant, in a brilliant analysis of our entry into modernity. See Gilles Deleuze, *Kant's Critical Philosophy* (trans. Hugh Tomlinson and Barbara Habberjam, Minneapolis, MN: University of Minnesota Press, 1984).

13 The classic theoretical exploration of this is Said, *Beginnings*. However, this present study is, as we will see more clearly below, more indebted to the thinking of Hannah Arendt on the relation between beginnings and freedom or autonomy.

14 Simon Schama, *The Embarrassment of Riches* (New York, NY: Knopf, 1987). The anglophone response to Proust, in these terms, is Joyce, who also famously proved to be something of an irritation to a quintessential 'English' critic, F.R. Leavis. For more on this, see Docherty, *The English Question*, pp. 3–29.

15 'Preface to *Lyrical Ballads*', in William Wordsworth, *Poetical Works* (ed. Thomas Hutchinson, revised by Ernest de Selincourt, Oxford: Oxford University Press, 1975), p. 735.

16 Samuel Johnson will do something similar in order to trounce ideas of Optimism. See his 'Review of Soame Jenyns's "A Free Inquiry into the Nature and Origin of Evil"', in Samuel Johnson, *Rasselas, Poems and Selected Prose* (ed. Bertrand H. Bronson, New York, NY: Holt, Rinehart and Winston, 1971), pp. 219–20; and also see my commentary on this in Thomas Docherty, *On Modern Authority* (Brighton and New York, NY: Harvester and St Martin's, 1987), pp. 233–6.

17 In relation to this, see also my earlier piece, Thomas Docherty, 'Big texts', *Strategies of Reading: Dickens and After*, a special number of *The Yearbook of English Studies*, 26 (1996), pp. 249–60.

18 It would be true to say that this is not an entirely new phenomenon. Newspapers have always wanted to be giving us the new, as it happens; and, of course, in this they mirror some early developments of the modern novel, as in Samuel Richardson or Daniel Defoe. Newspapers take this to a limit in populist forms when they start to carry horoscopes, which give not what has happened but what will happen. There is a sociology of this that has its roots in Walter Benjamin's analysis of the role and function of readers' letters in newspapers. The analysis could be widened to deal with an entire philosophy of modernity and postmodernity, as in Vattimo, *La fine della modernità* and Gianni Vattimo, *The Transparent Society* (trans. David Webb, Cambridge: Polity Press, 1992), where he argues that some contemporary technologies encourage the belief in a kind of absolute presentism, the coming-to-itself of Hegelian Spirit, *Geist*, as in real-time news TV programmes.

19 Beckett, *Molloy, Malone Dies, The Unnamable*, p. 386.

20 Giorgio Agamben, *Il linguaggio e la morte* (Torino: Einaudi, 1982).

21 For an interesting and relevant exploration of skin in relation to our surveillance societies, see Sofsky, *Privacy*, p. 39: 'The shell of the skin represents the outline of the body. It holds the individual in an indivisible possession.' This is constantly under threat by increasingly invasive technologies, argues Sofsky; and these now look within the body itself, as when we are X-rayed or body-searched going through airports and the like.

22 I am partly indebted to discussions with Jim Byatt.

23 See Norman O. Brown, *Life against Death* (Middletown, CT: Wesleyan University Press, 1959).

24 Andrew Marvell, *Complete Poems* (Harmondsworth: Penguin, 1972).

25 Giorgio Agamben, *Homo Sacer* (trans. Daniel Heller-Roazen, Stanford, CA: Stanford University Press, 1998), p. 4.

26 Benjamin, *Illuminations*, pp. 219–54.

27 Agamben, *Homo Sacer*, p. 10.

28 See Maurice Blanchot, *The Work of Fire* (trans. Charlotte Mandell, Stanford, CA: Stanford University Press, 1995), p. 319.

29 We may see the possibility here of an analysis of a present predicament. In the so-called 'war on terror', everyone is potentially militarized, in that everyone is affected in a daily life by a series of norms concerning 'security' that now shape and restrict our actual living. It is worth noting also, in passing, the rhetorical slippage at stake in Bush's declaration of this war. The 'war on terror' is a bit like earlier metaphorical wars, the 'war against polio' for example. In earlier usage of the metaphor, those involved were aware that they were speaking metaphorically; Bush's mistake might be regarded as a linguistic error: he took a metaphor for a reality, and then really declared war. In the absence of a specific target, Iraq was made to fill the vacuum.

30 Jacques Derrida, *The Gift of Death* (trans. David Wills, Chicago, IL: University of Chicago Press, 1995), p. 41. For the Levinasian background to this, see my commentary in Docherty, *Aesthetic Democracy*, pp. 31–8.

Chapter 6 Confession and Democracy

1 John Le Carré, *Our Kind of Traitor* (London: Viking, 2010), p. 95.

2 Macmurray, *Conditions of Freedom*, p. 59.

3 M.L. Rosenthal, *Poetry and the Common Life* (Oxford: Oxford University Press, 1974), p. 125. He traces the phenomenon, in his detailed analysis, back at least as far as Wyatt. We might also think that some earlier work in English writing obviously suggests itself, such as Gower's *Confessio Amantis*.

4 Rosenthal, *Poetry and the Common Life*, p. 131.

5 For a thorough exploration of this issue, see George Bornstein, *Transformations of Romanticism in Yeats, Eliot and Stevens* (Chicago, IL: University of Chicago Press, 1976); and, for what remains a classic formulation of the theoretical issues, see Jacques Barzun, *Classic, Romantic and Modern* (London: Secker and Warburg, 1962).

6 For an interesting history of music that aligns this minimalism with a certain moment of bureaucratic repetition in a society whose administered norms induce silence, see Jacques Attali, *Noise* (trans. Brian Massumi, Manchester: Manchester University Press, 1985).

7 In passing, it is worth recording that this period also sees an ostensible appeal to the common life within the Catholic Church, emerging through the Second

Vatican Council between 1962 and 1965. It is probably needless to add that this is significant also for Kennedy, in terms of his Catholic background.

8   It should thus recall Lyotard's response to Augustine anxiety about responsibility for sins committed in infancy, and that I discussed in Chapter 1 above. There, we had a sin committed but not by a subject; and here we have a confession made, but not by a subject. The confessing I is displaced on to a narrated 'he', 'she' or 'we'.

9   M.L. Rosenthal, *The New Poets: American and British Poetry since World War II* (Oxford: Oxford University Press, 1967), p. 28.

10   Rosenthal, *The New Poets*, p. 61.

11   Rosenthal, *The New Poets*, p. 26.

12   de Man, *Allegories of Reading*, p. 280.

13   Seamus Heaney, *Human Chain* (London: Faber), p. 71.

14   Theodore Roethke, *Collected Poems* (London: Faber and Faber, 1966), p. 195.

15   John Berryman, *Selected Poems* (London: Faber and Faber, 1972); see especially 'Dream Song 14', 'Life, friends, is boring', p. 73.

16   For an important discussion of this in terms of its consequences for democracy, see Alain Touraine, *Qu'est-ce que la démocratie?* (Paris: Fayard, 1994), pp. 204–6: 'The subject brings together identity and technique, constructing herself or himself as an agent capable of modifying her or his environment and of making her or his life experiences into proofs of freedom' (my translation).

17   Richard Nixon, 'First Inaugural Address', *Bartleby*, http://www.bartleby.com/124/pres58.html [accessed 10 February 2012].

18   'Song of Myself', in Walt Whitman, *Leaves of Grass* (New York, NY: Airmont, 1965), p. 79.

19   Giorgio Agamben, *Profanations* (trans. Jeff Fort, New York, NY: Zone Books, 2007), p. 74.

20   Roberto Esposito, *Communitas* (Paris: PUF, 2000), 20; my translation.

21   Esposito, *Communitas*, p. 20.

22   Pascal, *Oeuvres complètes*, p. 550 (série II of the '*papiers non classés*'; fragment 418 (or 233 in the earlier Léon Brunschvicg numeration).

23   Docherty, *Aesthetic Democracy*.

24   Henry James, *The Altar of the Dead and Other Tales* (London: Macmillan, 1922), p. 3.

25   J. Hillis Miller, 'The History of 0', *Journal for Cultural Research*, 8: 2 (2004), p. 132.

26   Miller, 'The History of 0', p. 135.

27   Edith Wharton, *A Backward Glance* (New York, NY: D. Appleton-Century, 1934), pp. 366–7.

28   See Agamben, *Remnants of Auschwitz*, p. 17. The question of witnessing is taken up in more detail later in this chapter.

29   J. Hillis Miller, *Speech Acts in Literature* (Stanford, CA: Stanford University Press, 2001), p. 6. For Miller, the beginning in question is the title of J.L. Austin, *How To Do Things with Words* (ed. J.O. Urmson, Oxford: Clarendon, 1962); and in this present piece, I shall also return to a consideration of both Miller's title and mine, 'zero' and 'one', but will do so partly via Austin.

30   The issue here also relates to matters of translation, where we routinely speak in the voice of an other. This will be the starting point for Chapter 7.

31   Said, *Beginnings*. While Said is concerned with what we might think of as 'authority', Miller, I shall contend, is and has been concerned with 'autonomy' and with the possibility of the 'event'. For an explanation of the precise sense of

the 'event', see Alain Badiou, *L'être et l'événement* (Paris: Seuil, 1988); but see also the work of Lyotard, especially Jean-François Lyotard, *Peregrinations* (New York, NY: Columbia University Press, 1988), where he makes explicit the issues surrounding the event that shape and dominate almost all of his work, including the most celebrated work around the 'postmodern'. For a fuller explanation, see also my piece, Thomas Docherty, 'Just Events', in Thomas Carmichael and Alison Lee (eds), *Postmodern Times* (DeKalb, IL: Northern Illinois University Press, 2000), pp. 53–66.

32 For the best example of this, see the work of Said's early protégé, Davis, *Factual Fictions*. This book is a brilliant deployment of Saidian thought, applied to the beginning of the novel; and, in it, we also see Said's fundamental intimacy with a Foucauldian logic.

33 Kermode, *The Sense of an Ending*, p. 67.

34 Miller has frequently been at pains to stress this sheer difficulty of reading. A typical remark would be that in J. Hillis Miller *The Ethics of Reading* (New York, NY: Columbia University Press, 1987), pp. 3–4, where he writes that 'Reading itself is extraordinarily hard work. It does not occur all that often. Clearheaded reflection on what really happens in an act of reading is even more difficult and rare. It is an event traces of which are found here and there in written form'. For a fuller examination of these and related issues, see my 'On Reading', in Docherty, *The English Question*; and see also Chapter 4, 'Dilatory Time', here.

35 At the root of this lies Hegel. In the Introduction to *Aesthetics*, Hegel stresses that such an invention is tied firmly to freedom; and I shall return to the politics of this later in the present work.

36 J. Hillis Miller, *Poets of Reality* (Cambridge, MA: Harvard University Press, 1965), p. 10. See also J. Hillis Miller, *The Disappearance of God* (Cambridge, MA: Harvard University Press, 1963).

37 Pascal, *Oeuvres complètes*, p. 557; my translation.

38 Lucien Goldmann, *Le dieu caché* (Paris: Gallimard, 1955).

39 For a fuller theorisation of this, see Docherty, *Reading (Absent) Character*.

40 Kant might have thought of this as the difference between the synthetic and the analytic a priori. For a fuller explanation, see the introduction to Docherty, *Postmodernism*.

41 J. Hillis Miller, *Ariadne's Thread* (New Haven, CT: Yale University Press, 1992), p. 21.

42 See J. Hillis Miller, *Fiction and Repetition* (Oxford: Blackwell, 1982); but see also the preface to Miller, *Ariadne's Thread*, pp. ix–xi, where Miller, in acknowledging that the theme of *Fiction and Repetition* spawns many other texts, is explicit about how things 'get out of hand' as he writes, especially as he writes his 'beginnings' or introductions; or, how, in my own terms, his writing becomes an *event*.

43 Miller, *Speech Acts*, p. 13.

44 Miller, *Speech Acts*, p. 19.

45 Edward Said, *The World, the Text, the Critic* (London: Faber, 1984), p. 28.

46 de Man, *Blindness and Insight*, pp. 187–228.

47 I argue this in detail (though not in terms of the one and the zero, of course) in Docherty, *After Theory*, pp. 119–26.

48 It is worth noting, in passing, that the title of the lectures that shaped Austin, *How To Do Thing with Words*, was 'Words and Deeds'; and also that there

is a vital interest in this issue within the hermeneutic philosophical tradition, very different from that of Austin, as testified to by, for example, Hans-Georg Gadamer's 'Logos and Ergon in Plato's Lysis', reprinted in Hans-Georg Gadamer, Dialogue and Dialectic (trans. P. Christopher Smith, New haven, CT: Yale University Press, 1980), pp. 1–20.

49 Gottlob Frege, The Foundations of Arithmetic (trans. J.L. Austin, Oxford: Blackwell, 1953). Frege's work, it should be recalled, was reviewed extremely negatively by Georg Cantor, though it is also usually agreed that Cantor had paid the work scant attention prior to reviewing it. Yet more significantly for the purposes of the argument later in the present paper, Frege was somewhat of a political reactionary, a monarchist who despised the very idea of socialism and even of democracy.

50 James Joyce, A Portrait of the Artist as a Young Man (ed. Richard Ellmann, London: Granada, 1977), pp. 191–4.

51 James Joyce, Stephen Hero (ed. Theodore Spencer, revised John J. Slocum and Herbert Cahoon, London: Triad Panther, Granada, 1981), p. 190.

52 Joyce, A Portrait, p. 192.

53 Pascal, Oeuvres complètes, p. 506. We should perhaps compare here the formulation of Jameson, The Political Unconscious, p. 102, that 'History is what hurts'. Jameson arrives at this formulation by means of a reading of two profoundly theological thinkers, Spinoza and Althusser; and, interestingly, history, in being 'what hurts', is defined as that which 'refuses desire and sets inexorable limits to individual as well as collective praxis, which its "ruses" turn into grisly and ironic reversals of their own intention'. It does this, leading intentions or beginnings awry, because it is an 'absent cause', like a Pascalian Deus absconditus or like the zero as I am formulating it in this present argument.

54 de Man, Blindness and Insight, p. 211.

55 de Man, Allegories of Reading.

56 Hannah Arendt, Eichmann in Jerusalem: A Report on the Banality of Evil (New York, NY: Viking, 1963).

57 Frege, Foundations, pp. 49–50. All intercalated comments are mine.

58 Jacques Rancière, Hatred of Democracy (trans. Steve Corcoran, London: Verso, 2006), p. 52.

59 See Martha C. Nussbaum, Cultivating Humanity (Cambridge, MA: Harvard University Press, 1997). For a counter-argument to Nussbaum, see Docherty, For the University.

60 Touraine, Quest-ce que la démocratie, pp. 27–8.

61 Benjamin, Illuminations, p. 224.

62 For a fuller background to this, see Gianni Vattimo, The Transparent Society, especially the discussion of Popper's 'zero-model', p. 24.

63 Maurice Blanchot, Friendship (trans. Elizabeth Rottenberg, Stanford. CA: Stanford University Press, 1997), p. 69.

64 Blanchot, Friendship, p. 71.

65 Benjamin, Illuminations, p. 225.

66 Benjamin, Illuminations, p. 225.

67 Catherine Belsey, 'From Cultural Studies to Cultural Criticism?', in Paul Bowman (ed.), Interrogating Cultural Studies (London: Pluto Press, 2003), p. 24.

68 I explore all this further in two recent books: Docherty, For the University; Docherty, The English Question.

69 Benjamin, Illuminations, p. 243.

70 Touraine, *Qu'est-ce que la démocratie*, pp. 209–10.

71 Frances Hutcheson, *Philosophical Writings* (ed. R.S. Downie, London: Everyman, 1994), p. 15. See also my commentary on this in Docherty, *Criticism and Modernity*, p. 86 ff.

72 Macmurray, *Conditions of Freedom*, p. 2.

73 Macmurray, *Conditions of Freedom*, pp. 3, 52.

74 Touraine, *Qu'est-ce que la démocratie*, pp. 23, 204.

75 Macmurray, *Conditions of Freedom*, pp. 79–80.

76 The other philosopher shaping this thinking is Badiou. See, especially, the chapter 'Philosophie et amour' in Alain Badiou, *Conditions* (Paris: Seuil, 1992); but see also Badiou, *Petit manuel d'inesthétique*; and Alain Badiou, *Abrégé de métapolitique* (Paris: Seuil, 1998). For Badiou, there would be an interesting parallel between Miller's 'zero' and the figure of Christ as mediated by Saint Paul: see Badiou, *Saint Paul*.

77 J. Hillis Miller, *On Literature* (London: Routledge, 2002), p. 127.

78 Miller, *On Literature*, p. 131.

79 Pascal, *Oeuvres complètes*, p. 356.

80 Agamben, *Remnants of Auschwitz*, pp. 104–5.

Chapter 7 Witnessing and Literary Confession

1 J.M. Coetzee, *Summertime* (London: Vintage, 2010), p. 249.

2 Seamus Deane, *Reading in the Dark* (London: Jonathan Cape, 1996), p. 103.

3 Deane, *Reading in the Dark*, p. 108.

4 Deane, *Reading in the Dark*, p. 108.

5 J.M. Coetzee, *Youth* (London: Secker and Warburg, 2002), p. 10.

6 Agamben, *Remnants of Auschwitz*, p. 45.

7 Agamben, *Remnants of Auschwitz*, p. 45.

8 This relates back to arguments advanced by Holocaust-deniers, who claimed that, because it was impossible to produce anyone who had actually been in the gas-chambers, therefore we had no conclusive proof that the chambers existed. I discuss the response to this, especially as mediated by Jean-François Lyotard, in the introduction to Docherty, *Postmodernism*.

9 Agamben, *Remnants of Auschwitz*, p. 120.

10 Jacques Derrida and Maurice Blanchot, *Demeure and The Instant of my Death* (trans. Elizabeth Rottenberg, Stanford, CA: Stanford University Press, 2000), pp. 33–4.

11 Theodor W. Adorno, *Notes to Literature: Vol. 1* (ed. Rolf Tiedemann, trans. Shierry Weber Nicholsen, New York, NY: Columbia University Press, 1991), p. 187: 'Auschwitz also means this much: that man, dying, cannot find any other sense in his death than this flush, this shame.'

12 In passing, it is worth noting that Adorno finds the exposure to the foreign something that makes him blush. We should place this alongside Agamben, *Remnants of Auschwitz*, p. 104.

13 See Gilbert Carr, 'Robert Scheu's *Die Konversation in der Ehe*. An exercise in translation', *Jahrbuch der Germanistik in Ireland*, 2 (2007), pp. 47–60. The cited passages come from p. 58. I am immensely indebted to Gilbert Carr for drawing this text to my attention and for discussing it with me.

14 Agamben, *Remnants of Auschwitz*, p. 18.

15 Blanchot, *The Work of Fire*, p. 303.

16 Blanchot, *The Work of Fire*, pp. 313–14.
17 Jorge Luis Borges, *Labyrinths* (Harmondsworth: Penguin, 1978), pp. 66–7.
18 Borges, *Labyrinths*, p. 99.
19 Borges, *Labyrinths*, p. 99.
20 Augustine, *Confessions*, pp. 208–9.
21 Brooks, *Troubling Confessions*, p. 1.
22 Brooks, *Troubling Confessions*, p. 6.
23 Quine, *Pursuit of Truth*, pp. 3, 5, 6.
24 Brooks, *Troubling Confessions*, p. 2.
25 'The logical form of action sentences' in Donald Davidson, *Essays on Actions and Events* (Oxford: Oxford University Press, 1980); for a fuller exploration of 'correspondence theories' related to Tarski-style theories, see the essays in Donald Davidson, *Inquiries into Truth and Interpretation* (Oxford: Oxford University Press, 1984), especially the first five essays grouped under Chapter 1, 'Truth and Meaning'.
26 Both are included in Jean-Jacques Rousseau, *Ecrits politiques* (Paris: Livre de Poche, 1992).
27 Rousseau, *Ecrits politiques*, p. 94.
28 Pierre Teilhard de Chardin, *Comment je crois* (Paris: Seuil, 1969), p. 117; my translation.

Chapter 8 My Language!

1 Bennington and Derrida, *Jacques Derrida*, p. 303. This is the text that contains Derrida's own confessional work, 'Circonfession'. See my commentary on it in Docherty, *Aesthetic Democracy*, Chapter 1.
2 Arendt, *Between Past and Future*, pp. 92–3.
3 Arendt, *Between Past and Future*, p. 93.
4 Arendt, *Between Past and Future*, p. 106.

Selected Bibliography

Publications

Adorno, Theodor W., *Notes to Literature: Vol. 1*, ed. Rolf Tiedemann, trans. Shierry Weber Nicholsen, New York, NY: Columbia University Press, 1991.

Agacinski, Sylviane, *Le passeur du temps*, Paris: Seuil, 2000.

Agamben, Giorgio, *Il linguaggio e la morte*, Torino: Einaudi, 1982.

Agamben, Giorgio, *Infancy and History*, trans. Liz Heron, London: Verso, 1993.

Agamben, Giorgio, *Homo Sacer*, trans. Daniel Heller-Roazen, Stanford, CA: Stanford University Press, 1998.

Agamben, Giorgio, *Remnants of Auschwitz*, trans. Daniel Heller-Roazen, New York, NY: Zone Books, 2002.

Agamben, Giorgio, *The Time that Remains*, trans. Patricia Dailey; Stanford, CA: Stanford University Press, 2005.

Agamben, Giorgio, *Profanations*, trans. Jeff Fort, New York, NY: Zone Books, 2007.

Agamben, Giorgio, *What is an Apparatus?*, trans. David Kishik and Stefan Pedatella, Stanford, CA: Stanford University Press, 2009.

Arendt, Hannah, *Crises of the Republic*, New York, NY: Harcourt Brace & Company, 1972.

Arendt, Hannah, *Between Past and Future: Eight Exercises in Political Thought*, Harmondsworth: Penguin, 1993.

Attali, Jacques, *Histoires du temps*, Paris: Fayard, 1982.

Attali, Jacques, *Noise*, trans. Brian Massumi, Manchester: Manchester University Press, 1985.

Auerbach, Erich, *Mimesis*, trans. Willard R. Trask, Princeton, NJ: Princeton University Press, 1968.

Augustine, *Confessions*, trans. R.S. Pine-Coffin, Harmondsworth: Penguin, 1961.

Augustine, *City of God*, trans. Henry Bettenson, Harmondsworth: Penguin, 1980.

Auster, Paul, *Sunset Park*, London: Faber, 2010.

Badiou, Alain, *L'être et l'événement*, Paris: Seuil, 1988.

Badiou, Alain, *Conditions*, Paris: Seuil, 1992.

Badiou, Alain, *Saint Paul: La fondation de l'universalisme*, Paris: PUF, 1997.

Badiou, Alain, *Abrégé de métapolitique*, Paris: Seuil, 1998.

Badiou, Alain, *Petit manuel d'inesthéthique*, Paris: Seuil, 1998.

Barzun, Jacques, *Classic, Romantic and Modern*, London: Secker and Warburg, 1962.

Baudrillard, Jean, *Fatal Strategies*, trans. Philip Beitchman and W.G.J. Niesluchowski, London: Pluto Press, 1990.

Bauman, Zygmunt, *Modernity and the Holocaust*, Oxford: Polity Press, 1989.

Beckett, Samuel, *Proust*, London: Chatto and Windus, 1930.

Beckett, Samuel, *Molloy, Malone Dies, The Unnamable*, London: John Calder, 1959.

Beckett, Samuel, *Proust and Three Dialogues*, London: John Calder, 1969.

Belsey, Catherine, *Desire*, Oxford: Blackwell, 1994.

Benhabib, Seyla (ed.), *Democracy and Difference*, Princeton, NJ: Princeton University Press, 1996.

Benjamin, Walter, *Illuminations*, ed. Hannah Arendt, trans. Harry Zohn, London: Fontana, 1973.

Bennington, Geoffrey and Derrida, Jacques, *Jacques Derrida*, Paris: Seuil, 1991.

Berryman, John, *Selected Poems*, London: Faber and Faber, 1972.

Blanchot, Maurice, *The Work of Fire*, trans. Charlotte Mandell, Stanford, CA: Stanford University Press, 1995.

Blanchot, Maurice, *Friendship*, trans. Elizabeth Rottenberg, Stanford. CA: Stanford University Press, 1997.

Blanchot, Maurice, *Faux pas*, trans. Charlotte Mandell, Stanford, CA: Stanford University Press, 2001.

Blumenberg, Hans, *The Legitimacy of the Modern Age*, trans. Robert M. Wallace, Cambridge, MA: MIT Press, 1983.

Borges, Jorge Luis, *Labyrinths*, Harmondsworth: Penguin, 1978.

Bornstein, George, *Transformations of Romanticism in Yeats, Eliot and Stevens*, Chicago, IL: University of Chicago Press, 1976.

Boutang, Pierre, *Le temps*, Paris: Hatier, 1993.

Brooks, Peter, *Troubling Confessions*, Chicago, IL: University of Chicago Press, 2006.

Brown, Norman O., *Life Against Death*, Middletown, CT: Wesleyan University Press, 1959.

Butor, Michel, *L'emploi du temps*, Paris: Minuit, 1957.

Carr, Gilbert, 'Robert Scheu's *Die Konversation in der Ehe*: an exercise in translation', *Jahrbuch des Germanistik in Ireland*, 2 (2007), pp. 47–60.

Coetzee, J.M., *Youth*, London: Secker and Warburg, 2002.

Coetzee, J.M., *Summertime*, London: Vintage, 2010.

Critchley, Simon, *Very Little, Almost Nothing*, London: Routledge, 1997.

Davis, Lennard J., *Factual Fictions*, New York, NY: Columbia University Press, 1983.

Deane, Seamus, *Reading in the Dark*, London: Jonathan Cape, 1996.

Deleuze, Gilles, *Kant's Critical Philosophy*, trans. Hugh Tomlinson and Barbara Habberjam, Minneapolis, MN: University of Minnesota Press, 1984.

Deleuze, Gilles, *Bergsonism*, trans. Hugh Tomlinson and Barbara Habberjam, New York, NY: Zone Books, 1988.

Deleuze, Gilles, *Spinoza*, trans. Robert Hurley, San Francisco, CA: City Lights Books, 1988.

Deleuze, Gilles, *Pourparlers*, Paris: Minuit, 1990.

Deleuze, Gilles and Guattari, Félix, *Qu'est-ce que la philosophie?*, Paris: Minuit, 1991.

de Man, Paul, *Allegories of Reading*, New Haven, CT: Yale University Press, 1979.

de Man, Paul, *Blindness and Insight*, London: Methuen, 1983.

Derrida, Jacques, *Writing and Difference*, trans. Alan Bass, London: Routledge, 1978.

Derrida, Jacques, *Margins: of Philosophy*, trans. Alan Bass, Brighton: Harvester Press, 1982.

Derrida, Jacques, 'Circonfession', in Geoffrey Bennington and Jacques Derrida, *Jacques Derrida*, Paris: Seuil, 1991.

Derrida, Jacques, *The Gift of Death*, trans. David Wills, Chicago, IL: University of Chicago Press, 1995.

Derrida, Jacques and Blanchot, Maurice, *Demeure and The Instant of My Death*, trans. Elizabeth Rottenberg, Stanford, CA: Stanford University Press, 2000.

Descartes, René, *Discours de la méthode*, ed. E. Gilson, Paris: Librairie Philosophique J. Vrin, 1970.

Descombes, Vincent, *Modern French Philosophy*, trans. L. Scott-Fox and J.M. Harding, Cambridge; Cambridge University Press, 1980.

Docherty, Thomas, *Reading (Absent) Character*, Oxford: Oxford University Press, 1983.

Docherty, Thomas, *John Donne, Undone*, London: Methuen, 1986.

Docherty, Thomas, *On Modern Authority*, Brighton and New York, NY: Harvester and St Martin's, 1987.

Docherty, Thomas (ed.), *Postmodernism*, New York, NY: Columbia University Press, 1993.

Docherty, Thomas, *After Theory*, revised 2nd edn, Edinburgh: Edinburgh University Press, 1996.

Docherty, Thomas, *Alterities*, Oxford: Oxford University Press, 1996.

Docherty, Thomas, 'Big texts', *Strategies of Reading: Dickens and After*, a special number of *The Yearbook of English Studies*, 26 (1996), pp. 249–60.

Docherty, Thomas, *Criticism and Modernity*, Oxford: Oxford University Press, 1999.

Docherty, Thomas, 'Just Events', in Thomas Carmichael and Alison Lee (eds), *Postmodern Times*, DeKalb, IL: Northern Illinois University Press, 2000, pp. 53–66.

Docherty, Thomas, *Aesthetic Democracy*, Stanford, CA: Stanford University Press, 2007.

Docherty, Thomas, *The English Question; or, Academic Freedoms*, Brighton: Sussex Academic Press, 2008.

Docherty, Thomas, *For the University*, London: Bloomsbury Academic, 2011.

Eliot, T.S., *The Sacred Wood*, London: Methuen, 1966.

Esposito, Roberto, *Communitas*, Paris: PUF, 2000.

Fiedler, Leslie A., 'Archetype and signature: A study of the relationship between biography and poetry', *Sewanee Review*, 60 (1952), pp. 253–73.

Fish, Stanley, *Surprised by Sin*, Cambridge, MA: Harvard University Press, 1967.

Forster, E.M., *Aspects of the Novel*, Harmondsworth: Penguin, 1927.

Frege, Gottlob, *The Foundations of Arithmetic*, trans. J.L. Austin, Oxford: Blackwell, 1953.

Gadamer, Hans-Georg, *Dialogue and Dialectic*, trans. P. Christopher Smith, New haven, CT: Yale University Press, 1980.

Gide, André, *Journal des Faux-monnayeurs*, Paris: NRF Gallimard, 1927.

Gorz, André, *Farewell to the Working Class*, trans. Mike Sonenscher, London: Pluto Press, 1982.

Gorz, André, *Critique of Economic Reason*, trans. G. Handyside and C. Turner, London: Verso, 1989.

Habermas, Jürgen, *Legitimation Crisis*, trans. Thomas McCarthy, London: Heinemann, 1976.

Habermas, Jürgen, *The Past as Future*, ed. and trans. Max Pensky, Cambridge: Polity Press, 1994.

Hardt, Michael, *Gilles Deleuze*, London: UCL Press, 1993.

Harvey, David, *Cosmopolitanism and the Geographies of Freedom*, New York, NY: Columbia University Press, 2009.

Harvey, David, *The Enigma of Capital*, New York, NY: Profile Books, 2010.

Heaney, Seamus, *Seeing Things*, London: Faber and Faber, 1992.

Hegel, G.W.F., *Phenomenology of Spirit*, trans. A.V. Miller, Oxford: Oxford University Press, 1977.

Heidegger, Martin, *Poetry, Language, Thought*, trans. Albert Hofstadter, New York, NY: Harper Colophon, 1975.

Hume, David, *A Treatise of Human Nature*, ed. Ernest C. Mossner, London: Penguin Classics, 1984.

Hutcheson, Francis, *Philosophical Writings*, ed. R.S. Downie, London: Everyman, 1994.

James, Henry, *The Altar of the Dead and Other Tales*, London: Macmillan, 1922.

Jameson, Fredric, *The Political Unconscious*, London: Methuen, 1981.

Johnson, Samuel, *Rasselas, Poems and Selected Prose*, ed. Bertrand H. Bronson, New York, NY: Holt, Rinehart and Winston, 1971.

Joughin, John and Malpas, Simon (eds), *The New Aestheticism*, Manchester: Manchester University Press, 2003.

Joyce, James, *A Portrait of the Artist as a Young Man*, ed. Richard Ellmann, London: Granada, 1977.

Joyce, James, *Stephen Hero*, ed. Theodore Spencer, revised John J. Slocum and Herbert Cahoon, London: Triad Panther, Granada, 1981.

Judt, Tony, *The Memory Chalet*, London: Heinemann, 2010.

Kermode, Frank, *The Sense of an Ending*, Oxford: Oxford University Press, 1966.

Kermode, Frank, *The Genesis of Secrecy*, Cambridge, MA: Harvard University Press, 1979.

Kermode, Frank, *Not Entitled*, New York, NY: Farrar, Straus & Giroux, 1999.

Kierkegaard, Søren, *Either/Or*, trans. Alastair Hannay, Harmondsworth: Penguin, 1992.

Klein, Naomi, *The Shock Doctrine*, Harmondsworth: Penguin, 2007.

Kristeva, Julia, *Le temps sensible*, Paris: NRF, 1994.

Lejeune, Philippe, *Le pacte autobiographique*, Paris: Seuil, 1975.

Lemon, Lee T. and Reis, Marion J. (eds and trans), *Russian Formalist Criticism*, Lincoln, NE: University of Nebraska Press, 1965.

Levenson, Michael H., *A Genealogy of Modernism*, Cambridge: Cambridge University Press, 1984.

Levinas, Emmanuel, *Le temps et l'autre*, Paris: Quadrige/PUF, 1991.

Lowell, Robert, *The Dolphin*, London: Faber and Faber, 1973.

Lyotard, Jean-François, *Just Gaming*, trans. Wlad Godzich, Manchester: Manchester University Press, 1985.

Lyotard, Jean-François, *Le différend*, Paris: Minuit, 1983.

Lyotard, Jean-François, *Peregrinations*, New York, NY: Columbia University Press, 1988.

Lyotard, Jean-François, *The Inhuman: Reflections on Time*, trans. Geoffrey Bennington and Rachel Bowlby, Cambridge: Polity Press, 1991.

Lyotard, Jean-François, *Signé Malraux*, Paris: Grasset, 1996.

Lyotard, Jean-François, *La confession d'Augustin*, Paris: Galilée, 1998.

McEwan, Ian, *The Child in Time*, London: Picador, 1988.

MacIntyre, Alasdair, *Three Rival Versions of Moral Enquiry*, London: Duckworth, 1990.

Mack, Peter, *Elizabethan Rhetoric*, Cambridge: Cambridge University Press, 2002.

Mack, Peter, *Rhetoric and Reading in Montaigne and Shakespeare*, London: Bloomsbury Academic, 2009.

Macmurray, John, *Conditions of Freedom*, Atlantic Highlands, NJ: Humanities Press, 1993.

Marvell, Andrew, *Complete Poems*, Harmondsworth: Penguin, 1972.

Mendilow, A.A., *Time and the Novel*, New York, NY: Humanities Press, 1952.

Miller, J. Hillis, *The Disappearance of God*, Cambridge, MA: Harvard University Press, 1963.

Miller, J. Hillis, *Poets of Reality*, Cambridge, MA: Harvard University Press, 1965.

Miller, J. Hillis, *Fiction and Repetition*, Oxford: Blackwell, 1982.

Miller, J. Hillis, *The Ethics of Reading*, New York, NY: Columbia University Press, 1987.

Miller, J. Hillis, *Ariadne's Thread*, New Haven, CT: Yale University Press, 1992.

Miller, J. Hillis, *Speech Acts in Literature*, Stanford, CA: Stanford University Press, 2001.

Miller, J. Hillis, *On Literature*, London: Routledge, 2002.

Miller, J. Hillis, 'The History of 0', *Journal for Cultural Research*, 8: 2 (2004), pp. 129–39.

Montaigne, Michel de, *Essais*, 3 vols, Paris: Garnier-Flammarion, 1969.

Moretti, Franco, *The Way of the World*, trans. Albert Sbraggia, London: Verso, 1987.

Nancy, Jean-Luc, *The Experience of Freedom*, trans. Bridget McDonald, Stanford, CA: Stanford University Press, 1993.

Nancy, Jean-Luc, *Being Singular Plural*, trans. Robert Richardson and Anne O'Byrne, Stanford, CA: Stanford University Press, 2000.

Newman, John Henry Cardinal, *The Idea of a University*, ed. Martin J. Svaglic, San Francisco, CA: Rinehart Press, 1960.

Nussbaum, Martha C., *Cultivating Humanity*, Cambridge, MA: Harvard University Press, 1997.

Parrinder, Patrick, *The Failure of Theory*, Brighton: Harvester, 1987.

Pascal, Blaise, *Oeuvres complètes*, Paris: Seuil, 1963.

Pascal, Blaise, *Pensées*, ed. Louis Lafuma, Paris: Seuil, 1962.

Pascal, Blaise, *Pensées*, ed. Léon Brunschvicg, Paris: Flammarion, 1976.

Perec, Georges, *Les choses*, Paris: Julliard, 1965.

Pouillon, Jean, *Temps et roman*, Vienna: Gallimard, 1946.

Poulet, Georges, *Etudes sur le temps humain*, 3 vols, Edinburgh: Edinburgh University Press, 1949; Paris: Plon Méaux, 1964.

Poulet, Georges, *Proustian Space*, trans. Elliott Coleman, Baltimore, MD: Johns Hopkins University Press, 1977.

Portoghesi, Paolo, *Postmodern*, trans. E. Shapiro, New York, NY: Rizzoli, 1983.

Quine, W.V., *Pursuit of Truth*, Cambridge, MA: Harvard University Press, 1990.

Rancière, Jacques, *Hatred of Democracy*, trans. Steve Corcoran, London: Verso, 2006.

Rancière, Jacques, *Moments politiques*, Paris: La Fabrique, 2009.

Ricoeur, Paul, *Temps et récit*, vol. 2, Paris: Seuil, 1984.

Robbe-Grillet, Alain, *Dans le labyrinth*, Paris: Minuit, 1958.

Roethke, Theodore, *Collected Poems*, London: Faber and Faber, 1966.

Rosenthal, M.L., *The New Poets: American and British Poetry since World War II*, Oxford: Oxford University Press, 1967.

Rosenthal, M.L., *Poetry and the Common Life*, Oxford: Oxford University Press, 1974.

Rosset, Clément, *L'objet singulier*, Paris: Minuit, 1979.

Rousseau, Jean-Jacques, *Confessions*, trans. J.M. Cohen, Harmondsworth: Penguin, 1953.

Rousseau, Jean-Jacques, *Ecrits politiques*, Paris: Livre de Poche, 1992.

Said, Edward, *Beginnings: Intention and Method*, New York, NY: Basic Books, 1975.

Said, Edward, *The World, the Text, the Critic*, London: Faber, 1984.

Sartre, Jean-Paul, *Being and Nothingness*, trans. Hazel E. Barnes, New York, NY: Philosophical Library, 1956.

Schama, Simon, *The Embarrassment of Riches*, New York, NY: Knopf, 1987.

Serres, Michel, *Eclaircissements: Entretiens avec Bruno Latour*, Paris: Garnier-Flammarion, 1994.

Sofsky, Wolfgang, *Privacy: A Manifesto*, trans. Steven Rendall, Princeton, NJ: Princeton University Press, 2008.

Stevens, Wallace, *Collected Poems*, London: Faber and Faber, 1984.

Swift, Jonathan, *Gulliver's Travels and Other Writings*, ed. Louis A. Landa, Oxford: Oxford University Press, 1976.

Teilhard de Chardin, Pierre, *Comment je crois*, Paris: Seuil, 1969.

Touraine, Alain, *Qu'est-ce que la démocratie?*, Paris: Fayard, 1994.

Vattimo, Gianni, *La fine della modernità*, Milan: Garzanti, 1985.

Vattimo, Gianni, *The Transparent Society*, trans. David Webb, Cambridge: Polity Press, 1992.

Veeser, H. Aram, *The Confessions of the Critics*, London: Routledge, 1996.

Villon, François, *Poésies complètes*, Paris: Livre de Poche, 1972.

Virilio, Paul, *Vitesse et politique*, Paris: Galilée, 1977.

Virilio, Paul, *Défense populaire et luttes écologiques*, Paris: Galilée, 1978.

Virilio, Paul, *Guerre et cinema*, Paris: Editions de l'Etoile, 1984.

Virilio, Paul, *L'horizon negative*, Paris: Galilée, 1984.

Virilio, Paul, *L'espace critique*, Paris: Christian Bourgois, 1984.

Virilio, Paul, *Esthétique de la disparition*, Paris: Galilée, 1989.

Virilio, Paul, *L'inertie polaire*, Paris: Christian Bourgois, 1990.

Virilio, Paul, *L'écran du desert*, Paris: Galilée, 1991.

Virilio, Paul, *L'art du moteur*, Paris: Galilée, 1993.

Wharton, Edith, *A Backward Glance*, New York, NY: D. Appleton-Century, 1934.

Williams, William Carlos, *Paterson*, Harmondsworth, Penguin, 1983.

Woolf, Virginia, *The Common Reader*, London: Hogarth Press, 1925.

Woolf, Virginia, *Moments of Being*, ed. Jeanne Schulkind, London: Triad Panther, 1978.

Woolf, Virginia, *Selected Essays*, ed. David Bradshaw, Oxford: Oxford University Press, 2008.

Žižek, Slavoj, *The Puppet and the Dwarf*, Cambridge, MA: MIT Press, 2003.

Films

Bresson, Robert, *Une femme douce*, 1969

Chaplin, Charlie, *Modern Times*, 1936.

Coppola, Francis Ford, *The Conversation*, 1974.

Wenders, Wim, *Paris, Texas*, 1984.

Index

5876621R00124

Printed in Great Britain
by Amazon.co.uk, Ltd.,
Marston Gate.